Routledge Revivals

The Functioning of the Yugoslav Economy

In this volume, Stojanović draws together several essays by Yugoslav economists to an English audience. Originally published in 1982, these works present and analyse the issues that faced Yugoslavia's economic development and the functioning of their economic system at the time of writing through a wide selection of views. Not only does this work provide an insight into Yugoslavia's economic policies, the reader is also granted an insight into the social climate under which these essays were written. This title will be of interest to students of Economics and History.

The Functioning of the Yugoslav Economy

Edited by
Radmila Stojanović

Routledge
Taylor & Francis Group

First published in 1982
by M.E. Sharpe, Inc.

This edition first published in 2016 by Routledge
2 Park Square, Milton Park, Abingdon, Oxon, OX14 4RN
and by Routledge
711 Third Avenue, New York, NY 10017

Routledge is an imprint of the Taylor & Francis Group, an informa business

Publisher's Note
The publisher has gone to great lengths to ensure the quality of this reprint but points out that some imperfections in the original copies may be apparent.

Disclaimer
The publisher has made every effort to trace copyright holders and welcomes correspondence from those they have been unable to contact.

A Library of Congress record exists under LC control number: 82000770

ISBN 13: 978-1-138-63861-7 (hbk)
ISBN 13: 978-1-138-63862-4 (pbk)

THE FUNCTIONING OF THE YUGOSLAV ECONOMY

Edited with an Introduction
by Radmila Stojanović

M. E. Sharpe Inc.
Spokesman

80 Business Park Drive, Armonk, New York 10504

First published in Great Britain in 1982 by Spokesman
Bertrand Russell House, Gamble Street, Nottingham NG7 4ET.
Spokesman ISBN 0 85124 337 1

Published simultaneously in *Eastern European Economics*, Vol. XX, no. 2, and no. 3-4.

Library of Congress Cataloging in Publication Data

Main entry under title:

The Functioning of the Yugoslav economy.

Translated from the Serbo-Croation (Roman)
Includes bibliographical references. 1. Yugoslavia—Economic conditions—1945- —Addresses, essays, lectures. 2. Yugoslavia —Economic policy—1945- —Addresses, essays, lectures.
I. Stojanović, Radmila.
HC407.F86 330.9497′023 82-770
ISBN 0-87332-207-X AACR2

Printed in the United States of America

TABLE OF CONTENTS

INTRODUCTION

In presenting this collection of essays by Yugoslav economists to the American public, I would like to call the readers' attention to a few points.

First of all, one must bear in mind that Yugoslavia is the first country in the world attempting to develop a system of management entirely different from the one existing in other socialist countries, especially the Eastern European ones. This task, viewed historically, is neither easy nor short in duration, even if concurrently performed by a greater number of countries sharing each others' respective experiences. If a single country finds itself in this position due to specific social and political circumstances, its development course can hardly be expected to be smooth. Very frequently, we are in a position to try out a variety of methods when performing a certain kind of social activity, only to arrive at the appropriate one (appropriate at least for a specific time period) through the process of elimination.

One cannot manage ever more complex social systems by using old management parameters, old methods and institutions. The path leading to the new is like a long obstacle course. Experience of the world, particularly of its most developed part, reveals slowly but ever more clearly the difficulty of managing development through only two channels — the state and political parties; for all social interests, diverse and in conflict among themselves, cannot thus be adequately expressed. We have introduced a third channel — self-management through elected workers' delegates.

A variety of interests and goals can thus be perceived and expressed far better. However, this approach at the same time opens a wide range of new actions and problems — from the expression of the variety of interests and goals, to social coordination through different forms of social negotiation.

Not only is Yugoslavia a multinational country, a fact which also has a bearing on the complexity of the formulation and implementation of development policy, but it is also a country of vast disparities in the levels of development of its smaller territories, each of which has its own specific historical and cultural heritage. Extending full equality to the nations under such conditions raises numerous questions in selecting a uniform strategy of development, in planning all future social development, in planning joint penetration of the world market, in establishing the unity of the internal market, etc.

The complex international economic and political situation, with repercussions felt in all, especially small, countries, makes individual solutions to problems difficult.

The reader will learn here not only about the numerous problems facing Yugoslav economic development, and especially the functioning of our economic system, but also about the wide spectrum of views, evaluations, and solutions offered to particular problems, as presented by the authors of these essays. The reader will also acquire a more thorough understanding of the social climate which gives rise to such diversity in conception, in assessment of the current state of the economy, as well as in recommendations concerning policy for future development. Only practice will show which judgment will remain valid in the not-so-distant future. And not only practice in our country, but also, gradually, in those other countries that decide to follow this or a similar road.

Here and there the patient reader will perhaps find certain elements which will seem to him to be unnecessary remnants of the old system, as well as points that will become possible in practice only at some level of development higher than the current Yugoslav level. This is, it seems, a normal occurrence when one is searching for a new way of managing the development of a society that is one's own.

Many illusory concepts we have already dispensed with, or which we will yet have to abandon, although they have still not been identified, will one day be of great use to those countries undergoing similar development in search of a new form of management. It is therefore probably equally interesting and useful to analyze our successes as well as our failures, for they both form a part of the general treasury of human knowledge.

Belgrade,
December 1980

Radmila Stojanović

THE FUNCTIONING OF THE YUGOSLAV ECONOMY

1 THE SOCIAL AND ECONOMIC BASIS OF SOCIALIST SELF-MANAGEMENT IN YUGOSLAVIA

Kiro Gligorov

1. Historical Background

The roots of self-management in Yugoslavia can be found in the nature of the country's revolution, in the strong support it has had among the working masses — workers and peasants alike — in the social changes successfully brought about, and in the experience gained during the first years of socialist development.

Throughout the war of liberation there existed national liberation committees which operated on the freed territory as bodies of governmental authority. They took care of economic, educational, judicial, and other social matters. Their democratic nature, independence, and operating efficiency in work and decision-making provided valuable experience for many participants. Later on it was this cadre and its experience that made it possible to set up the essentially new governmental and social foundations of a socialist community. For this reason the study of the national liberation committees' activities during the war and immediately after its end is a valuable source of knowledge about the creation of a new society from the bottom up and about the committees' enormously significant initiative and work methods, which relied on independent activity and mobilization of the masses, who directly took part in social events.

With the nationalization of almost all the more important means of production and the creation of the governmental authority of the new state, administrative management of the economy was introduced. The ruined condition of the country and its reconstruction required a high degree of centralization of governmental powers and authority in managing the economy. This was particularly evident in the centralization of accumulation and all other financial resources, in detailed centralized planning, and in giving priority to the development of basic industries and the industrialization of the country. Such an approach required the full mobilization of material and human resources. State ownership over the means of production, centralized economic power and decision-making, together with centralized control over almost all of national income, became the basis for the growing power of the state in the Federation and in its authorities and bodies in the republics and autonomous provinces. The governmental apparatus expanded very rapidly and became very influential in regulating economic life in particular. In addition, the development of production relations based on state ownership was considerably influenced by the experience and example of the USSR.

Taking into account the multinational nature of the Yugoslav community and the different levels of development of the republics and autonomous provinces, the strengthening of the state in general and of its center in particular had, inevitably and rather promptly, to entail considerable economic, political, and national repercussions. After centralism, with its mistakes and usurpations, had been exposed to criticism, attention was very quickly directed to analyzing the nature of state ownership, state management of economic enterprises, and the consequences for social relations resulting from the strengthening of bureaucracy and the danger of the state becoming a power over and above the society. Thus under centralism the worker could remain a wage laborer and become the object of an omnipotent state instead of continuing to be the subject of revolution.

Neither the very significant economic results achieved in the reconstruction of the ruined country nor the great initial successes in industrialization were sufficient to eliminate contradictions in the creation of socialist types of social relations. Centralism, on the one hand, and the multinational nature of the Yugoslav community and its federal constituents, on the other, inevitably came into conflict with every act of strengthening the center of the state. These were the developments which, together with the state management of economic enterprises at all levels and the strengthening of the state in general, not only suppressed the independent decision-making and democratic regulation of social matters widely practiced since wartime. These factors also provoked resistance in the working class, among working people in general, and among the cadres still unaffected by the process of bureaucratization and still accustomed to more independent activity adapted to the particular local conditions and the national, cultural, and social characteristics of the places in which they worked.

After greater excesses of bureaucratic deterioration occurred, the Communist Party of Yugoslavia and its leadership began to critically appraise the experience in the administrative management of the economy, the role of the state, and the place and role of the party. It was time to return to the original texts and ideas of the classics of Marxism and to examine methods of liberation of the working class in its struggle to control all economic relations and the entire social organization and to decide on its own about the conditions, means, and results of its work. The conflict with the Cominform and a closer acquaintance with current practices of building socialism in other countries were additional factors which speeded up the process of formulating our own judgments about the past development of socialism and of searching for answers to the growing contradictions in Yugoslav society.

The ensuing conflict had its roots in earlier periods of the revolutionary movement in Yugoslavia, especially after Comrade Tito came to head the party in 1937, in the war and postwar periods, and in the peculiarities of the Yugoslav revolution. Under the new circumstances of conflict with the Cominform and the need for Yugoslavia to rely on its own strength in the struggle for bare existence, social thought, faced with the need to seek solutions to emerging contradictions, considered all issues intensively and critically, lifting taboos and freeing itself from prejudices and dogmas. Statism, centralism, state ownership, and the wage-labor status of the worker, who depended on the state and who had removed the private capitalist only to find the state as his new ruler, a state that assumed control, in his name, over the means of production — all this was subjected to thorough criticism. On the basis of this criticism the idea of workers' self-management was gradually born.

2. The Central Issue: The Position of the Workers in the New Production Relations

By nationalizing and expropriating the means of production owned by the private proprietor, the worker, as the subject of the new production relations based on social ownership and self-management, has made the state itself unnecessary as the owner of the means of production, the manager of economic enterprises, and in particular, the appropriator and distributor of the proceeds of workers' labor. In this way it has been possible to start a historical process which should enable the worker to manage social means, exercise control over surplus value, and abolish the duality under which the wage portion of income has been disposed of by the worker and the surplus labor portion of income has been controlled by the proprietor.

Let us point out some of the most important economic and social consequences arising from the surrender of enterprises to worker management. In the first place, what is essential here is the change in the nature of ownership of the means of production and the ensuing "disempowering" of the state. The means of production managed by workers become social ownership. They are not, therefore, subject to any group or other form of collective ownership by workers but are owned by all of society, while the workers who work with them perform direct management, maintenance, and utilization of them. Therefore social ownership may be differentiated from the classic notion of private capitalist and state ownership in the sense that what is socially owned belongs to the whole society and does not belong to any individual or any group or collective of individuals. Ownership thus conceived provides the basis for the new socialist self-management relations in Yugoslavia.

The social character of the means of production and the worker's labor determine his social status and enable him to control the income and surplus value he creates. The socially owned means of production and income are the material basis of self-management and of the dominant position of the worker in the self-managed socialist society. Without them he would not have a real basis on which to build his position and influence in society. Only in this way does the worker cease to be a materially dependent wage laborer unable to exercise decisive influence on the course of social events. For this reason the Yugoslav Constitution declares such rights of the worker inalienable because they constitute his material and social position and enable him to play a decisive role in society.

However, the realization of the workers' inalienable rights does not end with their proclamation in laws and regulations. This process calls for social struggle, which has been underway for thirty years in Yugoslavia. Even so, a self-managed society is not immune to technocratic usurpations or to enroachments on workers' income and meddling by the state in self-management. For this reason the state should be more a guardian of the inalienable rights of workers and of self-management relations in production than a direct regulator of such relations, which should be increasingly controlled by a consensus of participants in self-management. In the case of Yugoslavia, this is the way in which the state is withering away and in which its powers are being reduced to those areas in which they are still needed and will continue to be for a long time (defense, security, foreign policy, unity of the system, and the like).

What is new and specific in an organization of associated labor in comparison with an enterprise managed by a private proprietor or one managed by the state? In the Yugoslav system of self-management, an organization of associated labor is a free association of workers — of their labor and social means. On the basis of such association, each organization acquires a full economic and legal identity. Such a status results not only from the need to respect social division of labor but also from the need to determine as objectively as possible each organization's results of business activity and its contribution to the growth of the social product and the social productivity of labor.

Since the means of production are socially owned, the right to exercise control over them entails the obligation and responsibility to preserve their integrity and renew them through simple or extended reproduction. For this reason, full respect has to be paid to the economic function of the means of production as well as to their rational utilization. The working collective (associated labor) may dispose of the means of production, replace them, or sell them, but always under condition that full attention is paid to preserving their undiminished value. Otherwise, the value lost must be replenished from the income of the working collective itself.

The same principle also applies to the valuation of work performed. It cannot be haphazard but must be justified by realized income and be based on the principle of distribution of income in accordance with work performed. Like any independent businessman, each organization of associated labor must also achieve a certain amount of accumulation, so that it can invest, either alone or with other interested organizations, its own or borrowed funds in the expansion of production. Investment decisions have to be based on prior feasibility studies, which should show whether a proposed capital investment will pay off in more products and higher income. In other words, all factors of production have to be duly evaluated and contained in the price which, in principle, should reflect general market conditions at home and abroad.

Each organization of associated labor is a complete businessman, an independent entity which under general economic conditions of production, and in accordance with its plan and market requirements, every day strives for income out of which it will satisfy the individual and common needs of its workers and the general needs of society. The income of each organization of associated labor is, at the same time, its own and social income. The income must be earned, and the distribution of that income must serve to satisfy the needs I just mentioned.

The state, in its various forms, has a limited right to impose taxes to satisfy general social requirements (defense, security, government administration, and the like), so that all other general social needs are covered by distribution which takes place either in the economy or in mutual relations (repayment of loans, etc.) or within the jurisdiction of each working collective (in case of distribution of net income to personal incomes and accumulation).

Thus an organization of associated labor in Yugoslavia is a specific entity which has managed to win autonomy with respect to the state. The new status of workers, which is based on social ownership, enables organizations of associated labor to be independent and to acquire economic power by having control over the means of production, their labor, and realized income. Therefore they may have inalienable self-management rights and at the same time be responsible both for their existence and for the progress and prosperity of the whole community. Their social status is obviously new, unique, and undoubtedly dominant in the society precisely because it is based on self-management and social ownership.

3. Economic Laws of Socialist Self-management

The new relations of production exert a decisive influence on the character of commodity production inherited from the past and make necessary the entire transitional period of the building of socialism. The contribution of each organization of associated labor is determined in the market through prices formed in accordance with economic conditions prevailing on domestic and foreign markets. To overlook such objectively given conditions of the development of self-management would lead to subjectivism, undermine the independence of organizations of associated labor, and impair the objective assessment of business results. Therefore the market and commodity production, with their favorable effects, do exist in the economy of self-management.

It should be pointed out, in this regard, that the changed relations of production make it possible to overcome, or at least mitigate, the impact of volatile market conditions by planning business activity, establishing closer cooperation among organizations of associated labor, or voluntarily combining them to form bigger entities.

In this way Yugoslav experience shows that associated labor possesses powerful resources which do not allow commodity production to transform self-management and its participants merely into group-owned enterprises competing in the market. With a meaningful application of planning and with the new relations of production, commodity production becomes an indispensable part of the whole economic mechanism because it stimulates the initiative of workers and of self-managed organizations and encourages economic competition for higher income on the basis of greater production, increased productivity, and improved quality. In other words, the means of production have been socialized; but the individual and collective contribution of workers, i.e., of organizations of associated labor, must be objectively measurable if the economic interest of producers is to be promoted as much as possible. In addition, the function of planning is to establish those conditions of work and income-earning which cannot be foreseen from a narrow perspective, to create conditions for balanced development, and to establish prerequisites for the elimination of economic and other contradictions by inspiring personal creativity and workers' interest and by motivating their social responsibility for the entire material and social development of the community. Moreover, objective economic laws, social production powers, and ever more developed self-management social relations are simultaneously at work. They limit, gradually transform, and eventually eliminate the inherited laws, thus providing more room to express and substantiate new categories and institutions of self-managed socialist relations of production and the system of self-management itself, which is being built on the basis of such developments. To suppress commodity production, or even eliminate it, under present conditions would, now and for a long time, unavoidably lead to statism and to the limitation of workers' self-management rights. This would mean turning away from self-management and going back to the state and state ownership.

The self-managed socialist economy in Yugoslavia pursues a policy of respect for the division of labor and strives for the widest possible cooperation with other economies. Its opening up to the world is seen as a condition for more rapid progress and as exposure to the favorable influence of higher productivity in more developed economies. It is seen as a chance to absorb the advances of scientific and technological progress through cooperation and exchange in the marketplace. Basically, the orientation of the economy is antiautarkic because it respects the need for free exchange of goods, knowledge, and technology, as well as the free flow of development capital.

However, one cannot forget the inequitable relations inherent in the present international economic order or the need to change it. The more developed economies of the industrialized countries use the existing economic order to acquire superprofits by means of unequal exchange of commodities and other forms of monopolistic activity on the world market. Therefore it is necessary to be more active in international markets and to make continuous efforts to increase work productivity and the profitability of business operations in the domestic economy in order to reduce the degree of inequity in trade with the economies of other countries. Simultaneously, continued efforts should be made worldwide to change unjust relations in the existing international economic order.

For this reason, planning of the domestic economy, as an ever more important factor in the establishment of long-term connections with other economies, particularly with the economies of developed countries, can be the right way to cause a gradual change in the present situation, to increase and strengthen the forces of those countries whose vital interest is to change the existing unjust relations by establishing new standards of behavior in international relations and world markets, and to make a practical contribution to changing the existing economic order by introducing new forms of business activity and more equitable relations in trade, the exploitation of natural resources, and technology transfer. The development of the self-managed economy in Yugoslavia is becoming a more integral part of such an approach to international economic relations.

4. Direct Self-management and Forms of Association of Organizations of Associated Labor

One of the major questions that arises in the self-managed organization of society concerns the size and nature of its basic self-managed cell — the basic organization of associated labor. The criterion for the appropriateness of such an organization is whether its size, rights, and obligations enable the worker to participate directly in making decisions essential for the life and development of the organization, and whether the necessary material and social conditions have been provided. The organization must be of a size that enables the worker to have direct insight into its condition and problems, while at the same time there must be full awareness of the economic and technological conditions required for its independent existence.

Economic and social preconditions for the functioning of self-management organizations have been secured statutorily in the Constitution, which stipulates that realized income belongs to the basic organization of associated labor, that no special use of accumulation from its income may be made without its consent, and that all newly created income resulting from the funds utilized with the consent of basic organizations of associated labor must belong to such organizations. In other words, the concentrated funds belong to the basic organizations of associated labor in the same way as do the results obtained from joint employment of the funds. Every instance of expropriation of income earned by organizations of associated labor is an unconstitutional act and a punishable usurpation. Only within constitutionally specified limits and on the basis of law may a portion of income be taken by taxes for general social requirements, or may a legal obligation to pool resources in case of an extraordinary social need be imposed (such as building power plants and lines).

However, the legal status of an organization of associated labor does not in any way diminish or negate the need to form larger and more complex organizations of associated labor in response to economic and social necessity. There is no doubt about the need to form complex organizations and to concentrate accumulation.

In defining the character and outward features of basic organizations of associated labor, our aim, first of all, was to strengthen the positions of workers and self-managed cells in order to prevent what had happened in the past, when complex organizations with central worker councils expropriated the workers' right to decide on the use of their income and accumulation. Such occurrences degrade the workers' direct self-management and give managers and the administration ways to secure for themselves an overwhelming influence in the process of decision-making.

The workers organized in basic organizations of associated labor have a primary interest in associating themselves in forms of organization that can help them, in their mutual relations and on the basis of self-management consensus, to effect the necessary concentration of accumulation, to adopt plans covering their common development, and to exert influence on other social decisions made within the political system of the self-managed society. In connection with this it must be noted that all forms of association, except the basic organization of associated labor, are derivative. Just as accumulation may be concentrated only on the basis of independent decisions of basic organizations, and just as concentrated accumulation may be used only subject to prior consent of all parties to the association, so the same basic organizations decide about jointly achieved results and about the distribution of realized income in accordance with the principle that each organization is entitled to share joint income proportionally to its contribution to the creation of such income.

Therefore the position and role of organizations of associated labor do not and must not lead to the atomization of society. As equal economic factors, the competent and materially well founded basic self-managed cells again emphasize the need to be interconnected and associated. Without a broad-based process of association there would be no solid foundation to concentrate the resources required for modern economic development to take place, because, at certain points, development requires the investment of huge resources that cannot be provided by one or a few basic organizations. However, the need to associate cannot be reduced solely to this. By associating and forming large associations, it becomes practicable and possible to plan jointly, do joint research work, and regulate many other important matters in a self-management way, so that many functions, instead of being performed by the state, are assumed by associated labor. This in itself considerably increases the opportunities and strengthens the influence of larger associations. Otherwise small organizations of associated labor can be manipulated very easily because they are unable to solve any problems without mediation and arbitration by the state.

The reduction of the functions of the state is a long historical process whose progress depends on continuous widening of the scope of self-management regulation and on gradually overcoming commodity production laws.

It is understandable that all economic decisions cannot be made within self-managed organizations however large or broad-based they may be. Those economic decisions which have a wider social significance and all other decisions which have a direct or indirect effect on the position of associated labor, its income, or social status must be made in institutions of the parliamentary political system. Basic organizations of associated labor elect from their own ranks delegates who participate in assemblies (parliaments) of sociopolitical communities (municipality, province, republic, Federation) and make very sensitive social decisions. In this way the political system finds its roots in the basic self-managed cells, while self-management in the production sphere, as the prevailing social relation, permeates all other social activities and the political mechanism and thus becomes an integral social relation.

The system of self-management constituted in this way emerges as the basic integrating factor in Yugoslav society. Under conditions of multinationality and different levels of economic, cultural, and social development of constituent subdivisions of society, the integrating factor is particularly important as the element which holds together the working class, peoples, and nationalities of Yugoslavia.

By gaining control over the means of production and the income resulting from their work, the workers have succeeded in changing the Yugoslav political system. The democracy which exists in production and work relations has been expanded to the political sphere — democracy in production has become the basis of political democracy in the whole society.

In the system of self-management there is a clear line which separates management and decision-making at the level of work collectives and worker councils from the functions of business and executive management, which must have their place and responsibility in the process of production and the current activity of economic organizations. Business management bodies and the managers of each organization have full independence in carrying out technological processes and current economic activities, while all decisions relating to distribution of realized income, cooperation with other organizations, and annual and multiannual planning are reserved for the whole working collective or its worker council, depending on the nature of the decision to be made. On this basis the manager, president of the management board, and management board members have independent authority in executing decisions which have been made, particularly in the production and technological process; but this authority is precisely limited with respect to the disposition of social resources, income, and accumulation. So clear a distinction between management and self-management rights is necessary to protect self-management rights from violation, to prevent the creation of an alliance between the technocracy and the bureaucracy and their usurpation of self-management, and at the same time, to permit the process of production and exchange to take place normally without interfering in executive functions.

5. Earning and Distributing Income

Realized income at the disposal of a basic organization of associated labor is defined as the income verified in the marketplace, provided that development has followed the plan and that basic economic trends are regulated. The unified Yugoslav market presupposes free movement of workers, commodities, and other resources existing in the market. Organizations of associated labor, freely and independently or through their associations, enter domestic and foreign markets as economic and legal entities that compete for higher incomes in local currency and foreign exchange. Prices are determined in the market in accordance with market conditions and under the influence of price movements on the world market. The influence of planning on the development and structure of the economy and changes in productivity and operating efficiency have a favorable effect on the formation and movement of prices and the stabilization of the market in general.

In accordance with the achieved level of development and productivity of labor, the monetary, foreign exchange, and customs-tariff policy determines the conditions under which all organizations of associated labor conduct business. The policy provides direct protection to domestic production, but only to an extent that does not eliminate the pressure of foreign competition and more productive foreign producers on domestic production. Under these conditions each organization of associated labor determines its prices alone, taking into account market conditions, or in accordance with a self-management agreement on prices made between interested producers and consumers. Those organizations of associated labor which do not sell their products directly in the market but cooperate in the production of final products as suppliers of spare parts and components determine prices of semifinished products and components by mutual agreement or receive a certain percentage of the total income realized from the sale of final products, i.e., they participate in the jointly earned income proportionally to their contribution to its formation.

The state is in a position to intervene in the price sector either to create more stable business conditions and curb inflation or to protect consumers from monopolistic and similar developments. Should such an intervention reduce normal income, then the administrative authority which has limited or reduced prices has to provide adequate compensation to the affected producers.

From the total income earned under such conditions, each organization of associated labor deducts all material expenses and depreciation of the means of production; it thus arrives at the income which remains at its disposal. This means that personal incomes are not deducted as production expenses because, under conditions of self-management, the worker functions both as the person who manages social resources and the one who invests his labor. For this reason, the contribution of each collective is not contained only in the labor it invests but also in the management and use of all the social resources at its disposal. In this way the division of income into wages and profits disappears because neither the private owner of capital nor the state as owner are interpolated into the process of production. The contribution of labor and the contribution of resources, as embodied in income, appear as realized, newly created value — the income at the disposal of the worker and his collective.

Although the limitations of private ownership which reduced the worker to a wage laborer have disappeared, and although the worker is in a position to dispose of the collective's income, this does not mean that the economic functions of income have also disappeared. The worker must respect the economic obligation to allocate part of the collective's income to consumption and part to accumulation. The division of income into accumulation and consumption is not a matter of free choice but an objectively given act which depends on the level of productivity of labor, in the case of consumption, and on the rate of accumulation required to secure further development. Therefore the right of workers to distribute income presupposes their economic and social responsibility to make the distribution in accordance with the need of the work collective to accumulate.

The association of more organizations of associated labor enables them to do business jointly in order to earn joint income. On the basis of a self-management agreement of associated producers, joint earnings are distributed in accordance with the criteria they themselves have determined to express the contribution of each participant to the value of joint products. This method of association and of earning and distributing income provides a natural basis for the concentration of resources, division of labor, and sharing of joint risks in business and development.

The results workers obtain through their labor and total business activity are the basis for distribution of income according to work performed and for the assessment of each individual's contribution. The criteria by which income is divided into personal income and accumulation are determined by self-management agreements of organizations of associated labor and trade unions. On the basis of adopted general criteria, each work organization stipulates in its own self-management agreement specific criteria of distribution and methods of measuring each person's contribution depending on the total results achieved by the basic organization of associated labor.

6. Solidarity and Mutuality in Yugoslav Self-managed Society

The effect of commodity production, the unequal composition of the means of production which workers manage and with which they work, workers' economic motivation, the influence of domestic and foreign markets, and the inherited differences in the level of development of the country's various regions all unavoidably generate differences which result in certain contradictions in society. Because of this the solidarity of the working class, peoples, and nationalities in Yugoslavia is an essential and integral part of socialist self-management. Without solidarity, economic and social differences would increase and cause considerable damage to the socialist character of society. At the same time, adherence to solidarity is one of the conditions which makes it possible to encourage to a greater extent workers' material interest in better observing the economic laws bearing on the development, formation, and distribution of income.

It should be understood that the limits of solidarity must be clearly marked. First of all, solidarity measures must not weaken anyone's interest in greater and more successful results of work. They must not nourish the unrealistic view that social differences can be eliminated at the expense of initiative and material interest in higher productivity, nor can they foster the illusion that one can live at the expense of other workers' solidarity. Therefore the purpose of solidarity must be to encourage those who receive it to make their own effort and activate their own resources; it must be merely a support to overcome problems of backwardness in development or external difficulties beyond the control of the work collective.

On this basis, and in addition to the solidarity manifested in the system of social insurance, education, health, etc., by which the whole working class and, in certain instances, all citizens are covered, and apart from some other instances of solidarity, such as solidarity housing construction and the like, it is possible to distinguish three basic areas of solidarity established constitutionally or by law:

a. The development of less-developed regions is a long-term problem whose gradual solution creates more equal conditions for workers to earn income and for economic equality of peoples and nationalities, republics, and provinces in Yugoslavia. The Constitution has established the obligation to form a common fund for more rapid development of less-developed regions, to which contributions are made by all organizations of associated labor at a specific percentage of their social product. Additional funds have also been planned for quicker development of social services in less-developed regions (education, culture, health, etc.). These funds are allocated to such regions from the federal budget, to which contributions are made for this purpose by the republics and provinces. The total resources contributed for all such purposes in the current five-year period exceed 3 percent of the social product of Yugoslavia. This mechanism of aid and solidarity, which also acts as a corrective to market effects, is an element of more rapid development of less-developed regions, an expression of the solidarity of the working class, and a fundamental factor in the cohesiveness of the Yugoslav peoples and nationalities. It provides sound economic foundations for self-management and, at the same time, avoids certain unacceptable effects of the market economy. It helps bridge the historical differences in development inherited from the past. In addition to this, the policy of accelerated development of less-developed regions has significant economic effects reflected in the widening of the Yugoslav market, the more even development of the economy, and its generally more rapid progress.

b. Solidarity in relations among work organizations is reflected in the aid extended to certain collectives, usually with the expectation of repayment. Sometimes it is a grant to organizations that have incurred losses because of worn-out means of production and old technology, or because of weaknesses in earning power that left insufficient funds to cover operating costs, expenses, and personal incomes. Reserve funds of work organizations are used for this purpose because they can, in part, be associated and can be coupled with bank loans and aid extended by sociopolitical communities. This kind of solidarity is realized on the basis of a rehabilitation program and evidence that the required changes will be made in production, technology, work organization, and personnel. In this way work collectives that have good prospects to overcome difficulties are helped to reorganize themselves without workers losing their jobs.

c. Solidarity in the case of natural disasters, such as earthquakes, floods, and the like, has already been shown in several instances. In the case of such disasters, all organizations of associated labor have, on the basis of laws enacted for this purpose, provided relief.

7. Contradictions of Self-managed Social and Economic Development

a. First of all, let us consider contradictions in ownership relations. As already stated, although workers manage the means of production and allocate income, both the means of production and income (surplus labor) belong to society. They are allocated by work collectives in accordance with their interests and requirements, but also taking into account the interests and needs of society as a whole. Here lies the link between the workers' inalienable self-management rights and their responsibility to the social community. This contradiction is not insurmountable because rational employment of the means of production and income is not contrary to social interests — it is the objective of the self-management system. Thus the system reveals its advantages as one possible realistic alternative for the development of socialism throughout the world.

Therefore group ownership and the privatization of social resources and income work against self-management. Commodity production and the market, to the extent to which they increase competition; the residual consciousness which still treats property either as "my own" or the "state's"; the petty-proprietorship mentality inherited from the past; and many other defects in specific mechanisms of economic activity, coupled with backward economic conditions — all these things strengthen tendencies to group ownership. However, such tendencies do not stem from the system itself but are the product of the laborious process of modifying inherited patterns of thought and identifying valid incentives that will join the interests of the individual and the collective to those of the society.

b. In the relations that exist in the process of management and decision-making in organizations of associated labor, among the tendencies that do arise, managerial usurpation is the most significant. It is manifested in efforts to manipulate self-management bodies, to impose decisions, to mislead through inadequate information, and to circumvent the self-management rights of the work collective and the worker councils. This tendency derives from the view that professionalism and competency in problem-solving are the only decisive factors in decision-making. However, the source of this viewpoint is actually the desire to gain power and control social resources and income without workers' self-management.

To justify such usurpation it is often argued that there must be unified decision-making in the process of production, that there is a need for efficient operation, that decision-making by workers is slow, that decision-makers are professionally incompetent for the decisions they make, and so on. However, the issues here are not, in fact, the unquestioned prerogatives which management bodies and managers have in the process of production and in the conduct of current business operations, nor are they concerned with professional assessment of problems. What is at stake are the key questions concerning development policy and income distribution, the fate of work collectives, and the interests of workers, without whom and against whose will no decision can be made with respect to their existence and the course of development of a self-managing society.

This problem will be overcome gradually by keeping workers constantly and adequately informed and aware of the nature of the problems their collectives face and, above all, by the vital practice and experience the working class is now gaining in the process of self-management.

c. The fact that the means of production are socially owned and that income and surplus value in the hands of working collectives represent a material power which, when pooled, can produce major results often misleads the economic and social authorities to adopt development programs and targets which are beyond existing possibilities.

In the process of planning it is often forgotten that resources belong to work collectives, that they can be allocated only by the will of the collectives, that big targets and large programs must be based on and originate from the plans of specific economic entities, and that the state has limited rights with respect to the redistribution of national income. For this reason there still exists a serious degree of subjectivism in the planning of development, just as there is voluntarism in the introduction of certain administrative measures through state intervention. In fact, in this tendency we see a desire to transform relations of social ownership into those of state ownership; but this cannot be done except by expropriating the self-management rights of the workers and work collectives. This results in spending beyond means, which causes market instability and affects price relations. Simultaneously, instances of concentration of accumulation against the will of workers, heavy borrowing, and the use of banking resources without the consent of associated labor or in alliance with state and political authorities lead to the creation of state capital and an alliance between managers and the state and political bureaucracy.

d. In Yugoslav society, which respects the plurality of interests, the reconciliation of individual, joint, and most common interests is of exceptional importance in resolving conflicts and in timely and efficient decision-making.

In addition, Yugoslavia is a multinational community, which requires full tolerance and respect for different national needs and interests. There is no doubt that free expression of different interests is a fundamental condition for democratization of society. The system of self-management is a social framework within which the different interests of workers and work collectives in production, distribution, and social services are mutually reconciled by way of self-management agreements, on an equal basis and taking into account that all people work with the means in social ownership and have equal economic and social status. As already stated, given the same relations of production and the equal social status of working people, there are many common elements which unite the working people and make them rely on each other. The working class also has a long-term interest in preserving and developing social relations, in which work is the dominant factor, and in securing material and social progress for itself and the community. The process of reaching agreement and consensus on different and common interests gradually eliminates administrative intervention and makes the state superfluous in many areas of income creation and distribution.

The delegation system may be regarded as an extension of self-management to the political sphere because it, like self-management, relies on the same social actors to elect delegates recruited from the basic self-managed cells. At every level, from the municipality to the Federation, delegate assemblies coordinate interests that are beyond the competence of organizations of associated labor, or even the largest associations of them. They deal with the problems and interests of the different sociopolitical communities — municipalities, provinces, republics, and the Federation.

The League of Communists of Yugoslavia and other political organizations represent an indisputable factor which creates an atmosphere of tolerance and democratic procedure. It promotes common principles which make it possible to resolve problems and conflicting interests through debate, argument, and the accentuation of common and general interests whenever these are brought into question or neglected.

As in any society, the resolution of conflicts is, of course, a laborious process which depends on people's attitudes and the choices they make, as well as on democratic traditions of tolerance, mutual respect, and regard for different interests.

e. The different levels of development of particular regions of Yugoslavia, as already mentioned, produce different interests and even different views on certain questions, including those of more general significance. This contradiction is long-term in nature, and it will inevitably play a very important role in political and social life. It also will be resolved through the delegate system, through perception of the close interdependence within which it must be approached, and through the accelerated general progress of the country.

f. A unified Yugoslav market is of exceptional importance in establishing economic and social links in our economy; but like any other market, it has certain inherent contradictions and weaknesses.

In the case of Yugoslavia, unfavorable market developments are manifested through the appearance of regional market boundaries, market fragmentation, and direct or indirect limitations on the free flow of social resources, so that the pooling of them tends to be limited to smaller regions. The right way to eliminate such unfavorable market developments is to develop the economy, to secure steadier regional development, and to promote the division of labor, cooperation, and association among economic organizations from different regions, wherever this is economically justified. An economic policy and changes in the economic mechanism that will encourage and facilitate economic activity in a unified Yugoslav market should contribute to the gradual disappearance of negative developments.

The self-managed socialist society is by no means an idyllic society. By allowing natural and direct expression of interests and opinions, the society appears as one with many contradictions and problems.

In a word, the self-management model is not without faults. It requires further exploration of its nature and internal laws. Answers to many problems are still unknown; and one could almost say with certainty that other societies, were they to choose the road of self-management under perhaps more favorable economic and social conditions, would find better answers to many questions that come up in the course of self-management and socialist development. That would encourage us to further explore more democratic and more humane forms of social organization.

2
PLANNING ECONOMIC DEVELOPMENT IN YUGOSLAVIA

Radmila Stojanović

I. Basic Features of Self-management Planning

The self-management system, which proceeds from the principle that each development decision ought to be made at that particular management level at which some given goal can best and most fully be observed, presupposes multilevel management, i.e., management at more levels than is the case with centralized systems. This fact, in turn, means at the same time that in determining the level of decision-making (both making and implementing decisions) a certain rule applies — a decision is to be referred to a higher level only when it cannot be fully and correctly comprehended and formulated at a lower level. Thus it is very important for the development of self-management to bear in mind the dangers of unnecessarily engaging a higher level, and not only the highest level; this is because it is totally irrelevant to the person who is deprived of the right to decide whether he has been supplanted by the next higher level or the highest.[1]

Two issues arise from this way of choosing a particular level of management:

a. What the goals of the higher levels mean to the lower levels under the conditions of self-management.

b. What the optimal decision is, and how it is reached.

The goals of higher levels (the state, whole regions, whole industries) do not represent obligatory goals that lower levels (e.g., an enterprise) must accept and include in their development programs; but such goals are constraints for them when they choose their own optimal variants. However, constraints in this case should be viewed actively not passively. In other words, if, for example, the goal of Yugoslavia as a whole were a certain decrease in the balance-of-payments deficit or an increase in employment over some given time period, then each enterprise would be obliged, during the independent formulation of its development goals, and even more during their implementation, to provide for the highest possible exports or the lowest possible imports, depending on the branch and on the anticipated expansion of the enterprise.

Understanding an optimum is a special problem. To the self-management system only the concept of a negotiated optimum is adequate, i.e., an optimum attained through a process of social negotiation. Or that solution is optimal which, as the best, most acceptable one, is determined in mutual negotiation by those directly concerned, regardless of whether they will gain or lose upon the attainment of a specific economic goal. And that is what, we emphasize, we are really concerned about — only those directly concerned should participate in the negotiation, for no one has the right to declare himself the sole legitimate interpreter of others' interests and goals.

The coordination of development goals on the basis of mutual negotiation can take place only if based on a correctly drawn draft of a project for attaining a certain goal. Thus, since the major part of every project consists of a cost-effectiveness analysis, costs and benefits must be treated as social costs and social benefits, and their calculation and expression must be unified. The unification of cost and benefit measurement is especially important for Yugoslavia because it is very diverse with regard to levels of development (such differences can be expressed in national income per capita, which in the extreme case of Slovenia compared to Kosovo reaches a ratio of 6 : 1); moreover, it is a multinational country in which sensitivity regarding project methodology is very great. Given regional differences such as ours, one very complex methodological question is what to consider as costs and what as benefits for a certain project. The underdeveloped regions, quite understandably, tend to include in a particular economic project certain subsidiary facilities in the sphere of public consumption (schools, health care, recreation, etc.), and at the same time their performance is lower than that in developed regions. Thus regional differences have a great bearing on the complexity of unifying cost and benefit measurement, which is then necessary for comparing investment variants and for selecting the optimal variant.[2]

The next feature of Yugoslav planning is the relationship between industrial and territorial planning. This simultaneously entails (a) planning that runs from the single enterprise to the industry as a whole, where the industry is often organized in the form of specific integration of all enterprises in order to divide the production program and coordinate mutual development; and (b) planning from the single municipality (commune) as the lowest territorial organization, to groups of a few nearby municipalities (smaller regions), up to the republics and provinces (there are eight of them), to Yugoslavia as a whole. The territory in this planning activity, of course, views the citizen primarily as a consumer, whose basic needs, including employment, have to be satisfied; while the industry, to the largest extent, views each employed person as a producer and as a creator of new material goods and services. Coordinating development programs between both industries and republics and provinces represents one of the most difficult and complex tasks in our entire system of planning. There is simultaneously a conflict between a stronger motivation for development (industry) and a stronger motivation for consumption (territory). That is, there is a conflict between a stronger motivation for accumulation and new economic investment (we have in mind primarily productive investment) and a stronger motivation to expand all forms of consumption (personal and especially public). By definition industry defends accumulation, direct investment, scientific and technical progress, integration, an increase in the productivity of labor, and lastly, remuneration in accordance with labor output. The territory inherently defends a certain level of consumption. An increase in consumption means an increase in general welfare, satisfying the needs of the largest possible number of citizens. Even with respect to an increase in new employment there exist two different attitudes: industry favors new employment to the extent to which new production and an increase in productive technology allow; a territory favors employment because it increases personal incomes and thus raises the standard of living. Industry favors an increase in welfare resulting from an increase in income per employed worker, and the territory favors an increase in welfare resulting from an increase in income per citizen. The very great power of a territory in the multinational state is the reason why in Yugoslavia there is so pronounced a motivation for consumption and so insufficient a motivation for new economic investment and integration. Hence it is a very complicated matter to coordinate industrial and territorial plans.

Self-management planning requires a very clear differentiation between the planning of development policy and the technology of planning. The former is a task for the elected self-management bodies at all six levels of management specified by the Constitution: (1) the section in a plant, which is the smallest organizational unit; (2) enterprises; (3) various forms of industrial and interindustrial integration of enterprises; and (4) municipalities, (5) republics, and (6) the federation. The technology of planning is a task for expert services, i.e., administrations for social planning and economic chambers — which are organized on a territorial basis but contain a corresponding industry division as well as corresponding expert enterprise services (the development sector — in our terminology). Given the differentiation I have described, the entire network of planning institutions in Yugoslavia is shown in the chart on page 27.

Finally, for a better understanding of Yugoslav planning, it should be noted that the basic criterion in selecting among different investment variants, and the basic success indicator of plan realization, is the level of earned gross income per employed person. This criterion is also the basic goal function of each individual enterprise.[3]

II. The Planning Procedure

The first step in formulating the midterm plan is to determine priorities for the next development period. On the basis of numerous foreign and domestic forecasts, and an analysis of the world and domestic economic situations, the Federal Executive Council makes a proposal to the Federal Assembly in the form of a General Program for Future Midterm Development. It is, in fact, a selection of priorities for future development. The General Program is first discussed by the Planning Board of the Federal Assembly; after corrections and supplements are made, it is presented at a plenary session of the Federal Assembly. Understandably, the program is the subject of extensive debate, for every region and industry wants priority. Of course, the General Program contains not only goal priorities but also a draft quantification of the goals for the planning period. The final quantification comes later, after data have been assembled on how much of each goal individual enterprises (i.e., various organizations which satisfy certain social needs) can undertake.

Planning of development policy			Planning technology
preparation of development plan		adoption of development plan	
territorial planning	industrial planning		
planning board of Federal Assembly	Federal Economic Chamber	Federal Assembly	Federal Administration for Social Planning
planning boards of republic and provincial assemblies	republic and provincial economic chambers	republic and provincial assemblies	republic and provincial administrations for social planning
planning boards of city and municipal assemblies	city and municipal economic chambers	city and municipal assemblies	city and municipal administrations for social planning
enterprise planning board (a body of the workers' council)	enterprise planning boards and associations	workers' councils	enterprise planning and development sector

Once the General Program for Future Development has been adopted by the Federal Assembly, it serves as the basic framework for drafting development plans simultaneously at all management levels. Each level draws its first drafts in at least two variants to allow for changes should it need to coordinate its plans with other subjects. Thus plans are drafted simultaneously not only by enterprises and their various associations (some of which encompass a whole Yugoslav industry, while others include an industry confined to one or two republics) but also by municipalities and republics as territorial units.

The initial negotiations over plan drafts follow two lines: territorial and industrial. That is, plans are coordinated by certain municipalities and their intermunicipal communities (groupings of many municipalities covering a small territory), and also by enterprises in the same industry. Thus republic and provincial plans (a total of eight territorial plans), as well as plans of individual industries, are gradually arrived at.

The main convergence of plan drafts moves from industrial to territorial units. On the basis of our current planning practice, the process is depicted graphically on page 29.

The primary coordination of plan drafts is followed by designing of projects on the basis of fundamental, i.e., strategic, goals. And on the basis of the projects there follows the process of social negotiation among individual actors which meet during the realization of the same goals.

Projecting development goals, i.e., project technique and project evaluation, is constantly evolving. This is so in spite of its exceptional role in the self-management type of planning. The reason for this is not primarily lack of experience in projecting, since a whole series of large projects has already been designed in Yugoslavia, applying the World Bank methodology. The reason lies in the great complexity of projecting in a relatively small country with pronounced regional disparities.

What is a cost or benefit in one region, and what therefore must be included in a project for that region, does not necessarily exist in another region; at any rate, the costs-benefits differ in value. The underdeveloped regions, for instance, are very heavily burdened by indirect (more precisely, secondary) costs, especially those costs related to the recruitment of a new labor force which must be brought to the cities, given housing, and provided with many subsidiary facilities (schools, health institutions, restaurants, etc.). In the most developed region of Yugoslavia, Slovenia, with a

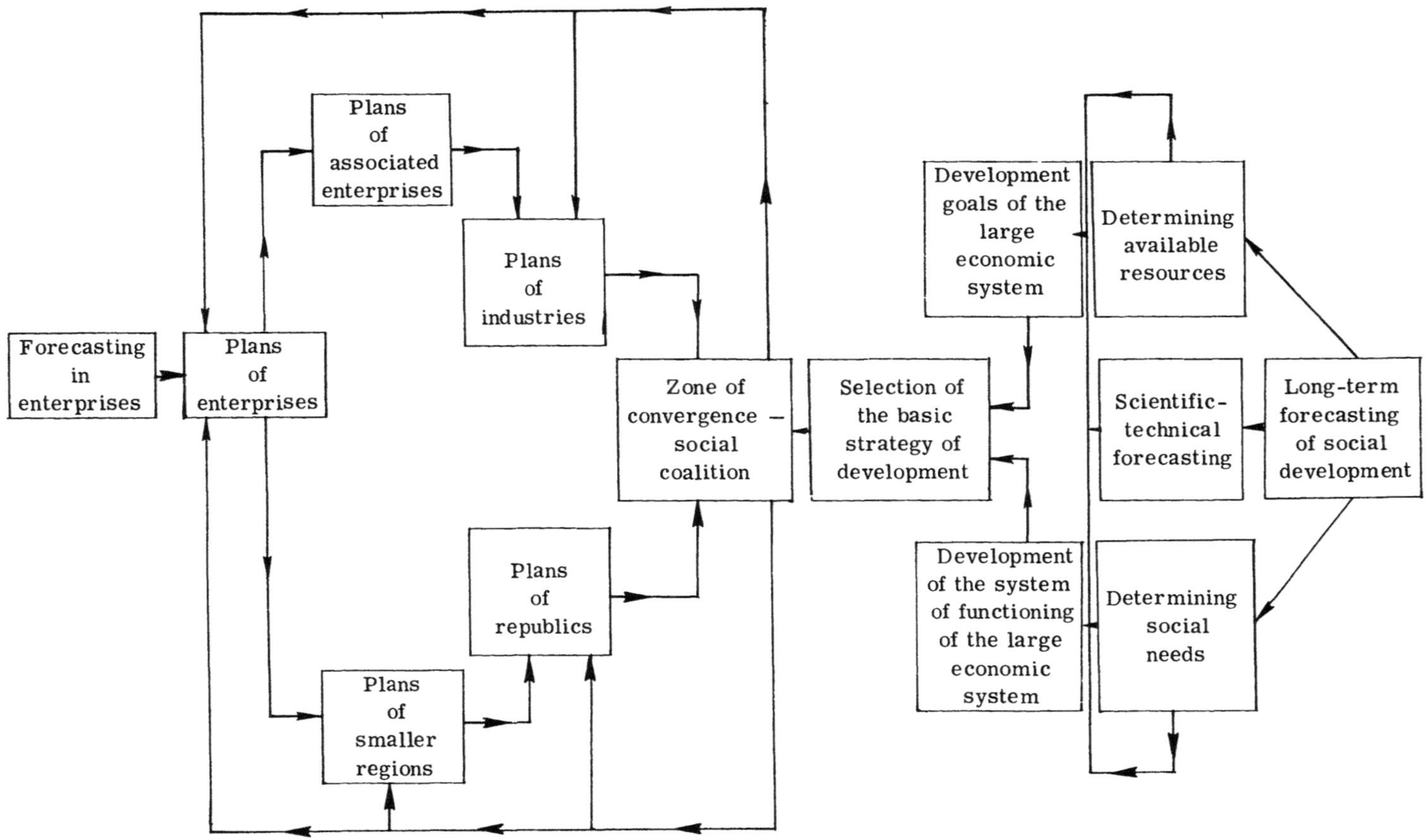

Forecasting in enterprises
Plans of enterprises
Plans of associated enterprises
Plans of industries
Plans of smaller regions
Plans of republics
Zone of convergence – social coalition
Selection of the basic strategy of development
Development goals of the large economic system
Development of the system of functioning of the large economic system
Determining available resources
Scientific-technical forecasting
Determining social needs
Long-term forecasting of social development

per capita income of over $5,000, it is sufficient to include in a project the cost of remuneration of the employed personnel and the cost of supplementary specialists' education (almost the only cost of continuing education in accordance with scientific and technical progress). Or let us take as an example the depreciation rate. At one time it was regulated by industry, i.e., an obligatory rate of depreciation was fixed for every industry. Very soon it was realized that regional differences were also manifested in the level of production techniques and the need for rapid modernization (especially that which was particularly capital intensive), while a region might have a great surplus of labor; and so a uniform rate of depreciation had to be dispensed with. A much more flexible attitude toward it has since been assumed. This flexibility, of course, carries the danger of slower technical progress; but amid such great regional differences, it is difficult to find a solution which is absolutely positive and equally acceptable to all.

For the purpose of comparison of project variants, some standardization of cost and benefit measurement is necessary. It is, in practice, a very clear, yet certainly not an easily accomplished task, because a certain cost or a certain benefit does not mean the same for regions at varying levels of development or for industries at different technical levels and in different positions on the market. It cannot be easily accomplished because it is a familiar aspiration of every enterprise to realize, through the sales of its products on the market, its entire individual labor output, i.e., to receive a gross income per employed worker which corresponds to his labor product. The differences in practice are such that this requirement can hardly be met; it is even debatable whether it is achievable in individual cases. For many reasons interindustrial and interregional transfers occur within the country, and even greater ones in international trade. The question of compensating those who through no fault of their own lose part of their gross incomes is thus constantly present and must play a role not only in projects but, even more, in social contracts and self-management agreements based on concrete projects.

Heretofore we have most often standardized in practice the following values that are significant for project design: (1) prices to be used in the project; (2) the accounting rate of foreign currency; (3) the accounting exchange rate, where the official interest rate of the National Bank of Yugoslavia is usually used; (4) the anticipated rate of inflation as given by the expert service of the National Bank of Yugoslavia. The following values have not been standardized up to now: the depreciation rate and the discount rate for discounting future costs and future benefits, for the purpose of comparison of projects upon selecting the optimal variant of the project. We have already stated why the depreciation rate has not been standardized. The discount rate, however, is in itself very controversial because the very notion of costs and benefits differs so much among the different industries and, especially, territories.

A special problem is the distribution of costs and benefits upon achieving some major development goal for which a project has been designed. In a multinational country one must be very sensitive to such distribution, so that someone does not reap greater benefits while at the same time incurring a smaller part of the cost. The problem is that another partner could experience the opposite: his costs could be relatively high, but his participation in the positive results of reaching the goal could be small. It must be taken into account that the underdeveloped regions, the basic industries, and agriculture (and especially certain segments of the population in such regions and industries) cannot bear a greater burden with respect to received benefits.

After the project variants for certain goals have been formulated (this usually holds true for strategic goals), and once the optimal variants have been preliminarily selected (the others remain as reserve variants), the process of social and self-management negotiation ensues. Social contracts are intended for large strategic goals which are of special interest to the whole country, while self-management agreements are made between enterprises in the same industry or enterprises linked in a production sequence (producers of resources–producers of equipment–producers of the final product), where in the case of certain products, trading enterprises participate as well. Of course, the process of social negotiation among the republics and provinces on the most essential goals in a given planning period is the most important and the most complicated procedure; it therefore requires further treatment.

Social negotiation occurs for the first time during the formulation of the General Program for Future Development, for it is then necessary to bring into accord different opinions on what our development priorities will be in the following planning period. However, the main role for negotiation in the Yugoslav system of planning starts after strategic goals have been selected and projects for them designed, in perhaps two variants.

While our experience in social negotiation is quite extensive, it is still an area with ongoing problems.

The first problem, which was very soon revealed by practice, is how to choose the right partners for negotiation. They should be those who directly participate in reaching the goal set. We have seen, on the basis of previous experience, that two things are necessary in approaching social negotiation: (1) a correct project design; (2) correctly chosen partners. Some social contracts were signed after a process of negotiating by actually competent partners, i.e., direct participants (for example, the social contract on the development of railway traffic, the development of production of nonferrous metals, the development of ferrous metallurgy, energy, etc.). That is to say, the contracts were signed by elected representatives from certain industries. But it was soon realized that the social contracts signed in the name of certain industries by representatives of the executive councils of the republics and provinces, and by representatives of the Federal Executive Council as counterparts, yielded no results. This happened because the presence of an enterprise which would have fulfilled the signed contract was not assured; moreover, some of the contracts were not even based on projects. Thus changes in practice were necessary, and today it is clear that the presence of direct executors of some development goal is of great importance.

The second problem, also revealed to us through practice, is how to engage certain representatives in the process of social negotiation. Partners are very diverse; some gain a great deal through the realization of a particular goal, some gain less, some are neutral (i.e., the zero case), some lose less, and some lose more. Of course, the attitudes partners assume during the process of social negotiation vary depending on the position of each individual partner. Those who lose a great deal, as well as those who gain a lot, stand in almost absolute conflict; in the case of average gains and losses, the conflict is somewhat more relativized, even more conspicuously so in the cases of small gains or losses. Therefore, if all partners promptly engage in social negotiation, i.e., from the very first iteration, then the number of iterations becomes too large, and the procedure of negotiation becomes too long, which in extreme cases may severely aggravate and even call into question a particular social contract.

Only after a great deal of practical experience and many delays in concluding social contracts did we gain some insight into the process of engaging certain partners in appropriate phases of negotiating. Those who lose a lot or gain a lot, i.e., who are very near the position +1 or −1, should not be brought in right away, if at all possible, for they hinder reaching a first variant of the text of a contract. Especially those who are at the −1 position, or near it, strive too hard to emphasize the question of who will compensate their losses. And once a discussion on compensation starts, that is, who has to pay whom, then the appraisal of the goal in question and ways to achieve it become secondary. Thus, according to past experience, negotiations should begin with partners who lose or gain moderately, excluding the zero case in the first iteration, because even a neutral partner, with his hesitant and frequently changeable stance, also contributes to a needless prolongation of discussions on controversial questions. It is best when the marginal as well as the neutral cases enter the process of negotiating only after the first draft of the contract has been drawn, where, on the basis of a previously selected optimal variant of the project, final negotiations can ensue. Most often this presupposes modest changes in the project itself. Although practice has shown that direct executors of goals on the one hand, and representatives of republics and provinces on the other (as well as the Federal Executive Council), should engage in negotiations, and that partners who lose, gain, or are neutral should be differentiated according to varying degrees of mutual conflict, and that the best methods of relativizing conflicts of development should be sought, it must nevertheless be said that performance in this area has not always been effective.

Namely, we again recall the aspiration of territories in a multinational country to be more powerful than industries, to participate more in the formulation of development strategy, and for that reason, to consider themselves competent enough for all types of social negotiation. Nevertheless, the different perceptions of economic and social development from the angle of the industry and the angle of the territory are sufficiently pronounced so that the variance must be respected during negotiations. This is the main reason why in the previous planning period only those social contracts were completely fulfilled which secured the agreement of both industry and territory (i.e., representatives of both on teams of experts that prepared the final texts of the contracts prior to their adoption by the respective self-management bodies).

The third problem, also very pronounced in social negotiations, is how to determine, on the basis of a project, the partners' actual gains and losses, as well as deciding on possible compensation for those who lost through no fault of their own. Here, as with goal projecting, very significant aid may be rendered by planning institutions, i.e., administrations for social planning and appropriate industrial sectors at economic chambers. Such help can take the form of necessary information supplied both on available resources by making resource balances, on balances of future needs and underutilized capacity, as well as on the construction of new capacity already begun or the expansion of existing facilities.[4]

Nevertheless, it often happens that during negotiations each partner deals mainly with his own data on how much he invests and how much he gains, and these data, as we have already noted, vary substantially regionally. Time and effort are needed to arrive at some common (not to say unified) position on each individual partner's losses and gains. Some people think that in analyzing who gains what and who loses what, one should not examine each project separately. Instead, all social contracts to meet goals contained in the General Program of the Federal Assembly for one midterm development period should be viewed cumulatively. Only after calculating the total sum of gains and losses for each partner (republics and provinces) can decisions on possible compensation be made. However, this attitude has not been accepted in practice because all republics and provinces are not always represented in all social contracts, that is, they are not all concerned in the same way about every goal. This question is discussed in practice for each goal for which a social contract is reached.

In analyses of why some lose while others gain, or, at least, why the differences in the gains are so great, different positions are often taken regarding the following two questions: first, is it in order to demand that so-called equal objective economic conditions be established to the fullest, especially, equal conditions for further development? Second, is the aspiration toward balanced growth of all parts of the economy, and of all the individual enterprises, justified and realistic? These two questions are always present in multinational countries![5]

Different objective economic conditions are the result of many factors, the most important of which are, without a doubt, the following: the previously attained level of development of the country as a whole; the various previously achieved levels of development of particular industries and particular regions, i.e., the entire different heritage; the differing positions of certain regions due to variations in present economic structures; the differing technical levels of certain industries; the different bearing of the international market on certain industries; and the various degrees of integration viewed intraindustrially and interindustrially, and thus the varying availability of the total mass of development resources, as well as the different possibilities of making use of economies of scale. All this objectively exists. An equal status for each and every industry, and even more so for each and every enterprise, is not possible. But self-managers want the same remuneration for the same amount of labor, and they demand that those differences in remuneration according to the results achieved which are not their "fault" be removed to the maximum possible extent.

The question is, therefore, to remunerate: according to the labor performed or according to the results achieved through the sale of one's products on the market? To the more developed it is more logical that payment be made according to results achieved, while the less developed prefer payment according to labor effectively performed. Were the less developed able to improve their economic position and the final results they achieved? To what extent does such an improvement depend on them, and where does the influence of so-called objective conditions begin? The complexity of the answers to such questions is enormous.

Second, looked at interindustrially and interregionally, does balanced growth exist at all? Is it at all possible; and if it is, then under what conditions?

While the first problem — equal remuneration for equally performed labor — has always been emphasized in particular by self-managers from less successful enterprises, the second problem — more balanced development of all parts of the country — has been posed by inhabitants of less developed regions.

Third, it is a well-known fact that totally balanced growth never occurs and never can, for some industries must always outpace others in development due to the different tempo of technical progress in individual industries. Moreover, the influence of individual industries on the general rate of economic growth, that is, on the rate of growth of material production and on the national income per capita, differs widely. This again causes disparate growth of individual regions in accordance with the distribution of industry among regions. In the longer run it does not mean that certain industries will always be the leading ones; their order changes as a result of scientific and technical progress and of changing international relations. But at any one time, somebody is always ranked first and somebody last.

And that is how we arrive at the fourth problem in social negotiation, i.e., to the question of compensating those who cannot realize even some minimal income. What should the compensation consist of, i.e., what forms can it assume, and who should give it? Even if all projects were so detailed as to show clearly who loses and how much, without personal "fault," through the realization of a projected goal, the question can be asked whether compensation should be linked to each individual goal or, as we have already mentioned, to a set of goals, which has as a consequence a greater number of discussions on compensation. Also, what form should compensation assume: only a monetary form, or the form of diverse aid during the projection as well as during the realization of a goal? Of course, here as well the differences are those between the more and the less developed: the less developed favor, almost exclusively, monetary compensation, while the more developed are also inclined to other forms of compensation (including aid in expert training of cadres).

Self-management negotiation between individual enterprises — between enterprises linked technologically in a production line or between producers and trading enterprises — is in practice a much simpler activity in the process of planning. Therefore cases of renewing old cooperation occur more often than cases of initiating new ties. However, if an old cooperation is at issue, it should be kept in mind prior to the conclusion of the agreement whether earlier cooperation with the enterprises dealt with was very successful, less successful, or possibly even unsuccessful. In other words, this past experience, so important in all forms of mutual negotiation, should be known. (This was noticed a long time ago by those who worked on cooperative game theory.) Depending on this experience (positive, neutral, or negative), it will be necessary to have as a basis of agreement not only appropriate variants of development programs and projects for essential goals but also analyses of who in the previous cooperation gained or lost, and how much.

Self-management agreements are formulated on the basis of the General Program for Future Development and thereafter coordinated with appropriate social contracts on the development of individual industries. That is, since the agreements are made (of course) between enterprises which are either only in production or in both production and trade cooperation, they do not encompass the whole industry, but the entire chain from the incipient to the final phase of production and marketing of some product. For this reason their coordination with social contracts which are concluded by industries is necessary. The role of the administrations for planning, and especially of chambers, in concluding agreements is reflected in the supplying of necessary information on time and quantity proportionality, as well as on resource coverage of projects. After coordination has been completed, the acceptance of the agreement by the appropriate self-management bodies of the enterprise ensues.

The development of the noneconomic sphere is an essential part of planning. Hence all services and all institutions which perform activities aimed at satisfying some specific needs of a nonmaterial nature formulate their respective development plans and take part in self-management agreements with enterprises benefiting from these services. Because of the pronounced inclination toward an increase in public consumption that we have noted, there is a tendency for the plans of these institutions to appear as integral parts of economic plans. Appropriate parts of development programs for services increasingly enter projects. Thereby these activities (scientific research, training of expert cadres, etc.) become more useful and more geared to the process of production; but in turn, production is not deprived of an inappropriate part of investment resources under conditions of insufficient domestic accumulation.

This process of linking plans of the noneconomic sphere with those from the economic realm in the whole of society, and especially the linking of trade with the sphere of production, is not so simple, for there is no direct connection between the expansion of material production and certain forms of noneconomic activities. For now, the actual procedure follows two lines: one part of the expansion of these activities becomes an integral component of large-scale development projects, while the other part enters development plans of corresponding territories and is financed from tax revenues on the incomes of citizens and enterprises.

Social and self-management negotiations together not only represent the basic means of attaining the final plan for development of the whole country but also the basic direction which the process of integration in the Yugoslav economy is following. At first glance, if integration were viewed in its legally formal aspect, i.e., as a joining of many enterprises into a combine, the impression could be obtained that the process of integration is going much slower than is actually the case. That is, information drawn from purely formal appearances provides an insufficiently correct and sometimes even an entirely erroneous view of certain social activities in practice — especially to outside observers. In Yugoslavia this occurs in the case of two essential social activities — planning and integration. It is true that the existing planning institutions (we have in mind primarily the administrations for social planning) have in many respects remained outside real life, for they reorganize themselves too slowly, and they are too slow to follow economic development and newly emergent problems. But others, for that reason, assume their roles. For example, as was already noted, economic chambers participate very actively in industrial planning. On the other hand, despite the relatively small number of formal integrational mechanisms at the national level (they usually stop at the frontiers of republics and provinces out of fear of an outflow of investment resources from their respective territories), integration actually appears in all those cases where contracts have been concluded for entire industries, at the same time having well-designed projects as a base.

III. The Control of Plan Implementation and the Evaluation of the Need for Corrective Measures

The road to the final development plan – General Program of the Federal Assembly–social contracts on strategic goals–self-management agreements – demands a special system for controlling plan implementation. The forms of control are numerous, and they are dealt with by a few institutions.

1. Of course, the basic form of control of plan implementation, i.e., of realization of contracts and agreements on certain goals, is effected jointly by the partners that concluded the contracts or agreements. Direct control is especially evident with agreements, for they are made between enterprises in the same production line. This control is continuous, so to speak, for every disruption in the connection line between producers that are technically connected (that is, between production and trade) is quickly noted.[5]

2. The second form of control of implementation of the social plan of Yugoslavia as a whole (and also of certain parts of that plan – the territories, industries, large integration groupings, etc.) takes the line of following success indicators. Such indicators are, of course, precisely determined and are controlled in different ways by five different institutions. They are: (1) administrations for social planning (planning boards); (2) economic chambers; (3) administrations for statistics; (4) social accounting services; and (5) banks. The first four of these institutions are organized at all management levels on a territorial basis – in municipalities, in intermunicipal communities, provinces, and republics,

and finally, at the federation level — and they constantly exercise control. Banks do so to the degree to which they are concerned as lenders (which is true for all commercial banks), or if it is within their competence to follow monetary trends (the National Bank of Yugoslavia and its republic branches).

The degree of competence of these institutions to react to the information supplied varies. One would expect the greatest intervention to be undertaken by the administrations for social planning and then by economic chambers. However, in our present practice this role is played by the social accounting services, which supervise complete financial transactions in enterprises and their associations and are authorized to prevent those financial transactions which are not in accordance with the existing financial regulations.[6] According to past experience, the chambers are still most effective in controlling development plan realization. They continuously conduct analyses of the realization of planning goals in industries or production groupings (production lines); their effectiveness is also greater in comparison with administrations for social planning because only a few success indicators are followed, and not a multitude of them, which sometimes obscures the essential point.[7]

3. The control of general economic flows is conducted through periodic analyses of the realization of selected development priorities as well as through analyses of the following important aggregate values: the total flow of accumulation, trends in balance-of-payments deficit, and trends in employment, that is, new employment. All this activity is performed by planning committees of the Federal Assembly and of republic and provincial assemblies, as well as by certain ministries in the government administration. Moreover, some of the aggregate values are also of special interest to certain sociopolitical institutions.

The volume of accumulation, the size of the deficit in the balance of payments, and the attained level of employment are, especially at this point in world development, essential for every country in the world; but their significance in small countries that are in the process of accelerated industrialization and that have a large supply of free labor power is especially pronounced. That significance is so great that it can freely be said that these three goals have absolute priority, i.e., that they are absolute development priorities, while all other priorities may be of varying strength and relative in importance. For that reason the quality of realization of the economic plan is best expressed by way of these goals. While following these three goals, certain points must be borne in mind in the current phase of Yugoslav development.

First, accumulation must be followed in both of its forms — as accumulation in real terms and as accumulation in monetary terms. We can say for certain that Yugoslavia, as well as by far the largest number of countries in the world, has for a long time paid much more attention to accumulation in monetary rather than real terms. As limits to growth manifested themselves in all their strength, it became clear that (apart from deficiencies in equipment, energy, raw materials, and food) an inadequate production structure, due above all to insufficient allotment of new investment to basic industries and agriculture, caused much deeper problems of accumulation — problems of deficiency of accumulation in real terms. To a large extent this is the case with Yugoslavia. The largest part of our imports consists of equipment, raw materials, and oil; the leap-frogging of their prices on the world market just further "melts" accumulation in monetary terms, which is already insufficient. The struggle for accumulation should therefore not be waged primarily in the sphere of national income distribution but in the sphere of new investment and its orientation toward technically modern equipment, raw materials, and new forms of energy.

Second, an increase in accumulation and an increase in new employment are often combined in the search for new ways to secure resources for development. It would be a great simplification to equate this problem with the growth of small private industries. The question here bears on a wider conception of what can be, and how it can be, left to private initiative in solving the problem of employment. Greater flexibility in providing new jobs is imperative; so it is necessary to determine through the plan those activities in which a greater degree of private initiative will be allowed, as well as desirable forms for private initiative to assume. Thus controlling the implementation of an entire program of new employment by means of mobilizing private resources would at the same time mean an inquiry into all the diversity revealed by practice.

Finally, the balance-of-payments deficit should be monitored in sectors of the economy and in republics and provinces. Also, as in the case of employment, various methods of association and cooperation with abroad should be followed, which will make possible more rapid resolution of the balance-of-payments situation.

Even though the monitoring of goals set by the plan also has its deficiencies, it must be said that it is more developed and more effective than the first form of planning activity, i.e., than the designing of projects for selected development goals and negotiating and making agreements on their basis. That is, while for the latter planning activity there exists an insufficient number of institutions (recall the lack of a special institute for forecasting, for example), in the former case their number exceeds what is needed (Social Accounting Service). Also, while in the former type of activity there is insufficient social regulation (recall that we still do not have the requisite uniformity of forecasting methodology or a uniform expression of needed indicators in projects), in the latter type of activity there is more such regulation than we would really deem necessary. Obviously, a process of transformation of the system of planning is taking place — a process marking the total disappearance of the previous system of planning and emergence and prevalence of self-management planning of all social development.

The use of corrective measures when it is determined that some of the goals anticipated by the plan remain unfulfilled varies, above all depending on whether the reason for nonfulfillment is external in nature (and demands our quick adaptation to a new situation) or is the consequence of internal, more or less foreseeable disruptions. Also, one sometimes comes to corrective measures because certain newly emerged disproportions are only recognized just before the plan is implemented, or the order of significance of inputs changes. Of course, the use of corrective measures, depending on their nature and magnitude, is sometimes also subject to negotiation between republics, provinces, and concerned industries. This follows because any correction not anticipated beforehand and included in the project changes the balance of power, i.e., changes the economic position of certain participants in the realization of a specific goal. This especially holds true for changes in the magnitude of some of the significant management parameters.

To be effective corrective measures demand a multivariant approach to development policy, at least two project alternatives, and of course, appropriate material reserves. All this must be borne in mind by self-management bodies during the adoption of plans for future development.

IV. Unresolved Problems

We can classify all open problems recognized up to now in our system of self-management planning into three groups: (1) problems related to the selection of development priorities; (2) problems which stem from the industry-territory relationship; and

(3) problems from the domain of planning methodology.

1. Selection of priorities in the medium-run development of the country. Here priorities are most clearly discernible, and, what is also very important, their persistence through the end of the planning period is a major problem of our planning. There are a number of reasons for this, of which we will cite only the most obvious ones. The selection of priorities is hindered in a multinational state by great disparities in the level of development of individual parts of the country, for, as we have ascertained, priorities differ in different territories; the very designation of priorities, and especially their strength, is subject to constant compromise under the conditions of self-management decision-making, especially if effective social control of their realization is not undertaken.

The selection of priorities is above all subject to a very complex procedure of negotiation between republics and provinces (industries are less evident in this phase). The attainment of an agreement on priorities was prolonged in the two previous five-year planning periods, and the number of priorities proved too large, which means that every one of them had thus been compromised. Regardless of some experience with previous plans, the formulation of the five-year plan for the period 1981-85 again shows that the selection of priorities remains the most complex problem for our planning in the medium run, for it is hard to make some republics and provinces relinquish some of their own priorities in favor of certain national Yugoslav goals. It is as though there are no counterpartners to the republics and provinces, in the form of associated industries within the process of negotiation, which would stimulate a greater selectiveness in choosing priorities. To a certain degree that is correct: at the Yugoslav level there is a lack of associated industries, especially of those which are the leading ones in the economic development of the country.

2. Thus we come to the second group of problems — problems which appear in the industry-territory relationship. We already stated that the basic goal-function manifests itself differently at the industry and at the territorial levels respectively (maximization of gross income per employed versus maximization of gross income per citizen); behavior also differs with respect to accumulation and consumption as well as to new employment. These factors combined demonstrate that the perception of development from the viewpoint of an industry and from the viewpoint of a territory differs. This occurs more or less openly in every country. But this obviousness is especially great in two cases: first, when differences in development among various territories are great, so

that different industries are represented differently in individual territories; and second, in a multinational country where sensitivity to the level of development is strong.

We had a period in our development when the organization of industries was stronger than territorial organization, and we experienced the shortcomings of industrial organization too powerful vis-à-vis territories. For example, in allocating new investments, industries acted according to the logic of the lowest costs of production, which prompted unequal territorial distribution in favor of the more developed territories. However, our current inadequate industrial organization reveals, it seems, far more deficiencies in new investment effectiveness than was the case before, even though it is obvious that the territory should not be underestimated as a development factor in a multinational state. Inadequate industrial organization (with a few exceptions — the electrical industry, ferrous metallurgy, nonferrous metals, railways, etc.) leads to slow intraindustrial and interindustrial integration, to insufficiently effective planning, and above all, to insufficiently emphasized priorities, to slower technical progress and application of scientific accomplishments, as well as, in particular, to an unnecessary increase in technological dependence on foreign countries. Industrial planning is necessary for more efficient development of goal setting. And such planning is, for now, the least developed part of our system of self-management planning, if we accept the division into industrial and territorial planning. Once more we emphasize: in a multinational country the normal aspiration of each territory to keep abreast with the country as a whole and not lag behind should not be hampered. For it is a positive aspiration from the standpoint of relations among nationalities. But if industrial organizations do not appear as sufficiently organized counterpartners, then integration will be slowed down, and less mobility of all productive factors, and especially of accumulation, will ensue, which will affect, in a familiar fashion, the general rate of economic growth. Finding the optimal relation between industry and territory is therefore essential in the process of planning; also essential are parallel growth and coordination of industrial and territorial planning, as well as methods which best maintain their balance. We are making vigorous efforts in this direction.

3. Planning methodology also has a few unresolved problems, the extent of which has essentially been perceived but whose solution will also require an appropriate amount of time, suitable in-

stitutions, and of course, adequate expert cadres.

First, a note regarding administrations for social development planning and their actual participation in the entire system of our planning. There is an old truism, verified many times in practice, that it is more difficult to radically change the manner of operation of certain institutions than to form an entirely new one that responds to new requirements. To a great extent this also holds true for our administrations for social planning. They do not engage in projecting technology (which is, beyond any doubt, the most important part of the technology of planning), even less in the unification of certain values used in projects; they also do not deal sufficiently with resource balances, i.e., degrees of their utilization upon realization of concluded contracts and agreements; they do not have an up-to-date and developed forecasting service, which would supply those working on projects with necessary information. This, of course, does not at all mean that a part of the work has not been taken over by the economic chambers; but it should be said that much remains to be done in this domain in the future. Inertia and routine, which sometimes appear in a powerful form in old institutions, will have to be eliminated by adequate social action. For again, the dubious and negligible utility of the so-called obligatory planning indicators cannot compensate for the lack of a modern project-estimating methodology.

To conclude this short exposition of the Yugoslav system of planning, two important points should be made. First, to an outsider it may seem that our system of self-management planning is being built quite slowly. However, one should not forget that we are the first and only country building a self-management system, and that we therefore frequently have to use the method of trial and error to determine what suits our new system, i.e., we have to make many attempts to decide what can and what cannot be successfully applied in practice. All this work would proceed a lot faster if there existed at least one more country with the same or a similar system, for the elimination of the tried and inadequate would be much faster.

Still, our experience is already a great deal richer, and our conclusions about the basic components of the system grow clearer.

Second, our new knowledge on the following issues should not be underestimated: how to approach negotiation of development goals and development policy in general; adequate social negotiation; the role of drafts of goals designed in at least two alternatives; relativization of conflicts due to various interests of specific regions or specific industries; and in particular, the optimal organization of industries and territories. Such knowledge already means a great deal in harmonizing individual and universal interests and goals, which is important in any social planning of future development. In short, the general line of development of self-management planning has become clear; more rapid and broader implementation of this line lies before us.

Notes

[1] Most frequently our discussions with authors from European socialist countries on the decision-making system diverge exactly on this point; this is because they usually maintain that they do not always have in mind the highest level but require at least one level above the one at which the problem occurred.

[2] Even this optimum should be viewed as relative in a country with large regional disparities, for if it were to be unreservedly implemented, an even greater gap could occur in the level of development, with familiar consequences for any country, especially a multinational one. Much world and Yugoslav research has shown that, sooner or later, the underdeveloped retard the growth of the whole economy due to disproportions in the development of certain industries.

[3] We note that the basic goal function of a Yugoslav economic enterprise — the maximization of gross income per employed worker — differs from the Soviet goal, which is maximization of gain from resources employed.

[4] According to current regulations, everybody is obliged to report a new investment that expands existing or constructs new capacity, so as to avoid excess capacity as well as the creation of bottlenecks.

[5] This method of planning the whole production line and the control of plan realization thereof is also practiced in some other countries, for the very technological process imposes it on a modern and more developed economy, in which so-called bottlenecks could be of too great a consequence for the entire economic development of the country, especially in the case of key industries and key products.

[6] Formed at one time to control the economic justification and a plan-based utilization of financial resources, and above all to protect accumulation so that it does not flow out into the noneconomic sphere in greater amounts than anticipated by the plan, the Social Accounting Service does not let the enterprise employ a more flexible policy of appropriation of gross income for personal consumption (salaries), public consumption (education, recreation, housing for the newly employed, etc.), reserves (material and monetary), and resources for new investments. Hence the proposed changes in the direction of limiting the rights of this institution, i.e., leaving to the self-management bodies in enterprises broader opportunities to administer the resources they have available.

[7] The administrations for social planning follow the realization of plans by means of seventy-three indicators, which proved to be too large a number, as well, in part, as an unnecessary duplication of effort with the statistical service.

3

INFLUENCE OF THE SELF-MANAGEMENT SYSTEM ON THE DEVELOPMENT OF THE YUGOSLAV ECONOMY

Jakov Sirotković

The development of the Yugoslav socialist self-managing socioeconomic system has created a new type of economy which has, in its turn, substantially influenced changes in earlier classifications of economic systems and interpretations of the economic categories customary in economic literature.

Although economic science in capitalist countries, considering their specific historical conditions, has been inhibited by a crude approach to the analysis of present-day socioeconomic trends, and although this approach seems to be disappearing rather slowly in other socialist countries, the specific character of the Yugoslav system, its consistency, and long-term nature could not be neglected.

Thus a theoretical study on organizational alternatives in socialist economies divides the latter into centralized and decentralized. Centralized socialism is further divided into controlled economies and the classic Soviet economy. Decentralized socialism is divided into the reformed classic Soviet system and market trade unionism, the latter implying the Yugoslav economy.[1]

Another general systematization of economic systems distinguishes traditional economies, market economies, and controlled economies in terms of their social mechanisms, and capitalist and socialist economies in terms of their systems of ownership of the means of production. This classification treats Yugoslavia as a socialist market economy.[2]

The Yugoslav economy has in recent years been the subject of an increasing number of studies in most socialist countries. Several serious analyses have pointed out its specific socialist character, based on social ownership, self-management, and socialist commodity production.[3]

However, one still feels the presence of Stalinist-oriented criticism which treats the Yugoslav solution as rightist revisionism, i.e., rather like a bourgeois economy or as market socialism; this criticism would disqualify it as socialist, since such critiques treat the market and commodity production as salient features of the capitalist mode of production. Although such analyses cannot be considered serious economics because of their entirely erroneous interpretation of the salient features and basic facts of Yugoslavia's socialist self-managing system, they should nevertheless be mentioned because of their unfavorable political impact on the normal, scientific study of present-day socialism.[4]

The salient features of Yugoslav economy, which make it a consistent unity and which provide for its specific character as compared with economies of other types, are primarily: social ownership of means of production (the salient feature of its economic structure); self-management of working people in enterprises and production (the salient feature of its economic system); and the focusing of the overall process of expansion of social forces of production on the continuous improvement of the material and cultural living conditions of the working people (the salient feature of its economic policy).

Although "the economic structure" is meant to suggest the totality of relations in production (social conditions or factors) and forces of production, the specific features of the Yugoslav economy stem from the relations in production or social conditions and are primarily related to the character of social ownership of the means of production.

In Yugoslavia the process of socialization of the means of production started as early as the War of National Liberation; immediately after the war social ownership of the means of production became dominant, while the share of private ownership has continuously decreased. Private ownership or the private sector of ownership of the means of production has to date been retained only in agriculture, where it still predominates, in the building trades and handicrafts, and only slightly in transportation, trade, the catering industry, and tourism.

This process can be illustrated by changes in the structure of the gross domestic product in individual activities. Qualitative changes have therefore affected not only social but material conditions. Moreover, the process of qualitative changes in the economic structure has also started in agriculture, as illustrated by the structure of the gross domestic product in agriculture (see Tables 1-3).

However, the decisive point for the development of socialist relations in production has been the emergence of the self-management system and its growth into the fundamental form of socialist production relations in Yugoslavia.

The emergence of self-management was associated with the simultaneous reduction of state functions and with the process whereby state ownership, as the initial form of socialist public ownership of means of production, was gradually transformed into social ownership managed by associated producers. Accordingly, the overall superstructure also had to be adjusted to new relations in the community, which resulted in adequate changes throughout the former. In the sphere of the economy this has had a decisive impact on the adjustment of the economic system and overall economic policy to the requirements of the self-managing community.

The fundamental aspects of the economic system, comprising the organizational forms, methods, and resources required for the running of socially owned production, have been substantially adjusted to the requirements of self-managing social relations.

This initially implies the development of organizational forms in the management of social activities as a whole, and particularly the development of such forms in the economy. Enterprises have become basic self-managing factors of economic activity, and the overall social superstructure has also begun to change in accordance with their interests. This has also brought about major changes in the functions of all agents of economic policy.

The conditions of economic activity in enterprises changed in accordance with the interests of the self-managing agents of economic policy. Where primary distribution is concerned, these conditions are primarily related to the objectivization of their economic position in the market; with regard to secondary distribution, they are associated with the development of such methods as would simultaneously provide an incentive for the best possible utilization of production forces and the fulfillment of the overall requirements of the society. The groundwork was also provided for the development of other methods (and resources) whereby the community can influence economic trends in an organized way;

Table 1

Yugoslavia's GDP per Type of Activity

Activity	1947	1952	1957	1962	1967	1972	1977
	(in millions of dinars; 1972 prices)						
Total	54,245	59,743	92,781	129,383	181,520	245,567	325,933
Manufacturing and mining	9,899	12,967	23,174	38,764	58,707	86,510	123,596
Agriculture	21,515	18,363	31,567	32,330	39,608	40,317	50,858
Forestry	2,669	2,225	2,008	2,404	2,461	2,598	3,031
Construction industry	7,218	7,460	7,318	13,525	19,346	25,991	34,386
Transport and communications	2,753	4,015	6,577	10,587	14,955	20,969	28,458
Trade	6,934	7,290	11,804	19,425	29,863	46,164	56,733
Catering and tourism	...[1]	2,675	3,221	3,838	5,282	7,663	9,282
Handicrafts	3,258	3,181	4,139	4,095	5,723	7,775	10,060
Public utilities				842	925	1,247	1,398
Water management[2]						726	1,026
	(in %)						
Total	100	100	100	100	100	100	100
Manufacturing and mining	18.2	22.7	26.0	30.0	32.3	35.4	38.0
Agriculture	39.7	31.8	34.1	25.0	21.8	16.5	15.6
Forestry	4.9	3.8	2.3	1.8	1.5	1.1	0.8
Construction industry	13.3	12.6	7.9	11.4	11.7	11.6	11.8
Transport and communications	5.1	6.8	7.1	9.2	8.2	8.4	8.5
Trade	12.8	12.3	13.8	15.9	17.7	19.8	18.6
Catering trade and tourism	...[1]	4.6	3.3	2.9	2.9	3.1	2.9
Handicrafts	6.0	5.4	5.5	3.2	3.3	3.2	3.0
Public utilities				0.7	0.6	0.5	0.4
Water management[2]						0.3	0.4

Sources: Statistical Yearbook of Yugoslavia, 1976, p. 81; Statistical Yearbook of Yugoslavia, 1978, pp. 81, 148, and 149.

[1] Counted in trade up to 1952.

[2] Counted in agriculture up to 1962.

Table 2

Structure of Productive Fixed Assets in Yugoslavia
1946-66
(net value; 1960 prices; in %)

	1946	1953	1957	1963	1966
Total	100	100	100	100	100
Social sector	71	79	81	85	87
Private sector	29	21	19	15	13

Source: Ivo Vinski, "Fixed Assets 1946-1966," Jugoslavenski pregled, 1968, no. 6, pp. 233-40.

this in particular bears on final distribution and the coordinated growth of the overall process of expansion of the social forces of production.

The complexities associated with the development of a system intended to additionally strengthen the self-managing rights of enterprises in controlling resources for the expansion of production capacity will not be discussed here. They are primarily related to a scheme of banking resource utilization which serves the direct interests of enterprises. A dynamic analysis of the growth of the capital formation capacity of enterprises reflects rapid progress. Thus, for example, in 1962 annual accumulation proper (resources distributed to operating funds) of enterprises would have permitted the doubling of their productive facilities only after 55 years; in 1964 the figure was reduced to 22.5 years, and in 1966 to 14 years.[5]

Economic policy, being an organized activity of the community in the economy, has also gradually adjusted to the requirements of self-managing society. This does not apply solely to formulating the goals of economic policy — the direct realization of socialist policy aimed at continuously furthering the material and cultural living conditions of working people; rather, basic progress in the rate and change of structure in internal distribution was due precisely to the new conditions in the community.

Since the implementation of the self-management system, the results shown in Table 5 have been achieved in characteristic periods of Yugoslav economic development with regard to the rate of growth of GDP and the basic categories of consumption.

Of particular significance in this picture are the growth ratios of personal consumption to GDP. If elements of public services

Table 3

Structure of GDP in Yugoslav Agriculture

(million dinars; 1972 prices)

	1952		1957		1962		1967		1972		1977	
	Amount	Structure (%)	Amount	Structure (%)	Amount	Structure (%)	Amount	Structure (%)	Amount	Structure (%)	Amount	Structure (%)
Total	18,363	100	31,567	100	32,330	100	39,608	100	40,317	100	50,858	100
Social sector	3,018	16.4	2,680	8.5	5,485	17.0	8,322	21.0	9,366	23.2	12,522	24.6
Private sector	15,345	83.6	28,887	91.5	26,845	83.0	31,286	79.0	30,951	76.8	38,336	75.4

The self-managing agents of economic policy in enterprises have gradually expanded the sphere of their competence in the economy and in the community, which has had a particularly pronounced bearing on the strengthening of their facilities and resources. Initially the say of self-managing bodies in controlling the results of their operations was quite slight; subsequent developments, however, have changed the situation to the point where they control most of the total realized income and, moreover, the greater part of the net product or national income (total income minus material costs and depreciation charges). (See Table 4.)

Table 4

Structure of Realized Net Product (Income)
(in %)

	1962	1965	1966	1967	1968	1969	1970	1971	1972	1973	1974	1975	1976
Realized net product	100	100	100	100	100	100	100	100	100	100	100	100	100
For public and welfare requirements	54.9	43.7	40.0	43.0	43.1	43.2	42.9	39.5	40.5	41.3	40.8	41.8	43.7
For organizations of associated labor	45.1	56.3	60.0	57.2	57.1	56.8	57.1	60.5	59.5	58.7	59.2	58.2	56.3

Sources: Balance-Sheets for 1965-1966, FSO (Federal Statistical Office), Studies, Analyses and Reviews, no. 39, p. 99; Balance-Sheets for 1962-1965, FSO, Studies, Analyses and Reviews, no. 39, p. 88, Belgrade, 1966; Balance-Sheets for 1966-1971, FSO, Studies, Analyses and Reviews, no. 61, Belgrade, 1972; Balance-Sheets for 1973, FSO, Studies, Analyses and Reviews, no. 73, p. 109, Belgrade, 1975; Balance Sheets for 1976, FSO, Studies, Analyses and Reviews, no. 91, pp. 84-85, Belgrade, 1975.

Table 5

GDP, Personal Consumption, Welfare Services and Public Expenditure, and Gross Investments
(average rates of growth, in %)

Period	GDP		Personal consumption		Welfare services and public expenditure		Gross investments in fixed assets	
	current prices	1972 prices	current prices	1972 prices	current prices	1972 prices	current prices	1972 prices
1953-60	14.3	8.0	14.0	7.9	6.6	3.3	14.5	9.5
1956-60	15.9	11.3	14.6	9.2	9.2	5.9	19.4	16.5
1957-66	19.5	7.5	19.3	7.0	15.5	6.8	19.2	9.4
1961-70	18.7	6.4	19.4	6.2	16.8	5.6	18.0	5.9
1971-76	23.7	5.0	24.2	4.5	28.1	7.0	26.1	6.5
1953-76	18.8	6.6	19.0	6.5	16.0	5.2	19.2	7.4

Source: _Balance-Sheets for 1976_, FSO, _Studies, Analyses and Reviews_, no. 91, Belgrade, 1977, pp. 70-71.

and housing, covered less by public expenditure and more by investments, were added to personal consumption, the trends of GDP and the standard of living in general would be even more favorable. These ratios differ qualitatively from those attained in the period of administrative economic control or in the capitalist, prewar Yugoslav state. Such ratios have not been achieved, even for shorter periods of time, in any other country regardless of its socioeconomic system.

The second characteristic element of Yugoslavia's economic policy under self-management conditions refers to trends in changes in its social and material structure.

The process of rapid development brought about changes in the material structure of production, which meant the strengthening of its socialist character (social to private sector ratios) and which provided for the implementation of the proclaimed socialist goals of economic policy in relation to the standard of living (industrial to agricultural output ratio). Moreover, particular emphasis should be placed on the fact that the rate of growth of agricultural production was relatively rapid, and that stable growth of agricultural production in the socialist sector was assured. Both are important, for they show to what extent economic policy is conditioned by the socialist character of social relations based on self-management, and how unfounded are the theses about the introduction of capitalist elements into the Yugoslav self-management system because of the strengthening of the commodity character of production.

Because economic-political decision-making in the self-management system is primarily based on autonomous decisions by enterprises, the rationality of the latter should also be considered; the more so as the critics of the self-management system thought that overall decision-making in matters concerning the expansion of production capacity could not be transferred to enterprises because of the danger of income being redistributed to personal incomes and personal consumption, i.e., because of the risk of reducing the capital-formation capacity of the national economy. Although this thesis is theoretically untenable to begin with, an empirical analysis of the behavior of the self-managing agents of economic policy only provides grounds for claiming that decision-making under the new conditions has become more rational than under the conditions of administrative centralism.

The economic rationality of the behavior of self-managing enterprises in the social sector can be seen in Table 6. The changes

Table 6

Distribution of Net Income to Personal Incomes and Funds within the Net Income Structure of Enterprises in the Social Sector (structure in %; current prices)

	1962	1964	1966
Net income, total	100	100	100
Personal incomes	72.2	65.8	64.6
Funds	27.8	34.2	35.6

Source: M. Korać, Analysis of Economic Position of Individual Industries, p. 33 and table 1, pp. 130-31.

demonstrated in Table 6 are due to the policy of enterprises in the period from 1962 to 1966. Personal incomes increased (at current prices) by almost two and a half times (244%), and the amount distributed to funds by almost four times (392%). The thesis of nonrational behavior by self-managing agents of economic policy is defended by pointing to the increase, in the same period, of the percentage of total realized income in the social sector of the economy distributed to personal incomes, i.e., from 31.4% in 1962 to 38.5% in 1966. However, supporters of this view appear to neglect the fact that the percentage distributed to funds increased in the same period even more rapidly, from 12.4% to 21.3%, i.e., by 8.9 percentage points, because of the increased share of net income of enterprises within the overall realized income of the national economy.[6]

International comparisons also confirm the efficiency and rationality of the Yugoslav self-management system. One such comparison for the period from 1950 to 1974 is shown in Table 7.

Of the capitalist countries, only Japan had a slightly higher average rate of growth of GDP per capita; among the socialist countries this was the case with Romania, Bulgaria, and the USSR.

In these comparisons particular significance should be attached to the fact that in the case both of Japan and of Bulgaria and Romania, economic policy was primarily focused on rapid increases in output and the capital-formation capacity. In this connection the rate of growth of personal spending and public services and housing lags considerably behind the overall rate of growth.

With an average rate of growth in excess of 10%, over a fifteen-year period (1952 to 1967) the average rate of growth of real

Table 7

International Review of Rates of Growth of Gross Domestic Product
(fixed prices; in %)

	1951-60		1961-70		1971-74		1961-74		1951-74	
	total	per capita	total	per capita	total	per capita	total	per capita	total	per capita
The world	5.2	3.3	5.5	3.5	5.7	3.4	5.4	3.4	5.3	3.3
I Countries with a centrally planned economy*	9.3	7.7	6.8	5.7	6.4	5.5	6.8	5.7	8.0	6.7
II Developed countries**	3.8	2.7	5.0	3.9	4.1	3.2	4.7	3.7	4.2	3.2
III Developing countries	...	...	5.3	2.7	6.4	3.9	5.7	3.1	...	...
I										
Bulgaria	9.1	8.1	8.2	7.4	7.6	7.1	8.1	7.3	8.6	7.7
Czechoslovakia	7.3	6.3	4.2	3.6	5.3	4.7	4.9	4.3	6.1	5.3
German Democratic Republic	10.8	11.6	4.4	4.4	5.4	5.3	4.9	4.9	7.8	8.2
Hungary	4.9	4.2	5.4	5.1	6.6	6.3	5.8	5.4	5.4	4.8
Poland	8.1	6.1	6.2	5.1	10.7	9.8	7.0	6.0	7.6	6.0
Yugoslavia	9.2[2]	8.0[2]	6.6	5.5	6.4	5.4	6.6	5.5	7.9	6.7
Romania	9.0	7.6	8.6	7.6	11.4	10.4	9.1	8.0	9.0	7.8
USSR (without the Ukraine)	10.4	8.6	7.2	5.9	5.7	4.8	7.1	5.9	8.7	7.3
II										
United States	2.9	1.2	4.6	3.3	3.3	2.5	4.1	2.9	3.5	2.1
Canada	4.0	1.2	5.6	3.7	5.6	4.2	5.6	3.7	4.8	2.4
Japan	8.0[6]	6.8[6]	10.5	9.4	6.8	5.5	10.0	8.8	9.0	7.8
Federal Republic of Germany	7.7	6.6	4.6	3.5	3.2	2.6	4.5	3.5	6.1	5.0

United Kingdom	2.7	3.5	2.8	2.3	3.1	2.8	2.8	2.3	2.8	2.3
France	4.4	3.5	5.7	4.6	5.2	4.3	5.7	4.7	5.1	4.1
Belgium	2.7[3]	2.0[3]	4.7	4.1	5.2	4.8	4.9	4.4	3.8	3.2
Sweden	3.6	2.9	4.4	3.7	2.8	2.4	4.0	3.3	3.8	3.4
Holland	4.6	3.3	5.5	4.1	4.1	3.1	5.4	4.1	5.0	4.4
Denmark	3.2	2.5	4.7	4.0	3.2	2.5	4.4	3.7	3.8	3.5
Italy	5.5[4]	4.9[4]	5.3	4.6	3.8	3.6	4.9	4.2	5.2	4.5
Austria	5.9	5.7	4.5	4.0	5.6	5.1	4.9	4.4	5.4	5.1
III										
Morocco	0.5[2]	−2.3[2]	3.9	1.0	4.7	1.5	4.2	1.2	2.3	−0.6
Tunisia	...	...	4.4	2.4	9.7	6.1	5.9	3.8	...	...
Uganda	4.5[5]	1.5[5]	4.7	2.1	0.6	−2.6	4.0	1.2	4.0	1.3
Bolivia	−0.3	−2.6	6.0	3.4	5.7	3.0	5.9	3.2	2.8	0.2
Chile	3.3	0.9	4.5	2.0	1.2	−2.0	3.9	1.6	3.6	1.2
Colombia	4.7	1.5	5.1	1.8	6.8	3.5	5.6	2.3	5.2	1.9
Mexico	6.3	3.0	7.3	3.8	6.3	2.8	6.9	3.4	6.6	3.2
Pakistan	...	...	5.2	2.2	3.7[1]	0.6[1]	4.7[1]	1.6[1]	...	...
Indonesia	...	...	3.0	0.4	7.3[1]	4.3[1]	4.1[1]	1.4[1]	...	...
Ethiopia	...	...	4.6[6]	2.4[6]	3.6	1.1	4.3	2.0	...	...

Sources: United Nations, Yearbook of National Accounts Statistics, 1969 and 1975.

*Net material product (NMP).

**Gross domestic product (GDP).

1 The data refer to the period up to 1973.

2 The data refer to the period since 1952.

3 The data refer to the period since 1953.

4 The data refer to the period since 1951.

5 The data refer to the period since 1954.

6 The data refer to the period since 1961.

workers' wages in Japan amounted to 4 to 5% per annum.[7] The high profit rate and cheap labor were the principal factors underlying Japan's rapid growth.[8] This case involves a traditional capitalist profit-motivated economic policy which provided for a very high average rate of growth of production owing to specific Japanese conditions.

The specific character and the content of the Yugoslav economy, as the unity of an economic structure, economic system, and economic policy, are based on self-managing socialist relations in production. These relations have developed as a new form of the socialist social system, whose inherent specific developmental stimuli and motives distinguish it qualitatively from any other past system of production relations.

The onset of self-management also marked the start of qualitative changes in the development of socialist relations in production and in decision-making with respect to the resources required for the expansion of production capacity. In this connection the development of socialist Yugoslavia can be divided into two stages: the first, involving the expropriation of the bourgeoisie through state authority, which concentrated and centralized the resources of the community for the development of the productive forces; and the second, distinguished by the transition to "association of labour and to a free, proper organization of its division."[9]

The self-management system started developing in 1950 on the basis of prior political decisions.[10] The example of the Paris Commune served as the foundation in the consideration of these historical decisions.[11]

In addition there had been a number of other, less significant experiences, although they were no more than attempts to introduce workers' management in individual enterprises and branches. The respective works of Marx, Engels, and Lenin, although primarily concerned with the analysis of the historical significance of the Paris Commune, offered the political leadership an initial theoretical foundation at the stage of introducing the self-management system in Yugoslavia.[12] Of particular significance was the interpretation of the Marxist theory of the state and of the withering away of the state under socialism.[13]

In spite of the foregoing, the initial stimuli during the introduction of the self-management system in Yugoslavia derived from the specific character of social and material conditions under which socialist Yugoslavia began to develop. This involved changes in the socioeconomic structure which were the logical consequence of the War of National Liberation and which, immediately after the Liberation, showed how very necessary it was to seek one's own path and to depart from the Soviet "model."[14] This led to the gradual deterioration of relations with the political leadership of the Soviet Union, to political pressure, and to the economic blockade of Yugoslavia.[15]

The development of the self-management system as the fundamental form of socialist production relations in Yugoslavia can systematically be divided into several basic stages.

The first stage started with the passing of the aforementioned law on workers' councils and workers' management of the economy and the simultaneous decentralization of state administration of the economy. Neither step, however, involved qualitative changes in relations of production, but they set the essential organizational prerequisites required to start these changes. Decentralization of administration of the economy meant only a vertical disintegration of authority but not yet the withering away of state functions in this sphere.

The second stage in the development of the self-management system started in 1954, with the introduction of the new economic system whereby enterprise self-management bodies were granted the right of autonomous decision-making with regard to the volume and structure of production. Market economy elements of greater importance began to appear in the system, and an entirely new set of instruments and measures was introduced, which for the greater part indirectly influenced the business policies of enterprises. In this stage enterprises mainly controlled the resources for normal operation and only part of depreciation. An element of incentive was introduced: profit, permitting the formation of resources for expansion of production capacity on a very limited scale and the increasing of wages above set limits according to the qualifications of the employed and the individual industries.[16]

The third stage in the development of the self-management system began in 1957, when the self-management bodies in enterprises acquired the right to control the resources intended for personal incomes. This actually involved autonomous decision-making with regard to the distribution of net income into personal incomes and funds, full freedom in decisions regarding the distribution of resources available to the enterprise for personal incomes, and limited control of the resources distributed to funds. In this stage the resources for expansion of production capacity were mainly controlled by central government bodies. This stage was decisive for establishing the foundations of self-managing society. That is, such changes in the system of production relations gave the self-managing bodies ascendancy over central government bodies in influencing both the approach to economic policy and its implementation. Economic policy was finally focused on improving the material and cultural living conditions of working people, this being its fundamental objective.[17] This objective is achieved by self-managing decisions on income distribution to personal incomes. Ever since, self-managing relations have developed by virtue of their own driving motives, and political decisions of government bodies as a rule have become dependent on the directly expressed interests of the self-managing agents of economic policy in the enterprises. This was also a stage at which the conflict of interest culminated between self-managing units, which mainly controlled the resources for normal operation, and the central agents of economic policy, which mainly controlled the resources for expansion of production capacity.

The socioeconomic reform of 1965 marked the start of the fourth stage in the development of the Yugoslav self-management system. The reform was essentially focused on the implementation of the principles laid down in the Constitution, i.e., the rights and the role of producers in matters regarding the expansion of production capacity.[18] This meant an orientation toward such changes in controlling the results of operation, particularly the distribution of surplus product, as would make the self-managing agents of economic policy in enterprises the basic agents of the overall process of expansion. In this connection a plan was drawn up for the period 1966-70 which considered the program of development precisely on this basis.[19]

Good results on these lines were achieved only at the outset of plan implementation; subsequently, however, the situation deteriorated and did not improve until 1970. Hence the five-year plan for 1971-75 again emphasized, among its basic goals, the strengthening of self-management relations and of their economic foundation, this being, after all, the constant goal of the Yugoslav socialist community.[20]

The fifth stage was ushered in by the constitutional changes of 1971 and 1974 (when the new Constitution was adopted), which introduced qualitative changes into production relations and the political system, and which also provided the starting point for corresponding changes in the economic system. Of particular significance in this period has been the establishment of basic organizations of associated labor, the basic organizational cells of the community, in which the workers control operation and expansion in their totality, and which in turn provide the foundation of the system of delegation of authority — the basis of decision-making at all levels within associated labor and on a broader, societywide scale. This stage can be said to have marked the end of one period in the development of the socialist self-management system, characterized by duality because of the still felt presence of state-socialist relations, and the beginning of a new period, distinguished essentially by the association of labor. It also promoted the development of socialist relations of production into a more elaborate form in which social ownership becomes predominant and in which technocracy and bureaucracy are losing their material and social positions. The overall system, political and economic alike, has been made subservient and adjusted to such relations of production, which means that the process also involves the establishment of a consistent socioeconomic system dominated by internal driving motives which by themselves, and with the support of the forecasts of the associated producers, lead to more stable development focused on the attainment of the natural interests and goals of the working class.[21]

Notes

[1]See B. Ward, The Socialist Economy — A Study of Organizational Alternatives, New York, Random House, 1967.

[2]See Gregory Grossmann, Economic Systems, Englewood Cliffs, New Jersey, Prentice Hall Inc., 1967.

[3]See L. F. Karinia, Iu. K. Kniazev and L. V. Tiagumenko, Ekonomika Iugoslavii, Moscow, "Ekonomika," 1966.

[4]See V. Mazur, Ekonomicheskii revizionizm. Kritika revizionistkoi vulgarizatsii politicheskoi, ekonomii sotsializma, Kiev, Ordena trudovogo krasnogo znameni izdatel'stvo politicheskoi literaturi Ukraini, 1976, pp. 140-240.

[5]See M. Korać, Analysis of Economic Position of Individual Industries Based on the Law of Value (1962 to 1966), Zagreb, Institute of Economics, 1968, p. 46; idem., Income Policy in Self-managing Commodity Economy, Aggregate Analysis of Economic Position of Individual Industries 1967-1970, Belgrade, Institute of Investment Economics, 1972.

[6]Ibid., pp. 32-33.

[7]See Saburo Okita, Causes and Problems of Rapid Growth in Postwar Japan, Tokyo, Japan Research Economic Center, March 1967; and V. Pertot, Japan at the Focus of Economic Policy, Zagreb, Sveučilišna naklada Liber, 1978.

[8]Only recently have the Japanese begun to ask that the government pay adequate attention to the interests of consumers in improving housing conditions and public utilities. Past government policies have been criticized for having been predominantly focused on production, neglecting everyday living problems.

It is a fact that so far, while industry, agriculture, and trade had a strong influence on governmental policy, this was not the case with consumers as a group.

In the early postwar years the government was mainly concerned with rehabilitating basic industries such as coal, iron and steel, fertilizers, power, and food. Subsequently the attention of the government was drawn to the policy of basic industry modernization, the establishment of new industries including petrochemistry, export promotion, the protection of agricultural production, etc. Monetary policies and banking practices were also mainly focused on production, as confirmed by the fact that thus far Bank of Japan loans have mainly been granted to manufacturers and traders, and not so much to consumers.

Thus the "production first" policy, in spite of some undesirable social repercussions, has certainly contributed to the rapid growth of production (Okita, p. 21).

[9]V. Bakarić, *Questions Regarding the Development and Building of Socialist Self-Managing Socio-Economic Relations in Production, and the Tasks of the League of Communists in this Sphere*, Komunist, 1973, p. 9.

[10]See J. B. Tito, "On Workers' Management of Enterprises" (policy statement at the National Assembly, Belgrade, June 26, 1950), in J. B. Tito, *Messages of the Revolution*, BIGZ, 1973, p. 110; and "Basic Law on Management of State-Owned Enterprises and Trade Associations by Work Collectives," *Official Gazette*, 1950, no. 43.

[11]See B. Kidrič, *Collected Works*, Belgrade, Kultura, 1961.

[12]See K. Marx, *Civil War in France* (with foreword by Engels).

[13]V. I. Lenin's *The State and the Revolution* was of particular significance.

[14]The problem of collectivization in agriculture was initially one of the central issues where agreement could not be reached. See V. Bakarić, *The Problem of Land Rent in the Transition Period*, Zagreb, 1950.

[15]The relevant documents were published in 1948, while economic pressure reached its culmination in the latter half of 1949. See V. Dedijer, *The Lost Battle of Y. V. Stalin*, Sarajevo, 1969.

[16]See J. Sirotković, *New Economic System of the FPRY*, Zagreb, Školska knjiga, 1954.

[17]See "Programme of the League of Communists of Yugoslavia," in *VII Congress of the LCY*, Belgrade, Kultura, 1958.

[18]See *Eighth Congress of the League of Communists of Yugoslavia*, Belgrade, Komunist, 1964, p. 231; and V. Bakarić, *The Socialist Self-managing System and Social Reproduction*, Zagreb, Informator, 1974.

[19]See "Social Development Plan for Yugoslavia 1966-70," *Official Gazette*, 1966, no. 28, chap. 1, par. 11.

[20]See "Social Development Plan for Yugoslavia 1971-75," *Official Gazette of the SFRY*, Belgrade, 1972.

[21]See J. B. Tito, *The League of Communists of Yugoslavia and its Efforts in Promoting the Development of Socialist, Self-Managing and Non-Aligned Yugoslavia, report at the XI Congress of the League of Communists of Yugoslavia*, Belgrade, Komunist, 1978; V. Bakarić, *Socialist Self-Management System and Social Reproduction*, vol. 2, Zagreb, Informator, 1978; E. Kardelj, *Social Ownership Contradictions in Present-Day Socialist Practice*, Belgrade, Radnička štampa, 1972; *Lines of Development of the Political System of Socialist Self-Management*, Belgrade, Komunist, 1977; *Free Associated Labour — Brioni Discussions*, Belgrade, Radnička štampa, 1978.

4

INVESTMENT POLICY

Dragomir Vojnić

1. Introduction

Throughout the postwar period Yugoslav investment policy has been oriented toward rapid growth of the material basis of Yugoslav society. Such an approach has been particularly evident during the developmental phase, which is based on the foundations of socialist self-management.

As in many other developing countries, industrialization was adopted as the basic method of Yugoslav development. Consequently it has become one of the basic characteristics of our investment policy.

Generally speaking, the entire postwar period has been characterized by intensive activity in the field of investing in and accumulating fixed assets. The result of this effort has been dynamic production growth as measured by the gross domestic product and national income and relatively rapid changes in some basic structural characteristics of the Yugoslav economy.

These rapid changes, especially in the socioeconomic structure of the population and in production, have led to a decline in the inherited great historical differences between Yugoslavia's economic development and that of other advanced countries.[1]

We will focus here on only the most important aspects of postwar investment policy: the investment rate, the investment structure, the economic efficiency of investment, and demographic investment. In doing so we will rely on statistical series for gross investment and gross domestic product computed in fixed 1972 prices,[2] as a basis. The period under survey is limited to the years the Yugoslav socioeconomic system has been based on the principles of socialist self-management.

2. Rates of Investment

As is well-known from the theory and practice of economic development, the process of investment in and accumulation of fixed assets is in a direct and functional interrelation with the process of expanded social reproduction, i.e., with the process of economic development. This is why the achieved rates of investment in and accumulation of fixed assets are significant criteria for the effectiveness of the investment policy and accumulation system in a developing country that operates on the foundations of socialist self-management. This point becomes clearer if we bear in mind the fact that many problems entailed in the system of self-management social planning flow from the goal of achieving specific socioeconomic development targets by means of an adequate rate and structure of investment. Naturally, such targets must be reached, in a socialist self-managed society, by the interaction of the social planning system and the part of economic policy related to investment policy.

The major motives for accumulation based on income maximization have had so great an effect that economic policy has had to try much harder to reduce investment to economically rational limits than to stimulate business organizations to accumulate and invest, i.e., to accelerate the process of expanded social reproduction and overall economic development. The incentives to capital accumulation contributed significantly to placing Yugoslavia among the countries with the relatively highest production growth rates in the postwar period, i.e., with the highest growth rates of gross domestic product and national income, and thereby in investment and fixed assets. This point is illustrated in Table 1.

If we analyze the rates of gross investment in the whole economy (Table 1), we see that the intensity of investment in Yugoslavia during the postwar period was relatively steady, considering the average values derived for time intervals of several years.

If the time intervals under survey are compared, we notice a tendency to accelerate investment intensity in fixed assets and to

Table 1

Rates of Gross Investment for Overall Economy and Social Sector of Yugoslavia, 1952-77 (in %)

Year	Social sector on a gross basis		Overall economy on a gross basis	
	total investment	economic investment	total investment	economic investment
1952	34.9	31.5	28.5	23.9
1953	39.9	34.6	30.2	23.8
1954	39.8	31.1	31.2	22.6
1955	35.7	29.0	26.6	19.9
1956	34.7	27.3	27.5	19.8
1953-56	37.4	30.3	28.7	21.4
1957	35.7	25.8	27.5	18.3
1958	36.8	25.8	31.0	19.6
1959	38.3	27.0	30.4	20.0
1960	39.3	27.4	33.9	21.5
1961	39.3	26.7	35.9	21.4
1957-61	38.1	26.6	32.1	20.3
1953-61	37.9	27.9	30.9	20.7
1962	43.7	28.8	29.1	23.1
1963	43.3	28.2	39.3	23.0
1964	44.2	29.5	40.5	24.4
1965	36.1	22.9	35.3	19.8
1966	30.9	21.1	30.6	17.9
1967	32.5	26.4	32.3	22.4
1968	34.8	28.3	34.3	24.0
1969	35.1	28.8	33.7	24.3
1970	35.3	28.5	34.1	24.6
1971	32.0	26.1	31.9	22.9
1972	28.9	23.0	28.3	20.4
1973	26.7	21.1	28.4	18.7
1974	28.0	21.9	30.0	19.9
1975	30.6	24.2	31.7	22.0
1976	33.2	25.7	33.0	23.2
1977	33.0	25.9	33.5	23.5
1962-77	33.2	25.3	32.9	22.1
1965-77	31.8	24.8	32.0	21.9
1953-77	34.0	25.8	32.5	21.8

increase gross domestic product in the second period in relation to the first. While the rates of total gross investment were 30.9 and 20.7% in the period 1953-61, they amounted to 32.9 and 22.1% respectively in the following period, 1962-77.

When analyzing the data, we ought to bear in mind that the scope of the survey did not include either investment in working assets or investment in inventory growth. If we take into account these investments as well, the share of total gross investment in the gross domestic product in some years would amount to over 40%.

We should also mention that this survey only deals with investment from domestic funds. The additional accumulation from abroad, which was relatively high in some years, is not included in the analysis.

If the scope of the survey is limited to the social sector, we can say that in recent years about one fifth of the gross investment in fixed assets of the social sector was realized through purchase from abroad, equipment bought on credit, and utilization of the part of financial credits designated for financing investment.[3]

Table 2 shows the rates of gross investment in Yugoslavia and

Table 2

Gross Investment Rates in Some Developed Countries
(in %)

Country	Rates of investment							
	1969	1970	1971	1972	1973	1974	1975	1976
Canada	21	21	22	21	22	23	24	23
France	25	26	26	26	24	25	23	23
West Germany	24	26	27	26	25	22	21	21
Italy	20	21	21	20	21	23	21	20
Japan	35	35	34	34	37	34	31	30
Great Britain	18	18	18	18	18	20	20	19
United States	17	16	17	18	18	18	16	16
Belgium	21	23	22	21	21	22	22	22
Denmark	22	22	22	22	23	22	20	22
Ireland	25	25	23	21	22	..	22	..
Holland	24	25	25	23	23	22	21	20
Norway	25	27	30	28	20	32	35	36
Sweden	22	22	21	22	22	22	21	21
Yugoslavia	34	34	32	28	29	30	32	33

Source: Statistical Yearbook 1975, New York, UN, 1978.

some developed countries in the period 1969-76. When comparing these rates, we must bear in mind that in view of different methods of calculating gross domestic product, the actual differences in the rates of investment between Western countries and Yugoslavia are somewhat smaller.

This article does not make comparisons with socialist countries because social bookkeeping in those countries does not apply the gross concept. A comparison on a net basis, however, would not change the general assessment of high rates of investment in Yugoslavia.

The fact remains that in the postwar period Yugoslavia has entered the group of countries with highly intensive investment activity. That intensity, in terms of the share of gross investment in the final allocation of the gross domestic product, varied in different socialist republics and provinces of Yugoslavia as shown in Table 3.

When comparing the intensity of investment by individual republics and provinces, it is clear that it is inversely related to the level of their development. This is quite in accordance with one of the primary aims of our investment and economic policy: to diminish historic regional differences in the level of economic development.

Particularly high rates of total investment in fixed assets were achieved in Yugoslavia in the periods 1964-68 and 1974-77. The first period embraces the socioeconomic reform begun in 1965, when the share of gross investment in fixed and working assets reached more than 40% of gross domestic product.

This is why one of the important tasks of the reform was to reduce the rates of investment and investment outlays. Along the same line, a special task of the reform was to improve the relation between investment in fixed assets and investment in working assets, because in the period 1964-67 investment in working assets and inventory growth amounted to over 10% of the total domestic product.[4]

The second period is the last five-year period, when the share of total investment outlays in the overall distribution of gross domestic product was over 40%. In 1974 and 1975 the share of investment in working assets was rather high and amounted to over 10% of the gross domestic product distribution. The relation between investment in fixed and working capital improved in the last three years, with a decline in investment in working capital. Since investment in fixed assets increased during the same period, the

Table 3

Rates of Yugoslav Gross Investment in 1972 Prices by Republics and Provinces, 1953-77
(in %)

Period	Republics									
							Serbia			
	all Yugoslavia	Bosnia and Herze- govina	Monte- negro	Croatia	Macedonia	Slovenia	total	Serbia proper	Kosovo	Vojvodina
1953-56 total	28.8	37.1	80.0	23.1	40.0	28.8	25.7	31.5	17.2	13.1
economic	21.4	29.6	64.2	17.0	29.3	20.8	18.4	22.0	13.1	10.5
1957-61 total	32.1	32.0	67.1	27.2	39.9	27.2	34.7	36.7	40.8	29.0
economic	20.3	20.1	53.7	17.1	26.9	15.8	21.9	20.7	32.3	23.1
1953-61 total	30.9	33.9	72.0	25.8	39.9	27.7	31.6	34.9	31.9	23.7
economic	20.7	23.6	57.6	17.1	27.7	17.6	20.7	21.1	25.1	18.9
1962-77 total	32.9	38.8	51.3	30.4	42.4	29.1	32.1	31.5	55.6	29.2
economic	22.1	25.2	40.2	19.8	29.6	20.3	21.4	20.5	39.0	20.2
1965-77 total	32.0	38.7	49.1	29.6	37.1	28.5	31.3	30.8	54.3	28.0
economic	21.9	25.4	38.8	19.6	27.4	20.3	21.4	20.7	38.5	19.5
1953-77 total	32.5	37.8	55.1	29.5	42.0	28.8	32.0	32.1	51.1	28.2
economic	21.8	24.9	43.4	19.2	29.2	19.8	21.3	20.6	36.4	20.0

total rates of investment rose, amounting to over 40% of the gross domestic product.

This is the reason why one of the primary tasks of the stabilization policy is to diminish such intensity of investment and thereby to reduce the rate of investment and investment outlays,[5] since all analyses and assessments of economic trends and economic policy indicate that high investment expenditures are one of the main causes of inflation.

3. The Structure of Investment

If we analyze the structure of gross investment in fixed assets in Yugoslavia in the postwar period, we can easily detect some characteristics of the economic and development policy. They relate particularly to the fact that industrialization has been one of the basic methods of economic development in Yugoslavia.

The data in Table 4 indicate that about two thirds of the total

Table 4

Structure of Overall Gross Investment in Yugoslavia, in 1972 Prices, 1953-77
(in %)

Sector	1953-56	1957-61	1953-61	1962-77	1965-77	1953-77
Industry and mining	45.8	29.9	35.2	35.0	35.6	35.0
Agriculture and fishing	9.5	12.9	11.8	7.5	7.1	8.3
Forestry and hunting	1.3	1.0	1.1	0.8	0.7	0.8
Construction	1.9	1.8	1.9	2.6	2.8	2.5
Transport and communications	11.5	13.1	12.5	13.0	13.5	12.9
Trade and catering	3.3	3.5	3.4	7.1	7.6	6.4
Crafts	1.1	1.0	1.0	1.1	1.1	1.1
Total economic activities	74.4	63.2	66.9	67.1	68.4	67.0
Housing and public utilities	19.5	28.5	25.5	25.3	24.2	25.4
Culture and social activity	3.6	4.6	4.3	5.3	5.3	5.1
Public services and government agencies	2.5	3.7	3.3	2.3	2.1	2.5
Total noneconomic activities	25.6	36.8	33.1	32.9	31.6	33.0
Total economic and noneconomic activities	100.0	100.0	100.0	100.0	100.0	100.0

gross investment in fixed assets in Yugoslavia in the postwar period under survey were invested in economic activities, and over one third in the sector of industry and mining.

If we limit the framework of the survey only to the productive sectors, then the share of gross investment in the fixed assets of industry and mining in total gross investment would increase to over 50%. The data in Table 5 show that such relations were relatively stable and did not change much over the period under survey. A considerable departure from this assessment is evident only in the period 1953-56, which were the years of intensive attempts to industrialize the country, as reflected in the very high share of gross investment in fixed industrial assets amounting to over 60%.

After gross investment in the fixed assets of industry and mining, the second largest share in the overall structure of gross economic investment relates to the sector of transport and communications, amounting to about 20%. This sector is also characterized by relatively stable fluctuations during the period under survey. As in the industrial sector, somewhat greater departures are noted

Table 5

Structure of Total Economic and Total Noneconomic Gross Investment in Yugoslavia, in 1972 Prices, 1953-77
(in %)

	1953-56	1957-61	1953-61	1962-77	1965-77	1953-77
Industry and mining	61.6	47.3	52.6	52.2	52.0	52.3
Agriculture and fishing	12.7	20.5	17.7	11.1	10.3	12.3
Forestry and hunting	1.8	1.6	1.1	1.1	1.0	1.2
Construction	2.6	2.9	2.8	3.9	4.1	3.7
Transport and communications	15.4	20.7	18.7	19.4	19.8	19.3
Trade and catering	4.5	5.5	5.1	10.6	11.1	9.6
Crafts	1.4	1.5	1.4	1.7	1.7	1.6
Total economic activities	100.0	100.0	100.0	100.0	100.0	100.0
Housing and public utilities	76.1	77.4	77.1	76.8	76.8	76.9
Culture and social activities	14.2	12.5	12.9	16.2	16.7	15.6
Public services and government agencies	9.7	10.1	10.0	7.0	6.5	7.5
Total noneconomic activities	100.0	100.0	100.0	100.0	100.0	100.0

only in the first three-year period, when the share was considerably lower.

Everything that has been said thus far about the structure of gross investment in Yugoslavia in the postwar period undoubtedly confirms our view that industrialization was the dominant method of the development concept and development policy during the whole period under survey.

In analyzing and assessing investment policy within the sector of industry, it is of particular interest to take into consideration the structure of gross investment in fixed assets by individual industrial complexes.

This can be easily illustrated with the data in Table 6, which show that over 30% of total investment in the fixed assets of industry and mining, in the period under survey, was in the power-supply complex, but that the intensity of such investment was considerably higher in the first years.

Table 6

Structure of Gross Investment by Individual Industrial Complexes in Yugoslavia, in 1972 Prices, 1953-77 (in %)

Industrial complex	1953-56	1957-61	1953-61	1962-73	1965-73	1953-73	1974-77*
Power	35.2	36.1	35.7	28.4	28.4	30.3	30.7
Basic metals	23.9	10.3	16.2	17.6	17.7	17.2	14.4
Equipment and durable consumer goods	10.2	11.9	11.2	14.2	13.9	13.4	14.3
Chemical industry	7.2	7.1	7.2	8.8	8.8	8.4	7.6
Building materials and nonmetallic industry	6.1	5.6	5.8	6.2	6.8	6.1	7.0
Food industry	5.0	8.7	7.1	7.7	8.4	7.6	9.2
Wood industry	5.2	7.5	6.5	6.7	5.9	6.6	7.8
Textile, leather, and rubber industry	4.1	8.6	6.6	8.2	8.1	7.8	7.5
Other industries	3.1	4.2	3.7	2.2	2.0	2.6	1.5
Total	100.0	100.0	100.0	100.0	100.0	100.0	100.0

Source: Dragomir Vojnić, Investicije i društvena reprodukcija, Zagreb, Informator, 1977, p. 61, table 9.

*The figures for the period 1974-77 are computed in current prices and are taken from Federal Bureau of Statistics, Announcements, Belgrade, 1975, 1976, 1977, and 1978.

Next in intensity of investment after the power-supply complex comes basic metals, followed by equipment and durable consumer goods, chemicals, etc.

Everything said about the investment structure so far refers to the average for Yugoslavia as a whole. However, as one would expect, the structure of gross investment in fixed assets by individual socialist republics and provinces tends to differ from the Yugoslav average, as illustrated in Table 7.

If we limit the scope of the survey to the relations between gross investment in fixed assets of productive and nonproductive

Table 7

Structure of Gross Investment in Yugoslavia and its Republics and Provinces, in 1972 Prices, 1953-77
(in %)

Sector	Republics									
	all Yugoslavia	Bosnia and Herzegovina	Montenegro	Croatia	Macedonia	Slovenia	Serbia — total	Serbia proper	Kosovo	Vojvodina
Industry	35.0	39.9	41.0	29.4	39.3	37.1	34.6	33.8	46.8	32.7
Agriculture	8.3	4.7	3.4	7.3	11.2	5.9	11.1	7.1	10.1	21.9
Forestry	0.8	1.9	1.2	0.9	0.5	0.9	0.3	0.3	0.3	0.3
Construction	2.5	2.6	1.5	2.6	2.9	2.9	2.2	2.4	1.9	1.8
Transport and communications	12.9	11.9	23.8	14.6	10.1	12.9	12.1	14.2	8.1	7.9
Trade and catering	6.4	4.0	7.4	9.5	4.8	8.0	5.1	5.3	3.3	5.1
Crafts	1.1	0.9	0.4	1.0	0.9	1.6	1.1	1.2	0.7	1.1
Productive sector	67.0	65.9	78.7	65.3	69.7	68.6	66.5	64.3	71.2	70.8
Housing and public utilities	25.4	26.9	16.1	28.2	22.4	22.0	25.6	27.3	21.2	22.4
Cultural-social activities	5.1	5.1	3.2	4.6	4.9	6.9	5.0	5.1	5.8	4.6
Government agencies and others	2.5	2.1	2.0	1.9	3.0	2.5	2.9	3.3	1.8	2.2
Nonproductive sector	33.9	34.1	21.3	34.7	30.3	31.4	33.5	35.7	28.8	29.2
Total	100.0	100.0	100.0	100.0	100.0	100.0	100.0	100.0	100.0	100.0

sectors, the greatest departure from the Yugoslav average would appear in Montenegro, Kosovo, and Vojvodina, where the proportion of productive sector investment in the total gross investment of productive and nonproductive sectors is considerably higher than the Yugoslav average. Great differences occur in the structure of gross investment in fixed assets between republics and provinces within total investment in both the productive and nonproductive sectors. Regardless of the fact that industrialization was the basic method of development and development policy in all republics and provinces, there were considerable differences in the intensity of investment in the field of industry and mining.

The highest above-average rates of gross investment in industrial sectors are noted in Bosnia and Herzegovina, Montenegro, Macedonia, and Kosovo. This is in accordance with the targets of Yugoslav development policy in this period, which were aimed at more rapid development of industry in the underdeveloped republics and the province of Kosovo.

Considerable differences in the intensity of investment in other sectors, particularly in agriculture and transportation, exist between republics and provinces depending on natural and acquired conditions, i.e., on structural characteristics and the phase of development. Departures in the structure of gross investment from the Yugoslav average are also evident in the nonproductive sector.

It can be generally said that the structure of investment is a reflection of basic elements in the development policy and the corresponding period of socioeconomic development. Along the same line, we ought to say that the structure of total, and in particular industrial, investment is influenced by a number of objective factors, such as the natural and acquired conditions of development, structural characteristics of a given phase of development, location and regional arrangement, etc. We need not emphasize that the structure of both total and industrial investment by individual republics and provinces has also been influenced by an active policy calling for more rapid development of underdeveloped republics and provinces, as well as by strategic considerations, etc.

Among the factors which can produce differences in the structure of gross investment in fixed assets of the overall economy and industry by republics and provinces, and thereby influence the allocation of productive resources and production facilities in republics and provinces, growing influence will attach to environmental protection in the future phase of our socioeconomic development. As the Yugoslav economy has entered the phase of functional interdependence of applied science, technology, and general technical progress, on the one hand, and economic development, on the other, concern for the human environment has become increasingly important when making decisions about the regional or geographic allocation of production facilities.

Considering various aspects of the investment structure, it is interesting to point out the technical structure of investment, as presented in Table 8. In the light of the statement that optimums in the technical structure of investment ought to be sought by means of maximizing the share of equipment (directly increasing the technical capacity of live labor and thus enhancing its productivity) and minimizing the share of construction work (in objectively given technical-economic conditions and limits), we note the tendency toward a moderate improvement in the technical structure of total economic gross investment in fixed assets of the social sector.

The data in Table 8 indicate a tendency to reduce the share of construction work and increase the share of equipment in the total technical structure of gross investment in fixed assets of the so-

Table 8

Technical Structure of Social Gross Investment of the Economy and Industry in Yugoslavia and its Republics and Provinces, in 1972 Prices, 1953-77 (in %)

Republics and provinces	period	total	construction work	equipment	others
Total economy					
Yugoslavia	1953-61	100.0	43.9	45.5	10.7
	1962-77	100.0	43.5	48.3	8.2
	1953-77	100.0	43.6	47.8	8.6
Industry					
Yugoslavia	1953-61	100.0	40.3	50.6	9.1
	1962-77	100.0	34.4	56.7	8.9
	1953-77	100.0	35.5	55.6	8.9

cial sector of the economy. If we limited the scope of the survey only to gross investment in industry, a similar tendency would be evident but, of course, at a different level. Regardless of the fact that the technical structure of investment is determined by the given phase of development and sectoral structure of investment, we can assess the tendencies discovered as positive.

The above-mentioned characteristics of investment policy in the period under survey resulted in rapid growth of fixed assets in the overall economy and industry. The growth index of the gross value of fixed assets for the whole period from 1953 to 1977 was 393. The average geometric growth rate was 5.9% per year.

If we limited the scope of the survey only to the gross values of fixed assets of industry and mining, we would get an index of 680 and an average geometric growth rate of 8.3%[6] per year. Hence over two thirds of the value of Yugoslav industrial equipment was purchased during the last fifteen years. The share of automatic and semiautomatic crankshafts was in the same proportion.[7]

All this indicates the great role played by technical progress and the application of science and engineering, and the corresponding technology, in the postwar period, particularly in Yugoslav industrial development. In addition to increasing employment, it has been one of the most important targets of investment policy.

4. Economic Efficiency of Investment in Terms of the Capital Coefficient

One of the important criteria for analyzing and assessing the results of an investment policy is the economic efficiency and social profitability of investment. Trends in capital coefficient values provide very relevant information for an analysis and assessment of the economic efficiency and social profitability of investment, as well as for an analysis of some essential aspects of the interdependence between investment and economic development.

The data on gross values of the marginal simultaneous capital coefficient are presented in Table 9. The survey refers to the whole period from 1953 to 1977, as well as to shorter time intervals within that period, and covers both the economy as a whole and individual sectors. Table 9 clearly shows great differences in gross values of marginal simultaneous capital coefficients among different sectors of the economy, i.e., different kinds of activities.

Table 9

Marginal Simultaneous Capital Coefficient of Yugoslavia, 1953-77
(1972 prices)

Sector	On a gross basis					
	1953-56	1957-61	1953-61	1962-77	1965-77	1953-77
Economy, total	3.7	2.3	2.7	3.9	4.1	3.6
Industry	5.4	3.4	4.1	4.6	4.9	4.5
Agriculture	1.6	2.5	2.2	4.5	4.5	3.5
Construction	-1.5	0.5	0.8	1.5	1.6	1.3
Transport and communications	6.1	5.6	5.7	7.9	7.8	7.4
Trade and catering	1.0	0.6	0.7	1.9	2.2	1.6
Crafts	0.6	1.0	0.8	1.2	1.2	1.1

Note: The marginal simultaneous capital coefficient is computed as the ratio of gross investments to the increase in gross domestic product.

We can say in general that the sectors with greater organic composition of resources (what in a figurative sense can be called a greater "specific gravity" of investment) have higher capital coefficient values. Consequently, the highest values of capital coefficients can be seen in the transport and communications, industrial, and agricultural sectors, while the values are considerably lower in other sectors. The lowest capital coefficient values are evident in the crafts sector.

The first conclusion drawn from these observations regarding trends in marginal simultaneous capital coefficients concerns the great differences in values of capital coefficients in different sectors of the economy. Another important conclusion drawn from the data in Table 9 concerns differences in capital coefficient values over shorter time intervals within the whole surveyed period. As regards the economy as a whole, the increase in the coefficients was from 2.7 in the first period (1953-61) to 3.9 in the following period (1962-77).

Such growth tendencies in capital coefficient values are evident in all sectors of the economy, but with varying intensity. The greatest intensity is found in agriculture, trade and catering, and construction, while it is somewhat smaller in the other sectors. The increase in industry was from 4.1 to 4.6, while in transport and communications it was from 5.7 to 7.9.

The flow of capital coefficient values was different in different republics and provinces. These differences will, however, be discussed in the following section, which deals with the rates of demographic investment.

The existing theoretical-methodological framework is still unable to provide very concrete and definite answers (in the sense of corresponding economic laws) that would explain the behavior of capital coefficients in different phases of development.

The assumption, however, remains that it is possible to produce a gradual stabilization (or even a decrease on a longer-term basis) of capital coefficient values in the future developmental phase. Our assumption is based on the fact that fragmentary observations of general opportunities to influence the flow of marginal capital coefficient values showed a clear interdependence of these trends and the quality of planning and decision-making. Therefore the quality of planning and decision-making in basic and other organizations of associated labor is of particular significance for enhancing the economic efficiency and social profitability of investment.

We can further say that the trends of social profitability and economic efficiency of investment are only a synthetic expression of the quality of numerous decisions on investment made and coordinated at various levels of self-managed organizations of associated labor. Such assessments are of particular importance for preparing a new five-year social plan for the period 1981-85. There are good reasons to assume that these preparations, as part of the operation of the self-management social system, will have a significant effect on changes in existing relations within the system of expanded reproduction in terms of enhancing self-investment (whose present share is one third), and the economic efficiency and social profitability of investment. This is, in fact, a unique process, simultaneously resulting in enhancing the quality of social relations and in introducing more qualitative elements into economic conditions.

The investment policy of the future developmental period must take into account all these questions, particularly the issue of the coordination of development plans and the question of improving the quality of investment decisions.

5. Rates of Demographic Investment

The rates of demographic investment in Yugoslavia, and its republics and provinces, from 1953 to 1977 have been computed as the product of marginal simultaneous capital coefficients and rates of population growth (Table 10). The figures in Table 10, which cover the whole period from 1953 to 1977, show that a specific rate of demographic investment of 3.6% is derived on the basis of the marginal capital coefficient of 3.6 and the rate of population growth of 1.0%. This further means that 3.6% of the gross domestic product must have been invested during the whole surveyed period in order to maintain the same per capita achieved level, considering natural population growth.

Since the rate of gross economic investment in fixed assets was 21.8% in the same period, the rate of economic investment for the whole period under survey, i.e., of the investment representing per capita reproduction of the gross domestic product, amounted to 18.2%.

One of the most relevant conclusions, drawn on the basis of an analysis of the relations presented in Table 10, is that 16.5% of the total gross investment in fixed assets of the economy should

Table 10

Rates of Demographic Gross Investment in 1972 Prices in Yugoslavia and its Republics and Provinces, 1953-77

	Yugoslavia	Bosnia and Herzegovina	Montenegro	Croatia	Macedonia	Slovenia	Serbia, total	Serbia proper	Kosovo	Vojvodina
K	3.6	4.4	7.2	3.2	4.5	3.1	3.4	3.4	5.8	3.1
P	1.0	1.5	1.3	0.6	1.4	0.7	1.0	0.8	2.5	0.7
S	21.8	24.9	43.4	19.2	29.2	19.8	21.3	20.6	36.4	20.0
Sd	3.6	6.6	9.4	1.9	6.3	2.2	3.4	2.7	14.5	2.2
Se	18.2	18.3	34.0	17.3	22.9	17.6	17.9	17.9	21.9	17.8
	S = 100.0									
Sd	16.5	26.5	21.7	9.9	21.6	11.1	16.0	13.1	39.8	11.0
Se	83.5	73.5	78.5	90.1	78.4	88.9	84.0	86.9	60.2	89.0

K — marginal simultaneous coefficient.
P — rate of population growth.
S — rate of gross investment.
Sd — rate of demographic investment.
Se — rate of economic investment.

have been made in order to maintain the same achieved level of per capita gross domestic product, taking into consideration population growth during the surveyed period.

Another significant question is the role, place, function, and character of demographic investment in the economic development of Yugoslavia during the period under survey. We can say in general that the specific values and rates of demographic investment in Yugoslavia as a whole during the period 1953-77 did not present any obstacles to the process of economic development but, on the contrary, acted as an important developmental factor.

This general assessment would, however, be slightly modified if the problem of demographic investment were treated from a regional aspect — it would be less favorable for certain Yugoslav republics and provinces.

Having dealt with the theoretical and methodological aspects of the problem of interdependence between investment and economic development, we can say that the factors that determine the rate and amount of demographic investment (i.e., the marginal capital coefficient [representing a general rate of demographic investment and population growth rate]) are, in a sense, inversely related to the level of economic development of the country as a whole or a specific region. The empirical research done on the basis of the practice and experience of our postwar economic development revealed such tendencies in the formation of concrete rates and amounts of demographic investment by republics and provinces.

Table 10 presents data on general and concrete rates of demographic investment. They clearly show that less developed republics and provinces have higher rates of demographic investment, and vice versa. More developed republics, such as Slovenia, Croatia, Serbia, and Vojvodina, have considerably lower rates and amounts of gross demographic investment than the less developed republics and the province of Kosovo. The lowest rates of demographic investment in the period 1953-77 are seen in Croatia, Slovenia, and Vojvodina, and the highest are evident in Montenegro and Kosovo.

In the discussion above on regional aspects of demographic investment, we pointed out certain relations and tendencies that emerged during the period surveyed. But if we consider specific time intervals within the surveyed period, we note considerable fluctuations in some relations and values when compared to the relations and values for the surveyed period as a whole.

For the purpose of this study, however, the most important

point is that the regional aspect of the analysis of demographic investment in Yugoslavia generally confirms the assumptions that the basic variables — the marginal capital coefficient and the population growth rate (the rate of demographic investment being their function) — are highly unfavorable in less developed countries and regions and in developing countries. Such a tendency is actually a general world phenomenon. Since Yugoslavia is historically a mosaic that represents the world on a small scale, the tendencies of capital coefficient behavior we have discussed (which even have certain characteristics of an economic law) can easily be demonstrated through the example of Yugoslavia and its republics and provinces.

Such behavior by capital coefficients in Yugoslavia and its republics and provinces indicates that an equal amount of investment does not make an equal contribution to economic development in different countries, in different developmental phases of the same country, or even in different regions of the same country in the same phase of development.

The differences in capital coefficient behavior were, in our specific case, the result of different structural characteristics of individual Yugoslav republics and provinces, as well as of different phases of development. These differences could have been influenced by relative prices and relations in primary distribution as components of the structural characteristics.

The behavior of the rates of demographic investment, however, can create a problem for countries with high capital coefficients and high population growth rates. Therefore some developing countries (China, India, and others) have undertaken special measures in the field of demographic policy and family planning.

We can positively state, without going into this complex group of problems, that they can be solved by the more rapid socioeconomic development of underdeveloped countries or developing countries — achieved primarily by applying the method of industrialization. This requires different economic relations between the developed and underdeveloped countries of the world than those that presently exist. Such relations would have to ensure a more intensive redistribution of gross domestic product and accumulation in favor of underdeveloped and developing countries. This is the main sense of the struggle of these countries for a new international economic order aimed at more just and more purposeful socioeconomic and political relations among the developed and underdeveloped parts of the world than those that presently exist.

There is no need to emphasize that the existence of demographic investment in a given economy signifies the process of reproduction on an expanded scale of the most important factor in any economy and society — the human factor.

In spite of considerable differences in the rates of demographic investment among republics and provinces, we cannot talk about demographic investment as a problem of development in the postwar developmental phase, considering the unity of the Yugoslav market and economic system.

One conclusion relevant for economic and development policy that can be made in connection with the existing distribution of demographic investment by republics and provinces in the previous developmental period is that such behavior of the rates of demographic investment slowed down the process of reducing the historic differences between more developed and less developed regions in the country. This further suggests an urgent need to continue the active policy of more rapid development, applying the method of industrialization of less developed republics and regions, especially the province of Kosovo.

6. In Lieu of Conclusions

Some basic characteristics of Yugoslav investment policy in the postwar period are summarized in this section.

Among a number of characteristics, we shall point out only the two considered most important. They are the great intensity of investment outlays expressed in high rates of gross investment, and industrialization as a basic method and strategic target of development and investment policy. The share of gross investment in fixed assets amounted to about one third of the gross domestic product during the whole period under survey. If we include investment in working assets, i.e., inventory growth, this share for certain time intervals within the surveyed period rose to over two fifths of the gross domestic product. This applies to the last developmental period within the current five year plan, 1976-80, as well. The share of total gross investment in fixed assets in industry and mining in overall gross investment amounted to 35%, and in gross investment in fixed assets of the economy, more than 52%.

These characteristics of investment policy entailed some advantages and disadvantages that emerged during the surveyed period. The advantages were very rapid growth of productive capacities and production, rapid employment growth accompanied by positive movements in the field of productivity of labor and technical progress, as well as some results in the policy of more rapid development of the underdeveloped republics and the province of Kosovo.

This consequently caused tremendous changes in the basic structural characteristics of the Yugoslav economy, particularly in the socioeconomic structure of the population, in the share of industry in the total gross domestic product, and in the changed living and working conditions of all Yugoslav citizens. This also applies to the field of the material basis and social superstructure.

The positive changes occurring as a result of investment policy can be summarized in the fact that Yugoslavia has lost the characteristics of an agrarian — industrially underdeveloped — backward, semicolonial country and become an industrial country at a medium level of development. The historic differences between Yugoslavia and the other developed countries of the world have thus been reduced.

The disadvantages of investment policy in Yugoslavia — of very intensive investment outlays — include stringency of financial resources to fund part of investment outlays, a large share of foreign funds and heavy indebtedness of the country, insufficiently coordinated investment in various interdependent and complementary programs and projects, the unsatisfactory quality of investment decisions, unsatisfactory trends with regard to the economic efficiency and social profitability of investment, and finally, the fact that the weaknesses of Yugoslav investment policy we have discussed represented one of the main generators of inflation and instability in economic trends. Therefore our economic, development, and investment policy will have to take into account all these experiences, particularly the weaknesses and mistakes, when it contemplates the upcoming development period, i.e., the new five-year plan, 1981-85.

Notes

[1] See Ivo Vinski, Kretanja društvenog proizvoda svijeta od 1910-1975, Zagreb, Ekonomski institut, 1978.

[2] See Investment in Capital and Working Assets (Social and Private) 1947-1973 in Current and 1972 Prices, Belgrade, Institute of Investment Economics and Zagreb and Belgrade, Institute of Economics, 1975; "Economic Flows of Yugoslavia in 1973," Studies, Analysis, and Reviews, no. 73, Belgrade, 1975, Federal

Bureau of Statistics, pp. 94-95, and Statistical Yearbook 1978.

[3]See Miroslav Prica, Formiranja i sektorska alokacija sredstava za finansiranje fiksnih radova, Zagreb, Ekonomski institut, 1975, p. 28.

[4]See the collective works, Aktuelni problemi privrednih kretanja i ekonomske politike Jugoslavije, Zagreb, Ekonomski institut, 1968, and Problemi provodjenja društveno-ekonomske reforme, Zagreb, Ekonomski institut i Informator, 1969, pp. 17-25.

[5]See Dragomir Vojnić, ed., Aktuelni problemi privrednih kretanja i ekonomske politike Jugoslavije, Zagreb, Ekonomski institut i Informator, 1978, pp. 21-35.

[6]These data are prepared on the basis of work by Ivo Vinski, Nova i stvarna vrednost fiksnih fondova privrede Jugoslavie od 1953-1976 u cijenama 1972, Zagreb, Ekonomski institut, 1978.

[7]See Dragutin Radunović, "Produktivnost rada u jugoslovenskoj privredi," in Produktivnost rada i efikasnost privredjivanja, Belgrade, Savezni ekonomski savet, 1977, pp. 13-28.

5

THE MONETARY AND CREDIT SYSTEM OF YUGOSLAVIA—REASONS FOR ITS FREQUENT CHANGE

Ivo Perišin

Very frequent changes in Yugoslavia's banking and credit system call for an explanation, particularly now that major new changes are again under way. An insufficiently informed or superficial observer, or one who makes no effort to look for the deep social, economic, and political reasons for these changes and the effects they are intended to achieve, might be left with an impression of reorganization for reorganization's sake or even of a reorganizational mania. Some pedantic students of these developments have counted about a dozen major reorganizations, which would seem to support criticism of an excessive frequency of change that undermines the stability of all organizational forms, all relations and instruments, and also creates staffing difficulties in the banking, credit, and monetary sphere. The critics find some arguments for their views in organizational solutions and policy instruments adopted at certain points and then soon abandoned when they proved inadequate. On this basis they readily conclude that practically all changes have been mere improvisations.

However, if one examines in detail the history of the continuous transformation of the Yugoslav banking and credit system over the past thirty years, and if one relates these changes to the aspirations of Yugoslav society and the objective conditions under which it has developed, one will soon find — even if one has no special liking for the Yugoslav model of socialist society and its goals — a deep rationale for this process. This approach will enable one to understand many of the developments, and even the occasional failures, which have all stemmed from a desire to achieve a thorough transformation of society and to build an adequate and necessary structure of banking and credit relations, different from the one existing at present in this or any other country. In considering these developments in Yugoslavia, as well as developments in other spheres of social life, it is always important to keep in mind the starting point and the ultimate objective.

The Yugoslav community of peoples was born in a tragic and devastating war; the economic basis of the country at the end of the war was either very backward or else totally destroyed; finally, the war left a legacy of great political traumas. This community, such as it was, opted for a socialist path of development and set itself highly ambitious economic, social, and cultural goals. As a multinational community burdened by very great differences in economic structure and levels of development between different constituent units, Yugoslavia — despite its great concern for national rights in the federal state — first opted for a state-controlled, centralist model of social and economic development. This model, with elements of strict centralization of resources and subordination in planning and decision-making, notwithstanding all political commitments and wishes to the contrary, could not but display the characteristics of a unitarist organization of society. This assessment suggests that the initially established model had to be changed quite quickly. The change was accelerated by the development of a critical attitude toward the Soviet model as a universally valid recipe for the construction of socialist society. Besides, there was a strongly felt need to seek original solutions better suited to Yugoslavia's needs — solutions, moreover, which would thoroughly democratize social relations in the spirit of socialism. This, in fact, was how the process of change began. It was originally motivated by elementary observations and needs, and later it continued toward increasingly complex social, economic, and political objectives.

Various factors were responsible for the gradual nature of the change. The vision of a self-managing organization of society was only just beginning to form. Yugoslavia's political relations with foreign countries were unsettled and uncertain, the objective difficulties of economic development were quite strongly felt, and the capital formation capacity of the Yugoslav economy was rather modest. Much has changed, much has been achieved and learned between 1950 and the present day. The old economic and political system, first monocentric and later polycentric, but always state-controlled and administrative, was more and more resolutely rejected, or at least efforts were made to reject it. New views and new relations gained increasing ground, necessitating a revision of earlier relations, institutional forms, and even ideas, many of which had first been regarded as quite adequate, even permanently valid. The development of a self-managing model of society raised numerous questions and required new solutions in all spheres of social and economic life. In particular, it required a new system of enlarged reproduction and its financing, which itself raised many issues, the most important of which concerned the relation between the plan and the market, the financing of enlarged reproduction, the system of prices, and, last but not least, the place, role, and organization of banks, credit, and monetary regulation. This was how the specifically Yugoslav process of transformation of society and its monetary, credit, and banking system actually began.

During the first twenty years of the development of self-management, the self-managing rights of the working people were defined more fully and with increasing precision. Self-managing relations in society thus gradually displaced other types of relations; but until the appearance of the most recent constitutional concept of self-managing socialist society, self-management, although the fundamental social relation, remained unable to displace other types of relations completely or at least reduce them to narrow and minimally necessary limits. Self-management was continually exposed to pressures from different quarters, such as administrative and centralist or liberalist and "technomanagerial." The reasons for this varied, but they were to be found primarily in the institutionally given material relations in the sphere of enlarged reproduction. These changed very slowly and with great difficulty, and they determined the material position of self-management and created the conditions for the emergence of diverse trends in society.

That is why the question of material relations in enlarged reproduction and in the formation and use of capital has never, in the thirty years since the proclamation of the working people's right to control the means of production, ceased to be the subject of more or less heated political and economic debates and polemics in Yugoslavia. During these thirty years the scope of self-management has been constantly widened. Self-management has been increasingly fully understood and adopted as a new yet viable social relation which constantly demands important and quite radical changes in social organization and in the prevailing material relations in enlarged reproduction. This has necessarily had clearly felt implications for all spheres of social and economic life and the social system, including the monetary, banking, and credit spheres.

This, then, is what necessitated the process of change in the banking and credit sphere. The process began immediately after the war, with the introduction of state controls in the fragmented banking system; today, thirty years later, solutions are sought that will bring the monetary and credit relations under the control of associated labor and establish in this sphere the kinds of social relations that should dominate the Yugoslav system of self-management. This fundamental issue — the social commitment to a system of self-management based on the principles of associated labor and enabling working people organized in their Basic Organizations of Associated Labor to decide freely on how to spend their corporate income — was barely sensed thirty years ago and was seen in oversimplified terms. The oversimplification affected the principles involved (which were at first hardly more than a vision) but also the operational details. In the banking and credit sphere, even the vision had to be created from scratch. The banking system, which in terms of its organization and in many other ways represents the "most elaborate product that the capitalist mode of production can attain," and, Marx continues, "also a form of general bookkeeping and distribution of resources on a social scale," could be used as a formal framework, provided that its social content could be changed. This, as the Yugoslav experience shows, is a much more difficult task than was at first thought.

A very complex process has been found to be involved in trying to realize the desire and need of socialist society to make use of an achievement of the previous society like modern banking. It has been quite difficult to give new content to this organism while preventing the danger of constant reproduction of something that is essentially a relation based on capital, which then naturally leads to such negative phenomena as "statism," bureaucratic hegemony, technocratic aspirations, or liberalist readiness to allow irrational market forces to operate freely, thus creating antagonisms between different parts of society and helping to set up centers of power and decision-making on enlarged reproduction outside the system of self-management. The influence of banking and credit relations on the overall reproduction in the country, which is decisive in the process of capital formation and allocation, was for quite some time insufficiently appreciated. The power of the banks and credit was underestimated and even misinterpreted. It was long thought, for instance, that the positions of the banks on the one hand and self-management on the other were determined by some other fundamental processes, primarily relations in the distribution of earnings between society and businesses. It was believed that an increased share of business firms in the distribution of corporate income would change the situation in capital formation and strengthen the material basis of self-management, and thus also its position vis-à-vis not only the state and its interventionism but also the banks and credits. By strengthening its financial position as a result of a more favorable distribution, the economy was expected to acquire control over the banks. However, such expectations proved unjustified in the long run. The decision-making power of Yugoslav banks (most of them small institutions by objective standards) continued to grow, with the economy becoming more and more dependent on them and their credits and falling deeper and deeper in debt.

The effect that these banking and credit relations had on all other relations, including those in the distribution of corporate income between the social community and the self-managing economy (necessitating strong government controls and interventionism in order to ensure a normal functioning of the processes of enlarged reproduction), remained largely unrecognized, though very strong, for a considerable period of time. The influence of banks and credit relations can be said to have been decisive, and yet it took quite long for it to become recognized as such. In the meantime, illusions were harbored and direction for action was lacking.

However, although the ideas and aspirations of the Yugoslav socialist society were freshly elaborated with each successive step in development, their main thrust has always remained the same. The objectives were more precisely defined at each point, and their formulations were more radical, with increasingly great emphasis being placed on the need to develop a self-managing social system and, as its constituent part, a self-managing system of social reproduction. The specific conditions, needs, and possibilities at each stage determined the speed of development, as well as the scope and depth of the aspirations on that path. But it is important to realize that despite sporadic vacillation, the main path was becoming more clearly marked with each successive step. This can best be shown by an analysis of progress thus far and of the distinct stages of development. Three such interrelated stages can be recognized.

The first stage, from 1946 to 1950, was rather short. It marked the establishment of the state-administrative system, as well as of the banking system in the new Yugoslavia. The aim during that period, following the liberation of the country at the end of the war, was to enable the state to acquire control over the entire system of enlarged reproduction, becoming the chief regulator and financer of reproduction. This could not but have an effect on the system and practice of state planning, state budget, and — connected with this — the system of capital formation and allocation and the monetary, banking, and credit system.

Two phases can be seen during this stage. The first, until 1948, was a period of nationalization of all existing banks and the fusion of all state short-term credit institutions with the National Bank of Yugoslavia. The only other bank in the country was the state Investment Bank for long-term financing, which was a mere technical and executive branch of the state budget. (The budget, at that time, included "a plan of the consolidated fund of state finances and of the use of these finances in accordance with the state economic plan.") The essence and purpose of the entire banking and credit system was thus very clearly defined: it rested on the state theory of money and credit, which was the dominant theory in that period and which was only gradually eroded in later years.

The second phase during this first stage, still clearly characterized by the state-administrative theory of socialism and monetary policy, lasted from 1948 to 1950. A feature of this phase was the encouragement of mainly local initiatives in the production and marketing of still scarce consumer goods. In this period, too, first attempts were made to diversify the credit institutions a little through the establishment of numerous municipal and savings banks and credit banks for farming cooperatives. However, the basic characteristics of the system remained unchanged.

The year 1950, which saw the inauguration of workers' management in Yugoslavia, marked the beginning of the <u>second stage</u>, during which new needs were felt, and the complexity of economic relations and processes, including monetary ones, began to be recognized. This was a period of tortuous and not always very successful search for new solutions, particularly in the banking and credit system. Again, this stage can be divided into several phases.

In the first phase, from 1950 to 1954, new solutions were sought along clearly self-managing lines, so that the state would no longer be the sole regulator and financer of development. This had some far-reaching, though still preliminary, repercussions for the role of the state plan, budget, and — in this context — capital accumulation, credit, and banking. Nonrepayable financing was gradually supplanted by credit relationships. But proper organizational solutions were not yet within reach. The National Bank of Yugoslavia became the only long-term and short-term credit institution, while at the same time the role of special investment funds controlled by the administrative authorities of political-territorial units were considerably strengthened.

In many respects this phase might be regarded as akin to the first stage: new attempts were admittedly made, but the theoretical and systemic framework was still as it was in the preceding period. Only the second phase, from 1954 to 1961, can be regarded as the true beginning of the new system, characterized by a genuine search for new solutions. This was the period when the principles of a market economy were more resolutely built into the system. Competitive bidding for available credit money was introduced at that time, and municipal and savings banks, as well as farming cooperative banks, were revived. Specialized all-Yugoslav banks were also formed, starting with the Yugoslav Bank for Foreign Trade, the Yugoslav Investment Bank, and the Yugoslav Agricultural Bank. A special Social Accounting and Auditing Service was established as well.

The phase which followed, from 1961 to 1965, was marked by a more radical orientation toward decentralization and development of commercial banking. First, the functions of municipal banks were strengthened, so that these banks formed the basic network of banking operation and assumed responsibility for almost all credits for the economy and private individuals. Next, business banks were established in all of the republics, while the already existing specialized banks, many of whose short-term operations were transferred to municipal banks, limited their operation to long-term credits, using the resources of the former (now abolished) General Investment Fund. The National Bank concentrated on its functions as a central bank, that is, implementation of the nationally agreed credit and money-issuing policies, provision of credits to commercial banks and supervision of their operations, and payment operations in the country and abroad.

In the next phase, from 1965 to 1971, new efforts were inspired by the need for more complex reforms. The business rationale was more strongly stressed throughout the economy, including banking. Social investment funds were abolished during this period, and their resources were transferred to banks for their credit operations. That was when business banks began to be classified into three classes: investment, investment-commercial, and commercial banks.

We thus see that strong aspirations for a business-oriented type of operation, greater responsibility, and more self-management also found their repercussions in the monetary and credit sphere. Both in the economy as a whole and in banking, principles of business efficiency came to the fore. In banking this meant the development of commercial banking business in which the crude and oversimplified concepts and models characteristic of the state-controlled economy were gradually eroded. But with the affirmation of market mechanisms and principles, technomanagerial attitudes came as a by-product. They continued to exist side by side with the self-managing aspirations and commitments and with the still surviving concepts of state controls and regulation, which were particularly strong in the monetary sphere and monetary policies in general. These were the roots of vacillation and conflicts throughout this period, manifesting themselves, among other things, in the clash of monetary constraints and autonomous market-motivated agents of enlarged reproduction. The flow of the expanded quantities of goods and money in the economy became increasingly irregular and more and more in conflict with the regulatory measures stemming from the monetary center. The instability of money flow, though a mere reflection of deeper relationships, became increasingly evident. At one point it found its expression in the lack of liquid funds, which simply meant that monetary constraints could no longer contain the pressure caused by the irregularity and disorder of the fundamental transaction flows; at another, the external manifestation was a flood of newly issued money, which alleviated the problem for a while but soon spent its force in the expansion built on old foundations.

The state-administrative system of regulation was gradually pushed into the background during this period, while the principles of business efficiency, emphasized in the economy as a whole and in banking, served to increase the power of banks. Their power began to grow now after a long period during which they had been viewed as financial and planning institutions of the state or as dispersed state coffers, the keepers of money belonging to the commune, to the republic, or to the federal government. As the power of banks continued to grow, they became more and more autonomous agents. This process was favored by the way in which money was brought under the control of the state and in which additional money was created to compensate for neutralized money and to put some additional money into circulation. This volume of money, of which only a small part was additional, newly issued money, and the bulk of which was money withdrawn from circulation, returned into the system as a new and always anonymous financing power of banks. What is more, this anonymous potential was partly a substitute for the potential which earlier had not been anonymous. The anonymity of the monetary potential was the first specific cause of the emancipation and increased power of banks over their depositors and of the depositors' dependence on banks at the time when formally, in terms of legal provisions, it was they who should have been controlling banks. The strength of banks as centers of power thus stemmed from a particular concept of money, a state-directed theory of money, and from the modes of creation and cancellation of money derived from that concept.

Thanks to the state-oriented concept of money and monetary system, the already felt functional power of banks received not only the necessary theoretical and ideological underpinnings but also new material strength. This strength was drawn from the fact that the system perpetually renewed the relationship of dependence through indebtedness. The state-oriented concept of money remained firmly rooted in Yugoslav practice until the most recent period, although it clashed directly with self-management and even with the nature of money itself. It was only in the most recent period that this concept began to be doubted and revised.

This brings us to the third major stage of development of the banking and credit system, beginning in 1971, during which the chief causes of economic-political and sociopolitical deformations were diagnosed, and attempts were made to lay new foundations for more consistently applied self-management, for greater responsibility, and for freer pooling of resources. A new, comprehensive, and consistent concept of self-managing organization of society was developed during this period. In the new concept, the monetary, banking, and credit system was no longer viewed as a separate entity divorced from the totality of social and economic relations; on the contrary, as a system it is incorporated into the whole in order to make it more complete, consistent, and efficient.

It should be admitted that the theoretical analysis of socialist society penetrated into the field of banking and credit relations only with the greatest difficulty, and for a long time this area remained rather vague and unexplained. It was vaguely felt that banking and credit relations, such as they were, were out of step with self-management; as already noted, it was believed instead that changes in the sphere of distribution and in the organization and management of banks would correct the situation. That is why a great deal of weight was given to changes in the management of banks and in the processes of policy decision-making in banks. Although the efforts toward — to put it simply — democratization of banking operations were a constant feature of development, they became particularly marked in 1971, when constitutional amendments were passed which were a prelude to a complex constitutional reform. New constitutional provisions emphasized the decisive role of basic organizations of associate labor in the banking and credit sphere as well. The Basic Organizations of Associated Labor were the banks' founders; it was these organizations that were meant to control banks, and the banks' earnings were to be distributed among those who had deposited their money in them.

It was found, however, that all the attempts, even those that sounded very radical (abolition of credit funds belonging to banks, return of resources to the economy rather than their accumulation in banks, changes in the management of banks, etc.), were not sufficient to change the essence of the old relations.

There was one unfavorable element which, together with an awareness of its causes, began to affect theoretical orientations and political commitments. This was economic instability. Instability, coupled with the inability of economic and political measures to cope with it successfully, again drew attention to defects in the process of capital formation and especially to the role of banks and credits in this process.

Yugoslavia's marked success in the economic, social, and cultural fields was marred by the growing trends of instability in the economy. They found their expression in the first place in very rapid price increases and in balance-of-payments deficits. Besides, difficulties in the establishment of linkages in the economy were increasingly strongly felt, with important economic and political implications. The purely political effort failed to produce satisfactory results, as did a combination of economic and political measures. Intensive research soon revealed the main generators of instability. Although many factors helped to generate instability — with an ambitious program of social and economic development that the resources of society could not sustain and certain irrational decisions being just two of them — the chief source of negative trends was the imperfect and inadequately developed system, in which the system of capital formation with its contradictions was the worst culprit. Although many of its features had changed in the history of self-management, moving from monocentrism to polycentrism, from state controls to genuine banking, the system of capital formation always preserved one characteristic — alienation of surplus labor, or accumulated capital, from direct producers and their self-managing organizations and its centralization in one or more centers controlled either by the state or by banks. Only the manner of centralization changed and the places to which accumulated capital was siphoned off; but the basic relation remained unchanged, as did the trends which stemmed from it. Accumulated capital, concentrated first in state investment funds and later in banks, remained alienated and was seen as a panacea for all problems. This stimulated everybody to incur debts and favored the emergence of consumerism. To put it differently, this fact was responsible for the kind of behavior among the agents of enlarged reproduction which paid no attention to their own resources and income or their own capital-formation capacity. The limits of indebtedness, and thus also barriers to expansion, were lost in the mist of expansionism. The balance between investment and accumulated capital could not be maintained under constant pressures, which resulted in the inflationary financing of various needs from new issue of money. Banks, for their part, were eager to siphon off as much surplus labor (accumulated capital) from the economy as possible so that they could finance new projects, thus making it difficult for the economy to cover not only its needs in capital assets and permanent revolving assets but also its needs in temporary revolving assets. This, in turn, created new problems in enlarged and simple reproduction which could only be solved with newly issued money. The banking mechanism of credit and deposit operations was stretched to capacity to multiply and transform money so that all the needs could be covered. The transformation of short-term into long-term investment resources grew apace. According to some calculations, as much as 30% of all investments in recent years was financed through such transformation. The share of investments in the gross material product of the country became very high.

Such activities on the part of banks and the credit relations designed to replace the state-administrative system and the system of central distribution of resources did not, in fact could not, lead to greater economic stability or to changes in social relations in enlarged reproduction along self-managing lines. The reasons for such developments had to be found. And the effort to find them revealed how correct and necessary the orientation toward self-management in a socialist society was; for under the conditions of social ownership of the means of production, it is quite easy for new expropriation of producers to take place — first by the bureaucratic state machinery and then by the technocratic class and different centers of financial power. This produces alienation in all spheres and induces a kind of behavior, even in the sphere of production, which tends toward irrational consumption and irrational development. For this reason the banking mechanism and credit relations began to be studied with greater attention and more critically, after they had spread to such an extent that they deprived the economic subjects of their freedom and independence through indebtedness and blocked the progress of self-management and the development of relations and moving forces that could contribute to stability in enlarged reproduction. Such studies showed that the relations and mechanisms prevailing in the monetary sphere were one of the chief sources of alienation of accumulated capital and blocked progress of self-management. It was this sphere that was found to be an alien body in self-management and a direct contradiction to stability. When the basic mechanisms were examined, the extent of centralization of resources effected through their workings became apparent. It was shown that banks had developed a powerful potential which figured as anonymous capital vis-à-vis the economy (though it was in fact owned by many and various subjects), and which served to build additional potential for which no cover existed. This also showed the genesis of almost total financial dependence of the economy on banks. At the center of attention of these studies there suddenly appeared the mechanism of credit and deposit operations of banks, which used to be regarded in earlier times as a mere technical matter. In the specific Yugoslav situation it had become a powerful mechanism of disappropriation of basic economic subjects and, consequently, a breeding ground of money and capital without cover which was then distributed to the dependent economic subjects scrambling to get as much of it as possible. From this there followed lack of responsibility and rationality, which was particularly strongly felt in the use of accumulated capital (i.e., in investments).

But this whole process of monetary and investment expansion cannot be fully understood unless one explains in a little more detail the nature of the financial dependence of the economic subjects. In those early days, when the means of production were first handed over to the workers' collectives to manage, the sources of financing for their permanent and temporary revolving assets were not placed under workers' control. Rather, the workers' collectives were forced to obtain this capital from banks in the form of credits.

Thus, from the outset they became debtors. Besides, they were obliged to take these credits on their interest-free accounts, and not as current account credits, which only increased their credit needs. Moreover, ostensibly to ensure financial discipline and facilitate record-keeping, they were obliged to keep these funds in a number of different accounts, from each of which disbursements could be made only for specifically listed purposes, which increased their credit needs even further. Also, they were obliged to have enough money in their accounts to meet their payment obligations at any given point. Across-account borrowing and mutual credit extension were administratively prevented. This again made the intensity of needs for banking credits greater. All this, coupled with relatively high obligations in the financing of various social needs, reduced the volume of available capital left to the firms and their ability to finance their expansion themselves; instead, it heightened their dependence on banks for all their financing needs in the sphere of enlarged reproduction. Thus, with the economy dependent on banks and a great deal of power being concentrated in them, banks naturally assumed responsibility for the financing of all economic growth. This is where one should seek the source of quantitative and qualitative disruption, which is the subject of so much discussion in Yugoslavia at present.

It is against this background, and with the aim of changing relations in economic growth, ensuring more stable development and fostering systemic relations which will make the economy more homogeneous, that reforms in the system have been introduced recently which should change the situation in Yugoslav banking and reduce credit relations to the necessary level, restricting them only to areas in which they are unavoidable.

The main concern is to make the economy less dependent on credits and to prevent the creation of money for purposes which would otherwise have to be financed with accumulated capital. These changes in the position of domination and dependence form part of a comprehensive reform of the system. They involve radical interventions in the very foundations on which the monetary, credit, and banking system rests. Intensive studies have been under way for several years, and a general approach has already been worked out, while the operational details and variants are still under study and are the subject of lively debates and polemics.

The first principle of the new approach is that the issuing function of banks should be limited and should be strictly related to the real commodity and monetary transactions of the Organizations of

Associated Labor. Some basic modalities for the linking of issuing functions with real commodity and monetary transactions in the economy have already been worked out. This, together with some other changes in the system of payment and use of financial resources, is expected to restrict the banks' crediting activities, reduce the dependence of the economy on credits, and subject the process of money supply for the economy more clearly to economic criteria. It is also expected that this will produce changes in the process of capital formation and give greater scope to self-financing and pooling of resources, which is bound to have an effect on the stability of the economy.

The changes are thus designed not only to prevent the creation of money and capital without coverage, which has become quite widespread, but also to forestall the formation of autonomous banking capital. Through the direct monetization of newly created value which has been socially recognized as such, that is, in the marketplace, issuing of money would be linked with the real processes of creation and marketing of products and services. Demonetization, that is, the withdrawal of money from circulation, would follow the same pattern. In this way the central bank would lose much of its interventionist scope, which it still has as a regulator of monetary flows. Such changes would necessarily have an effect on relations in the sphere of capital formation. The anonymous investment potential of the banks would have no chance of survival, since capital formation would be taking place in the economy and would be controlled by the basic economic subjects. Only then would they be able to play their self-managing role in enlarged reproduction. Finally, on the basis of this, they would be able to take control of the banks, which would thus become their financial associations in the true sense.

This approach foresees the appearance of a new type of banks that will be financial associations of associated labor. They will take the form, on the one hand, of so-called Company Banks (or Internal Banks), where a particular bank will serve one Complex Organization of Associated Labor (that is, one consisting of a number of Basic Organizations of Associated Labor, each of them being an independent entity); on the other hand, they will take the form of the so-called Basic Banks, where a particular bank will serve all the firms which are its members and which are linked by production and economic considerations they share territorially. The bank and its staff will be a mere service backup for the member firms.

The process of establishment of such banks started as soon as the approach described here was adopted, and formal adaptation has already been achieved. Their further substantive transformation will depend on the far-reaching changes in the existing issuing mechanism that were outlined above — changes in the mechanism of credit and deposit operations which still predominates and which will have to be replaced by the direct monetization of newly created value.

The fundamental question, therefore, is how to overcome the anonymity of the banking potential and give decision-making prerogatives to independent, self-managing subjects ready to engage in self-managing negotiations on all questions bearing on economic expansion. The possible solutions depart radically from the banking practice in Western European countries. Equally, they have nothing in common with credit relations in Eastern European countries. They are intended to reflect faithfully the characteristic features of the Yugoslav system based on self-management in basic cells of associated labor and in higher associations and communities of interest, including financial associations and those outside the productive branches of the economy. Self-managing decision-making on the totality of corporate income and the formation of higher self-managing organisms, communities of interest, and associations, which is an integral part of the process of self-managing association of labor, will enable direct producers, who now manage Basic Organizations of Associated Labor, to become associated producers and take control of the totality of social processes, including the process of enlarged reproduction and thus also the spheres which have so far been furthest removed from them, such as the sphere of credit relations, banking, and issuing of money. Only then will direct producers become sovereign self-managers, and only then will they gradually free themselves from the power above them and take power in their own hands.

This is the system as it is laid down in the Yugoslav Constitution. It is now being elaborated so that it can be fully implemented. There are still many obstacles along this path, and new solutions are required to overcome them. This is the reason for the transformation of banks, credit relations, and the monetary system as a whole.

A considerable amount of knowledge and experience has already been accumulated from practice and, at times, painful experience. Together with a wealth of positive achievements, this practice has also produced developments that are a reason for dissatisfaction now. It can now be said that the monetary system, the system of credit and deposit operations of banks, has not been just an indifferent mediator but also one of the major generators of unfavorable developments.

The time has now come to reform it radically. And this is what we intend to do.

6
THE BANKING SYSTEM

Branko Mijović

I. The Role of the Financial System

The role, functions, and structure of the banking system depend on the specific economic system of the country. The development and the changes in the economic system carried out in recent years have demanded an adequate readjustment of the financial system.

In the development of the economic system in Yugoslavia there was full continuity, so that each subsequent phase of development led to a widening of the functions of management and decision-making in the field of production and distribution of income by the working people and a reduction of the functions of the state and its bodies. In this respect one major characteristic is the choice of the basic organization of associated labor (hereinafter referred to as the company) as the starting base of self-management. Within the company the working people directly make decisions on all questions relating to production, distribution of income, investments, etc. Personal incomes, savings, employment, social contributions, and so on all depend on the success of the activities of each company. The market mechanism is one of the important criteria influencing the behavior of workers in a company.

Therefore income as the basic motive of the workers' behavior is of double importance: on the one hand, the level of personal consumption of workers and the level of resources used for expansion of production and employment depend on income; and on the other hand, opportunities for developing collective needs, as a constituent part of the total standard of living, such as pensions and health insurance, education, science, culture, social security, etc., depend on the level of income.

Companies in Yugoslavia are producers of goods. The market laws, as the expression of goods production, influence the rationality and efficiency of business activity. The market influences the structure of production and the allocation and more efficient use of savings. Under these conditions savings are accumulated by all those economic subjects which control income and participate in its distribution. From the point of view of the role of the financial mechanism, the fact that savings in Yugoslavia are not formed by taxation or any similar administrative method, but by the free decision of numerous decentralized economic subjects, has particular importance.

The role of the financial system in the Yugoslav economy is of great importance for the efficient functioning of the whole economic system and fulfillment of the objectives of economic policy. It all assumes construction of a financial mechanism, especially in the field of the structure of the financial institutions and financial instruments, that can meet the demand of the economy in the field of financing on the one side and in the field of monetary regulation on the other side. In the field of financing two important functions of the financial mechanism must be underlined: first, financial mediation which should ensure raising of additional resources for the needs of the economy; second, to be the initiator and organizer of combination of resources of companies and other organizations for the purpose of concentrating savings and their transfer within wider production entities, which promotes more rational and more efficient construction of larger productive capacities.

In the field of monetary regulations, the most important function of the financial mechanism is to maintain a supply of money adequate to establish a relatively greater equilibrium of economic movements both within the country and in the field of economic relations with foreign countries. Within this quantitative regulation, selective channelling of resources for the purpose of achieving the priority objectives of economic policy has an important place.

Changes in the economic system carried out in recent years also required adequate adjustment in the financial mechanism. These changes tended toward the construction of a financial mechanism that would, on the one hand, be more in line with the system of self-management and, on the other hand, would perform more efficiently the above-mentioned functions in financing and monetary regulation.

In the above sense the changes in the financial field have moved in two directions. First, in the implementation of monetary-credit policy, the changes have moved toward a closer connection between monetary regulation with the goods and money transactions of companies, so that the granting of credits is, to a greater extent, based on and connected with the real needs of the economy. The real goods and money transactions of companies should become the most important basis for creation and withdrawal of money. Second, in the field of banking organizations, the changes have moved toward greater integration of the banks and the financial sphere in general with the companies that have founded a bank. Companies that are founders of a bank make all the decisions about setting and implementing the business policy of the bank, but they also bear all the consequences and risks resulting from the banks' activity. Thus the companies within the bank form a relationship of interdependence, greater security, and joint responsibility. This provides them with maximum stability and the chance to meet their obligations at home and abroad on time.

Successfully attaining the above-mentioned objectives requires an adequate banking organization. Under the present conditions in Yugoslavia there is the following structure of financial organizations:

1. the central bank system;
2. commercial banks;
3. Yugoslav bank for international economic cooperation;
4. savings banks and other savings and loan institutions;
5. other financial organizations.

The establishment and operation of bank consortia and associations of banking organizations are also made possible by the law.

Below we shall discuss only the central bank system and the place and role of the commercial banks, for they are the basic institutions of the Yugoslav monetary system.

II. The Central Bank System

The Yugoslav economic system represents a specific combination of the market and plan elements. Under the conditions of decentralized and free decision-making by individual companies, money is assuming a more and more important role. Hence the determination and implementation of monetary policy in Yugoslav conditions have great importance for meeting the objectives of economic policy.

The objectives of monetary-credit policy are achieved through a system of national banks (the National Bank of Yugoslavia, six national banks of the republics, and two national banks of the autonomous provinces) which constitute the central bank system of Yugoslavia. All nine national banks act as an integrated central banking system. This integration results from the provision of the Constitution which defines their activities: (1) Yugoslavia is an integrated and indivisible money and credit area. The most important monetary principles, which result from the provision of the Constitution for the integrated Yugoslav market, are as follows: uniform money, a uniform monetary and foreign exchange system, and a uniform basis for the banking and credit system. (2) The National Bank as a money-issuing institution undertakes uniform measures and instruments of monetary-credit and foreign exchange regulation valid for the whole country and compulsory for all banks and other financial organizations, including the national banks of the republics and of the autonomous provinces.

Functions of the central bank

The most important functions of the National Bank of Yugoslavia, jointly with the national banks of the republics and of the autonomous provinces, are:

— regulation of the quantity of money in circulation;
— maintaining liquidity of the bank;
— maintaining liquidity in foreign payments;
— issuing bank notes and coins;
— performing bank operations for the federal government;
— special rights as regards control of implementation of measures in the field of monetary and foreign exchange policy by the banks.

The basic objectives of monetary-credit policy, as an integral part of economic policy, are determined by the Federal Assembly of Yugoslavia. On the basis of objectives and tasks set in such a way, the Federal Executive Council each year passes, on the advice given by the National Bank of Yugoslavia, a decision which defines more specifically the targets in the field of fulfillment of the quantitative as well as of the selective objectives of monetary-credit policy.

On the basis of independent decisions of the Council of Governors, the National Bank of Yugoslavia undertakes measures to fulfill the objectives and the tasks of the credit and monetary policy set. The Board of Governors (whose members are the governor of the National Bank of Yugoslavia and governors of the national banks of the republics and of autonomous provinces) directs all the activities of the National Bank of Yugoslavia. The Governor of the National Bank of Yugoslavia is *ex officio* also the president of the Board of Governors. The Governor of the National Bank of Yugoslavia is appointed by the Federal Assembly of Yugoslavia.

The National Bank of Yugoslavia is responsible in executing its work to the Federal Assembly, which also supervises its activities.

The National Bank of Yugoslavia does not establish direct relations with the commercial banks, while the national banks of the republics and of the autonomous provinces perform operational functions in connection with the implementation of the approved issuance, monetary-credit, and foreign exchange policy. Both the National Bank of Yugoslavia as well as the national banks of the republics and of the autonomous provinces directly control the implementation of measures of monetary-credit and foreign exchange policy.

Implementation of the monetary-credit policy

The structure of the instruments of monetary regulation is based on the existence of a multibank system. The multibank system implies monetary regulation based on the control of liquidity and bank credit potential. In implementating monetary and credit policy, the most important instruments and measures used by the National Bank of Yugoslavia are:

— determination of the level of the legal reserve requirements of banks and other financial organizations with the National Bank of Yugoslavia;

— issuance and withdrawal of treasury bills of the National Bank of Yugoslavia;

— buying through the banks of short-term securities issued by companies;

— granting of short-term credits on the basis of bills of exchange discounted by the banks;

— participation in bank credits for certain selective purposes;

— buying and selling of foreign exchange on the foreign

exchange markets in Yugoslavia;

— fixing of active and passive interest rates of the National Bank of Yugoslavia;

— limitation to the volume of bank placements is applied only if credit-monetary policy objectives cannot be achieved by other measures.

The implementation of monetary-credit policy implies on the one hand quantitative regulation of the supply of money in accordance with the real economic changes, and on the other hand performance of the selective tasks in accordance with the objectives and needs of economic policy for a definite period. The instruments of monetary regulation at the disposal of the central bank, which are outlined above, make possible efficient implementation of an adequate monetary-credit policy. But the implementation of monetary-credit policy in recent years has not been in total harmony with actual economic changes and the stabilization objectives of economic policy. In this respect it should be stressed that in the implementation of monetary-credit policy, in recent years there were periods of pronounced liberal elements or of excessive restrictive tendencies. This shows that existing measures of monetary regulation have not been efficiently enough applied in implementing the objectives and the tasks of monetary-credit policy. The lack of efficiency of monetary policy in achieving the forecasted movements of the supply of money raised numerous questions and stimulated discussions about the instruments of monetary policy.

The discussions on these questions have shown that one of the main reasons for the monetary policy's lack of efficiency in regulating the supply of money in circulation is the wide use of the issuance of money by the central bank in financing, on the one hand, a great number of selective-purpose projects by the commercial banks and, on the other hand, in covering the federal budget deficit. This sort of use of the issuance of money by the central bank has led to lack of flexibility in implementation of established monetary policy.

It can be concluded that in the coming period, monetary policy must become more efficient and flexible than it has been. Therefore a significant cut in the use of the issuance of money by the central bank for selective credits and for financing of final consumption (including the federal budget) would make possible more flexible regulation of the monetary basis and more efficient implementation of monetary policy in accordance with the stabilization objectives of economic policy.

III. Commercial Banks

The basis of the credit and banking system

In short, the most important features on which the credit and banking system have been created are as follows:

— starting from the principle of the free flow of money in the single Yugoslav market, every bank has the right to operate on the whole of Yugoslav territory and to establish commercial relations with companies regardless of their location;

— a bank is established by companies and other public legal persons. The social-political communities (communes, republics, autonomous provinces, and the federation) cannot be founders of a bank and cannot, therefore, take part in management;

— companies and other public legal persons are free to choose any bank. A bank cannot refuse an application for membership if the applicant accepts the self-management agreement of association in the bank;

— members of the bank — companies and other public legal persons — manage the bank, especially in planning the bank's business policy and its implementation. Since the members of the bank make all the decisions regarding the formulation and implementation of the bank's business policy, they bear all the consequences and risks which might result from the bank's activities.

Therefore a self-management agreement on establishment of a bank made by companies and other public legal persons has the character of a basic constituting act. In that respect the bank's activities have the character of the combining of resources by companies for the purpose of fulfilling their development plans, current tasks, and other joint interest.

The founders of a bank have to pay in their share of the equity and to guarantee the bank's liabilities. To ensure that banks will meet their liabilities, the Fundamental Principles of Credit and the Banking System Act prescribe strict penalties and sanctions for the purpose of maintaining banks' liquidity, including the responsibility of individuals in case of late meeting of the bank's liabilities. Also, the responsibility of a bank for correct and timely fulfillment of liabilities to foreign partners is particularly emphasized.

The structure of the banking system

The banking system includes two types of banks: commercial banks and savings and loan institutions. Here we will discuss the structure of commercial banks, which include: internal banks, basic banks, united banks, and the Yugoslav Bank for International Economic Cooperation.

There are in Yugoslavia 135 internal banks, 163 basic banks, and 8 united banks.

Internal bank. The internal bank is a closed-circuit bank established by companies (as well as other public legal persons) which are members of a complex socialist company. Within that complex organization independent companies are interconnected by their business activities in production and trade, as well as in development planning. The purpose of these banks is to perform banking and other financial operations for the needs of the members of these complex companies. In this sense, within these internal banks proposals are made for combination and concentration of resources to finance development plans, as well as for the most rational use of money resources for the current activity of its members. The internal bank performs all the financial activities which the law permits its member companies to do. Within this framework the bank carries out financing among its members and joint financial investments, and it prepares investment projects and proposals for borrowing in the country and abroad. Also, the internal bank can carry out some activities with third parties that are connected to the activity of its member companies, such as collecting savings to finance certain credits and the sale of goods by its members.

An internal bank cannot accept sight deposits, so it cannot issue bank money. For these reasons the measures of monetary regulation of the central bank are not applied to the internal banks.

The internal banks have management bodies like those of the basic bank. The internal banks can be members of basic banks.

Basic bank. The basic bank is a type of universal banking organization. It is the only banking organization which can perform all credit and banking operations in the country. Also, it is the only banking organization which can collect sight deposits. Therefore these banks are deposit banks that can carry out both short-term as well as long-term banking operations and make all payments at home and abroad.

The basic bank is a type of an open financial organization

founded by companies, internal banks, and other public legal persons. In a basic bank all categories of sources of finance appear: deposits of business and nonbusiness activities, savings and other deposits of individuals, as well as foreign credits.

The founders make a self-management agreement on establishing a bank. Every company and other public legal person may become a member of the bank insofar as it accepts the self-management agreement. The self-management agreement includes all the basic elements which, in addition to other matters, relate to business activity, ensuring of liquidity, responsibility and bearing of risks by members of the bank, rights, and manner of bank management.

The highest bank management body is the bank assembly, consisting of representatives of all the founders. The bank assembly decides on basic directions of bank business policy, interest rate policy, and distribution of the bank's income. The bank assembly also elects the executive board, credit board, and the bank director. The bank assembly makes medium-term plans and annual programs for the bank and sets the basic directions of business policy to achieve those plans and programs.

Compulsory funds in a basic bank are: the reserve, joint, and several liability and business funds. The reserve fund is used to ensure the current liquidity of the bank. The joint and several liabilities funds are designed to cover bad debts (unrecoverable claims). The business fund is used to finance the fixed assets of the bank, such as the bank premises and office equipment.

United bank. Two or more basic banks may establish a united bank. The united bank may carry out only those activities which have been transferred to it by the basic banks in their self-management agreement on founding of the united bank. Generally, the basic banks transfer to the united bank only the activities of joint interest. In that respect, first of all, one should point out credit operations and payments abroad as one of the most important activities of the united bank. For the purpose of more efficient performance of these activities, united banks may establish their representative offices abroad. Also, united banks appear as the initiators and organizers of raising and tying of domestic and foreign resources to the objective of financing major development programs, which are of special importance for the development of major economic regions.

For this purpose a united bank may act as an initiator for pooling of resources not only within its basic banks but also within other united banks. The united bank has to make available to the basic banks objective and timely analyses and information on economic trends in the domestic and foreign markets that are important in making decisions, especially those connected with development programs.

The united bank is managed by the basic banks which are its members and are responsible for all its liabilities. All other bodies of management of the united bank are similar to those of a basic bank.

The Yugoslav Bank for International Economic Cooperation

The Yugoslav Bank for International Economic Cooperation was established in 1978 by a separate federal act as a specialized banking organization. Its basic objective is to promote and expand economic cooperation with all foreign countries. In this respect this bank should stimulate and help the long-term production and financial cooperation of domestic companies with foreign partners for the purpose of a joint approach to third markets.

The self-management agreement on association in this bank, as a specialized bank for additional credits for financing of exports of capital goods and general improvement and promotion of economic cooperation with foreign countries, has been accepted by basic and united banks on the basis of decisions of the companies that are members of those banks.

The most important objectives of this bank are as follows:

— granting credits for export of capital goods, investment, and other projects in foreign countries, as well as granting credits for investments in own and mixed companies abroad;

— insurance against noncommercial risks and additional participation in insurance against commercial risks.

In cooperation with the commercial banks, the Yugoslav Bank for International Economic Cooperation participates in developing long-term cooperation for entry into foreign markets, organizes joint deliveries of equipment and other industrial plants with foreign partners in third markets, and expands investments by foreign partners in Yugoslav companies.

The financial resources for carrying out business activities by this bank are provided first of all by its founders. The bank also uses resources channeled to it by social-political communities and the National Bank of Yugoslavia. The bank also may use credits at home and abroad. Finally, the resources and liabilities of the Yugoslav Fund for Financing and Insurance of Exports were transferred to the bank, as were its activities.

Savings and loan institutions

There are three groups of savings and loan institutions: savings banks, the Post Office Savings Bank, and savings and loan cooperatives.

Savings banks. Companies and other public legal persons can establish savings banks. The business activity of the savings banks and savings and loan cooperatives is regulated only in general in the Law on Banks, and the detailed regulation of their organization and business activity is left to the legal provisions made by the republics and the autonomous provinces.

First of all, the savings banks collect funds from the people and grant credits to individuals for the improvement of their business activity, for housing, for purchase of consumer goods, as well as for other needs of the population. The savings banks can grant credits directly through banks for financing of certain needs on the territory of the savings bank.

The Post Office Savings Bank. Companies and other organizations within the post, telegraph, and telephone services have established the Post Office Savings Bank. This savings bank is a unique organization which operations throughout the country. It has its windows in every post office. The basic operation of this savings bank consists of collecting savings of the population at home as well as abroad. It cannot use resources for its own placements, except for a certain part of collected resources to finance P.T.T. companies. It is obliged to keep its remaining resources with certain banks.

The savings and loan cooperatives. The establishment and business activity of these organizations is regulated by legal provisions of the republics and of the autonomous provinces. First of all, they are organized within farmers' cooperatives and agricultural companies. These savings and loan cooperatives are used mainly to improve business cooperation with individual agricultural producers.

Association of banks

The Law on Banks provides the possibility for business and professional association of banking organizations. The most important are two forms of association:

— banking consortia;

— associations of banking organizations.

The banking consortia are used by the banks to obtain required resources at home and abroad and to finance certain important investment programs and projects. The consortia can include, besides domestic banks, foreign financial organizations. If only domestic banks take part in a consortium, they make a self-management agreement; and if foreign financial organizations also take part, then relations, rights, and liabilities among the parties are regulated by a contract.

Consortia can be established by united banks, basic banks, or internal banks. However, a consortium can include all three sorts of banks. That depends on the specific interests and needs for pooling resources.

A banking consortium is not a public legal person. When the purpose for which the consortium has been established is achieved and all liabilities under the agreement or contract are fulfilled, its activity ceases as well.

Associations of banking organizations. The Law on the Chamber of Economy of Yugoslavia states that all banking organizations must be members of the Association of Yugoslav Banks. The Association of Yugoslav Banks is a member of the Chamber of Economy of Yugoslavia. The Law on Banks provides institutional bases for voluntary associations of banking organizations both on a territorial principle and by type of banking organizations (e.g., associations of savings banks).

The Association of Yugoslav Banks is mainly meant to develop all sorts of mutual cooperation among banks and to coordinate their individual interests at home as well as abroad. In that respect the following can be pointed out as its main functions:

1. Improvement of business activity of the banking organizations by giving professional assistance, professional training of personnel, organizing research work in the field of money, credit, and general activities, and organization of the banks.

2. Organizing of work on implementation of special targets relating to banks but included in the Social Plan of the Federation or in the measures of current economic policy for the fulfillment of the plan. For the purpose of fulfillment of those tasks, banks undertake certain responsibilities by making a self-management agreement.

3. Cooperation with federal bodies of government in preparing

legal regulations in the monetary-credit field, as well as when certain tasks must be performed by the banks that result from the Social Plan and the measures of current economic policy.

4. Promotion of cooperation of banks with foreign financial organizations, as well as organizing agreements of banks on joint conditions for approaching foreign financial markets.

The association cannot perform operational credit and banking activities.

IV. The Business Policy of Banks

The role of the financial mechanism, as can be seen above, is of major importance in meeting the targets and objectives of economic policy. In this respect an adequate structure of financial institutions and financial resources required for their fulfillment in the creation of money and financial mediation is needed for efficient functioning of the economic system.

Here we will look more closely at questions relating to the determination and implementation of the business policy of banks, such as: planning of business policy, the role of banks in savings and investments, and the role of banks in pooling of resources.

Planning of business policy

In the Yugoslav economic system planning is not an exclusive function of the state; it is a right and duty of all companies, chambers of economy, banks, as well as social-political communities from the commune to the federal government. Irrespective of the fact that the companies are the main agents of planning, the plans of the banks have a special importance. On the basis of the plans of the banks it is possible to connect and adjust the individual plans of the members of a bank, to appraise the reality of the plans of the companies from the point of view of sources of finance, to initiate long-term pooling of resources of companies, and to link individual companies to the social ones.

The bank assembly, which is made up of representatives of all members of the bank, prepares the medium-term plan of the bank for a period of five years. Every year the bank assembly estimates the results of fulfillment of plans for the previous period and determines a program for the current year, with necessary measures for the fulfillment of the plan. These plans and programs, and especially the required financial resources for their fulfillment, the bank endeavors to bring in line with possibilities for raising funds. The basic sources for mobilizing funds for every bank are: money deposits, savings of the population, issuance of securities, credits from other banks, and foreign credits.

Relations, rights, and liabilities among the members of the banks, as well as basic directions of business policy of the bank, are determined in the medium-term plan of the bank. In this respect the plan includes the following:

— joint targets and directions of development for the members of the bank;

— the bank's opportunities in pooling and mobilizing resources for the fulfillment of plans;

— basic directions for channeling the bank's resources to match the needs of the companies for the available resources;

— the volume of foreign debts and conditions for issuance of bank guarantees;

— measures for maintaining the bank's liquidity and ways and means to bear risks for the bank's activities;

— interest rate and tariff policies for banking services.

The annual plan, or program, of the bank is approved every year by the assembly.

As has already been said, measures needed to meet the objectives set in the medium-term plan are provided for in the plan.

Guarantees for foreign placements

The system of guarantees and provision of security for foreign placements in Yugoslavia is regulated by legal provisions, specifically by the Law on Banks.

First, limits of borrowings for each republic and autonomous province are determined annually. Accordingly, banks can issue guarantees for foreign borrowings to their members only within those limits. That means that there is no possibility that a bank can borrow or issue guarantees above the determined limits. On the other hand, in accordance with Article 197 of the Law on Banks, the members of the bank are obliged to determine, in a self-management agreement on the establishment of the bank, an unlimited subsidiary responsibility among them for the liabilities of the bank. In Article 158 of the law it is stated:

> For its liabilities the basic bank is responsible with all resources at its disposal. If those resources are

> not sufficient to meet the liabilities, the members of the bank are also responsible for the liabilities of the bank with other resources, in proportion to the total resources at their disposal, and in the following order:
> 1. resources of the reserve fund;
> 2. money part of the business fund;
> 3. all other resources at their disposal.

As can be seen, the companies and the other members of the bank are responsible for bank liabilities with all their resources, which in practice means that the creditors cannot encounter a situation in which they would not be able to recover their claims.

A guarantee issued by a basic bank has the same legal force and security as a guarantee issued by a united bank. However, for a basic bank to engage in this sort of activity, it must fulfill certain conditions set by the national banks, and on that basis it will issue permissions.

Finally, it must be pointed out that Article 78 of the Law on Social Accounting Service provides that if a bank fully authorized to perform foreign operations does not fulfill its liabilities in an agreed period of time, the National Bank of Yugoslavia can issue an order to the service to transfer an appropriate amount of dinar resources from the account of the bank to the National Bank of Yugoslavia, which will fulfill the foreign exchange liability abroad.

The role of banks in financial mediation

The methods of forming savings and their use occupy a central position in understanding the role and importance of the financial mechanism in a country. Under Yugoslav conditions savings are not formed by taxes or other administrative methods, but by decentralized and free decisions of companies, the population, and other participants in the distribution of income.

The industrial companies are the main agents of economic development in the Yugoslav system. Therefore they are also the main agents of savings and investments. Under such conditions the question arises as to the motives which influence the behavior of companies in the field of distribution, sharing, and allocation of savings, and their more efficient use and mobility. In this respect the following factors, among others, can be mentioned:

— the workers of every company are interested in as high a level of saving as possible and in using their savings as efficiently as possible because, on the one hand, the enlargement of the material base and the stability of their work and employment and, on the other hand, the level of their personal income depend on them. The development of social services (health, education, insurance, science, culture, etc.), which form a part of their total social standard, also depend on their savings;

— the workers of one company do not act independently and are not isolated in the distribution of income. It is their right and duty to establish, in agreement with other companies, joint principles and standards of behavior for distribution of income;

— the income of a company, as well as the personal income of workers, does not depend only on their work and on the efficient use of savings in their company but also on the efficiency of work in other companies with which they have pooled their resources.

These and other motives for producers' behavior in the system of decentralized decision-making and in the distribution of income have promoted the maintenance of a high rate of gross savings.

Table 1

Social Product and Rate of Savings

	1974	1975	1976	1977	1978
Social product at current prices, in billions of dinars	407.3	503.0	592.3	722.6	901.3
Gross savings, in billions of dinars (with depreciation)	161.9	199.1	246.5	282.1	369.4
Percentage share of savings in social product	39.7	39.6	41.6	39.0	41.0

The structure of savings by sectors is of the greatest importance for understanding the role of the financial mechanism. In recent years about 50% of total gross savings was formed by companies, while at the same time these companies participated in 70% of total investments. The companies make up their lack of savings for the necessary level of their investment by transferring resources through the mediation of the financial market. The second half of savings is formed outside the companies. At the same time, it is of great importance that almost a third of total gross savings is formed by the population.

Such asymmetry in the distribution of savings and investments demands an efficient financial mechanism, which should ensure the transfer of the part of savings formed outside of the economy and put at the disposal of the companies.

Table 2

Self-financing of Companies
(in billion dinars)

	1974	1975	1976	1977	1978
Real investments (fixed assets and reserves)	125.9	148.5	157.9	229.1	277.6
Own savings	99.9	100.9	117.2	151.3	196.1
Rate of self-financing as a percentage	79.3	67.9	74.2	66.0	70.6

Investments by companies in financial property (sales on credit, money needed for current payments, unrecovered claims, etc.) have not been calculated here. If these investments are also taken into consideration, then the rate of self-financing is reduced from 70% to about 50%.

From the point of view of the role of the financial mechanism, the pattern of financial savings by individual sectors has a special importance. In this paper financial savings are understood to mean the difference between the available money savings of one sector and allocations for investments (fixed assets and reserves).

Table 3

Financial Savings
(in billion dinars)

	1974	1975	1976	1977	1978
Industrial companies	–26.0	–47.6	–40.7	–77.8	–81.5
Federation	–11.7	–12.6	–12.8	–12.5	–12.4
Other sociopolitical communities	2.4	0.6	4.7	–4.5	11.1
Other organizations	8.7	12.4	16.9	18.0	19.2
Population	16.8	24.8	32.0	36.7	61.8
Not allocated	–5.3	6.3	2.9	7.8	–14.5
Positive financial savings of domestic sectors	27.9	44.1	56.5	62.5	92.1
Foreign countries	15.1	16.1	–3.0	32.3	16.3
Total available resources	43.0	60.2	53.5	94.8	108.4

In the Yugoslav economic system, in which the formation and the use of savings are mainly done on the basis of free decisions of companies and of other participants in economic activities, it is a normal fact that the economic companies sector, as a basic agent of economic development, invests more than its own savings, while at the same time the population sector appears as the main source of supply of money resources.

However, the largest part of financial resource supply is short term. Against such a supply the demand for long-term resources is constantly increasing. Under such conditions a more active and a more adequate interest rate policy could yield positive results. The level of interest rates should be more in line with the need for greater stimulation of savings of all members in the distribution of income. While on the other hand, the structure of interest rates should be such as to stimulate to a greater degree time deposits of savings on longer term, which would to a greater extent satisfy the needs of companies for long-term resources.

Under Yugoslav conditions of demand constantly greater than the supply of financial resources, the functioning of the financial market is restricted, which often decreases the mobility and the most rational allocation of savings. On the other hand, banks are mainly organized on the territorial principle, which in certain cases leads to territorial shutting and cutting of financial flows.

The factors I have mentioned, along with others, are the reason for insufficient mobility and, therefore, also insufficient efficiency of savings. As has been said, gross savings in the Yugoslav economy are very high (gross savings amount to about 40% of the social product), but their use is not always very efficient. Factors which encourage the use of savings only within one company or a small region, regardless of the fact that they could be used outside these limits more rationally and efficiently, must be removed. In this respect greater application of the mechanism of pooling of savings could become an important factor in the increased integration of the economy and in more rational and efficient use of social capital than at present.

The interests of companies in combining their labor and resources may be numerous and various. For these reasons there is no obligatory form of combination of labor and resources. There must be freedom here for the organizations to find the form that best satisfies their interests. Those interests can be direct, such as taking part in joint income in proportion to invested resources, or indirect, such as ensuring a supply of raw materials, electric energy, improvement of technology, organization of joint research and laboratories, etc.

The combination of labor and resources can include three important elements:

— the return of the real value of the combined resources after a certain period of time;

— taking part in the achieved income in proportion to the invested resources;

— joint bearing of risks.

Pooling of resources, as a form of connecting and integrating the economy, most efficiently secures the movement of social capital throughout the territory of the country and contributes to increasing the rationality of investments. The material interests achieved through combining labor and resources can only secure the necessary concentration of resources in accordance with the needs of modern technical and technological development.

In this way all forms of combination of resources — from a basic organization, work organization, complex organization, up to the wider forms of association within production entities — aim at providing more rational use of social savings by integrating and connecting social capital. The mechanism of combination of resources is applied by self-management agreements and social compacts, which contain rules of behavior, purposes of association, basic principles of distribution of joint income, and modes of responsibility. All forms of association are in fact a question of voluntary and agreed subordination of individual and short-term interests to joint and long-term interests. Pooling of resources, as a form of rational use of social capital, is in the interest both of each individual company and the social community as a whole.

Banks can play an important role here. First, a bank should be the initiator of joint investments in specific major projects, not only among its members but also in large areas throughout the country.

In addition, a bank should provide professional assistance and the necessary analyses and information connected with such combination of resources. Finally, coordination and channeling of companies' programs are also achieved within a bank, because within a bank companies establish mutual dependence, joint responsibility, and greater security in their activities.

Banks should more and more become initiators and organizers of the pooling of resources and, in general, of greater mobility of total social capital. They should be institutions which organize the preparation of joint development plans both among their members and within major production units. In this respect banks should provide companies professional assistance in preparing and presenting development plans and should make available to them timely and objective analyses and information significant for making decisions.

7

BALANCE-OF-PAYMENTS POLICY

Branko Čolanović

In recent years balance-of-payments difficulties have appeared to be among the major economic problems of the national economy. The conclusions drawn by the country's political leadership in November 1979 pointed to "the trade and current-account deficits as a crucial problem for the country, one that has deteriorated to such an extent that it has become a restraint on further growth, negatively affecting the total complex of reproduction flows."

We are faced with a typical example of controversial feedback effects. First, the overall level of economic activity has caused the large balance-of-payments deficit, which has in turn negatively affected the level of economic activity.

The problem can be approached in two ways. First, the routine approach involves the usual practical changes in economic policy. We have all seen how the economies in many countries, even in the most developed, register successes on the one hand and failures on the other; growth in certain economic sectors over a period and then stagnation or decline in other sectors; sometimes high employment and demand and strong capital spending and then recession, unemployment, and an extremely high inflation rate. In this respect the Yugoslav balance-of-payments deficit can be seen on the one hand as a reflection of the very rapid growth of productive forces, a continuing rise in social standards and the standard of living, rapid growth in urban population and areas, etc. Or on the other hand the deficit can be seen as a problem that could be handled fairly swiftly by shifting to new economic, social, or political targets by means of various measures in the areas of fiscal, monetary, credit, foreign trade, or capital spending policies.

Similar problems are encountered in many other countries, both developing and developed. Consequently, the Committee for Economic Policy of the OECD, in its forecasts for 1980, pointed out that a majority of member countries is expected to register deficits in their current accounts.

In some countries deficits accounted in aggregate for a relatively significant share of their social product: in Ireland they amounted to 9.5% of the country's social product for 1979; in Greece, 5.5%; Denmark and New Zealand, 4%; Turkey and Sweden, 2.5%; Portugal, Norway, Belgium, and Australia, 2%; while Yugoslavia recorded deficits in its current account for 1979 at a level of 7-8% of its social product.

Other considerations may include the influence that deficits can produce on the further development of the sociopolitical system, strengthening the position and the role of associated labor in the sphere of the social reproduction and development of the self-management system in line with the Yugoslav model of a decentralized socialist economy.

It is obvious that large deficits limit movement toward various social objectives due to the numerous disturbances they cause in production, trade, and development, which in turn may necessitate state intervention. Yet Yugoslav doctrine consistently anticipates the withering of the state and its functions in the country's economic life, concurrently with the growing influence of the productive entities and their self-management associations on economic activity by means of their independent planning and decision-making, social compacts, and self-management agreements.

However, in this respect, we have witnessed stagnation, decline, serious difficulties, and to some extent, even painful conflicts. They can be partly attributed to a rather rapid process of de-etatization and the withering of certain regulatory functions of the state in the realm of economy, with the result that self-management economic organisms were not properly prepared for their new role; and the administration itself showed either reluctance or resistance to processes aimed at reducing its power, which is understandable. Large balance-of-payments deficits give the administration good reasons to expand in order to cope with various disturbances, structural inadequacies, bottlenecks, and economic disproportions. The balance of payments is a synthetic category, and enormous deficits in it are only a mirror in which the true difficulties of a particular development phase and the subjective weaknesses and mistakes of a particular economic policy are reflected in aggregate.

Res publica rediviva — if a state is considered a mighty structure of concentrated power in the area of planning, production, trade, and distribution of wealth, savings, etc., this is the last thing that would correspond to the essence of Yugoslav self-management socialism.

Balance-of-payments deficits are not a new issue for the Yugoslav economy. We encountered deficits for the first time in the early postwar period, as soon as the country started its programs of accelerated industrialization and social emancipation. Between the two wars Yugoslavia, as an underdeveloped agricultural country, had generally registered surpluses in its accounts. But during the whole thirty-five year period after World War II, our balance of payments showed deficits every year, with the exception of the period between 1972 and 1976, when, as a result of special efforts meant to change the balance-of-payments position of the country, we recorded deficits in two and surpluses in three of the years. This period coincided with the first international energy crisis, which severely affected the Yugoslav balance of payments. Viewed historically, it seems that we were not clearly aware of the enormous and continuing effect this problem had on Yugoslavia's external economic position. Adjustments to the new energy situation and necessary changes in the rate and pattern of development have been neither quickly sensed as necessary nor rapidly undertaken.

The 1979 international energy shock, which strongly affected the country, caught us unprepared to promptly undertake efficient countermeasures, since we are historically accustomed to very rapid growth in social product and employment. As a result, the deficit in the current account for 1979, in the amount of $3.7 billion, was a maximum in both relative and absolute terms.

We will not comment on the years preceding the Yugoslav economic reform of 1965-66, during which the country constantly showed deficits in its balance of payments. The economic reform was largely undertaken not only to orient the Yugoslav economy toward the international environment, to provide for its more complete involvement in international economic flows and the distribution of labor, and to provide new markets for Yugoslavia's growing industries on the one hand and a better assortment and quality of imports for Yugoslav markets on the other, but also to institute solid competition among Yugoslav companies and their foreign partners in order to generally improve the technology, organization, and productivity of the Yugoslav economy. The poor balance-of-payments position before 1965-66 was one of the direct reasons for the economic reform, while dinar convertibility was one of the general aims, although its specific nature and the period over which it was to be achieved were not precisely defined.

Actually, the economic reform brought considerable relief to foreign trade, the balance-of-payments deficit decreased, and the export coverage of imports increased to over 75%. However, the weak points of the strategy adopted became evident rather quickly. Yugoslav economic policy, accustomed during previous decades to high rates of growth in social product and employment, with 220,000 to 250,000 new jobs a year providing enough jobs for coming generations and the transfer of population from agricultural to nonagricultural sectors, now faced entirely new problems. The growth rate declined considerably, and instead of high new employment we registered an absolute downturn. Deflationary monetary policy cut inflation, but also capital spending. Since new jobs were not created, there followed a strong migration to European countries and to Australia and the United States. The highly active economies of those countries were able to absorb this migratory wave. Although the liberalization in foreign trade was not carried out very rapidly, organizationally it was nevertheless not accompanied by an adequate set of the measures and mechanisms developed countries use to explicitly or tacitly protect against unwanted imports. As a result, we had a steady deterioration in current accounts during the whole period from 1967 to 1971. The situation deteriorated to such an extent that in 1971, monetary reserves declined to an insignificant $180 million, which at the best at that time could cover two and a half weeks of imports.

The period 1972-76 was characterized by efforts to improve the balance-of-payments position. Economic policy concentrated on various measures aimed at the fundamental relief of balance-of-payments difficulties. They included, among others, strong stimulation of exports of goods and services from fiscal sources; improvement of export sales on favorable credit terms funded from the sources of the central bank; introduction of meaningful and selective controls on the import side; a series of dinar devaluations; heavy stimulation of private foreign-exchange savings; encouraging Yugoslavs working abroad to remit their savings to Yugoslavia; etc. These policies yielded results. Export coverage of imports, which had in the meantime declined, increased again to satisfactory levels, and foreign exchange invisibles rose considerably. Only the first international energy crisis in 1974 jeopardized these positive trends.

The table below shows a ten-year series of export and import movements and changing balance-of-payments positions for the period 1967-76. It is clear that two variables were significant

Year	Export coverage of imports (in%)		Net position at year end (in millions of $)
1967	73.3	deficit	126.6
1968	70.3	"	171.7
1969	69.1	"	241.8
1970	58.4	"	461.3
1971	55.8	"	473.8
1972	69.2	surplus	419.0
1973	63.2	"	485.0
1974	50.6	deficit	1,183.0
1975	52.9	"	1,032.0
1976	66.2	surplus	150

for the Yugoslav balance-of-payments position: export coverage of imports and the volume of revenues from tourism, transportation, and in particular, from remittances of Yugoslavs working abroad. The above series indicates that the first variable was subject to constant changes, reflecting on the one hand insufficient and inadequate domestic control of export and import flows and, on the other, the unfavorable effects of external prices.

One frequently hears that Yugoslavia has not thus far established a stable long-term export-oriented policy. The effort to enhance exports turned largely into a fight to find commodity surpluses that would remain available in domestic markets characterized by chronic high demand. On the import side some slowness was evident in establishing market-type mechanisms as the chief instrument to protect the country from excessive imports while relying on administrative controls only as a subordinate measure. Perhaps in this respect preservation of the nonconvertible quality of the domestic currency was among the most significant factors. In fact, at the end of the 1972-76 period, during which we recorded favorable trends in our balance of payments, the Yugoslav dinar was practically knocking at the door of external convertibility. The greater attention paid to balance-of-payments trends; the considerable improvements in export-import ratios, including more liberal importation; the significant success in keeping down inflation, which in 1976 was only 9%; the considerable increase in monetary reserves, which at the end of 1976 amounted to almost $3 billion; the successful start of operations of a domestic foreign-exchange market (an interbank institution enabling banks to mutually settle their demand-supply requirements, with the National Bank of Yugoslavia intervening if necessary); the continuing increase in invisibles due to the rise in foreign-exchange savings and remittances from Yugoslavs working abroad; and the trading of Yugoslav banknotes abroad at relatively stable rates that compared favorably with the official dinar parity — all these elements indicated that a decade after the 1965-66 economic reform, external convertibility of the dinar could have been achieved had the economic strategy continued to further provide effective policies and measures.

However, in the years following the first international energy crisis, economic policy did not operate adequately, since domestically very high rates of growth and employment were continued, and even worse, we recorded more rapid growth of personal consumption than of overall social productivity.

During the period from 1977 to 1979, Yugoslavia recorded a large balance-of-payments deficit in each year. In 1977 it amounted to $1.6 billion; in 1978, to $1.3 billion; and in 1979 it amounted to almost $3.7 billion. Such a severe deterioration in the balance of payments resulted in a steep decline in monetary reserves. In 1979 they decreased by $1.9 billion compared to 1978. Simultaneously, foreign borrowing increased in aggregate during the three-year period by $4.9 billion, raising the country's total external indebtedness to $15 billion. The debt service ratio considerably deteriorated to 27% in aggregate, or to 23% with respect to the convertible exchange area. Three years before, in 1976, the ratio amounted to 14 and 17% respectively.

It is not difficult to provide reasons why the economic position of the country deteriorated so sharply. First, we would point to a steep drop in export coverage of imports. In 1977 this ratio amounted to 54.5%, in 1978 to 56.7%, and in 1979 it fell to only 48.5%, mainly due to extremely high domestic consumption. Only in 1979 did personal consumption decline, due to a 1% decrease in real personal income. Nevertheless, capital spending, which remained enormously high during the whole three-year period, and which averaged much higher than in the past, and particularly than in other developing countries, peaked during 1979. The share of investment in fixed assets amounted to 36.5% of the social product in 1977, 39.5% in 1978, and in 1979 it was around 40%. Residential construction was also extremely intensive: in the amount of new housing construction compared to national income, Yugoslavia was first or second in Europe. The inflationary pressures emerging from the two investment sectors were the main reasons for a very rapid escalation of prices and import increases in real terms.

The prevailing terms of trade for Yugoslavia can also be taken as a second important reason. During the whole postreform period ending in 1976, Yugoslav export prices rose faster than import prices, with the exception of 1974, when Yugoslav export prices rose by 32% and import prices by 46%, largely due to oil price increases. Such favorable terms of trade contributed heavily to qualitative changes in the balance-of-payments position of the country during the five-year period 1972-76 in which Yugoslavia, as already mentioned, recorded surpluses in three years, uniquely for the whole postwar history of Yugoslav international economic relations. In 1977 import prices rose slightly faster than export prices, but in 1978 export prices rose considerably faster than import prices. In 1979 however, export prices increased by 15% and import prices by almost 20% due to a new oil price increase. In this respect the unfavorable terms of trade generally multiplied the negative effects of the increased physical volume of imports in 1979.

The third reason perhaps relates to the reforms in the foreign-exchange system which came into force in March 1977 with a new law on foreign exchange and credit operations abroad. The law, which had been prepared and discussed in many state and semigovernmental organs, inaugurated a significant decentralization of federal competence over international economic relations by transferring the responsibility for economic relations with foreign states to republics and provinces and introducing the principle that foreign exchange belongs to those who had ultimately earned it. It appeared, however, that this unique decentralization was not organized in a completely rational manner. It also appeared that republics and provinces showed less efficiency in the field of promoting exports, instead occupying themselves with creating import licenses and rights that exceeded the balance-of-payments potentials of the country. In the absence of an overall control system that could apply corrective measures, such behavior was a significant reason for a steep increase in the volume of imports after 1977.

On the other hand, we confront a quite new phenomenon. We have a nonconvertible domestic currency, on the one hand, and a liberal disposition of foreign exchange by the direct exporters on the other. Only further experience and examination could demonstrate to what extent and in what way the two elements could be consistent.

However, a decentralization of foreign trade decisions, through the transfer of competence to republics and provinces, appeared to be a significant factor causing difficulties in the initial years of the new foreign-exchange system. The essence of the problem lies in the fact that a strong rise in imports emerging from polycentrically organized competence resulted not only in the already-mentioned considerable decline in foreign exchange reserves, on the one hand, and an increase in external indebtedness on the other, but also in the failure of the Yugoslav foreign-exchange market to operate in the manner provided for by the current law. As a result there were considerable disturbances in the complex of reproduction, the material position of enterprises, the relations between various economic entities, the supply of commodities, etc. This experience points to the need for decentralization of foreign economic relations to be organized in a more appropriate way. The economic policy for 1980 has focused on this problem. It has been not only more active in its efforts to improve the balance-of-payments position of the country by means of various practical measures on the federal, republic, and provincial levels, but also in providing necessary improvements in the foreign-exchange system and the law on foreign exchange and credit operations abroad. This should remove institutional factors promoting economic disequilibrium in the country.

In general, the various factors that determine balance-of-payments movements can be divided into four groups. The first group relates to the long-term development trend, that is, to regular characteristics and typical phenomena which unavoidably appear in certain development phases.

The second group includes the international, economic, financial, and political environment, which can determine a country's balance-of-payments position over a certain period. The third group relates to various institutional solutions offered by prevailing foreign trade and foreign exchange systems producing different influences on the characteristics and overall stability of the country's balance of payments. Finally, practical economic policy measures, not only in the foreign trade sector but also in other sectors, may directly or indirectly determine the current balance-of-payments situation. We will briefly review these groups of factors and their role in shaping the Yugoslav balance of payments.

Yugoslav experience confirms the general rule that an underdeveloped country which undertakes the accelerated development of its industrial and other economic sectors, including the regional dispersion of productive forces as well as a major improvement in the social and cultural standards of its population, almost always faces balance-of-payments difficulties that may last for decades after its initial takeoff. In our case the problem was more difficult because we entered the period of accelerated development immediately after World War II, in which the economic potential of the country was almost destroyed, and we lost 11% of our population.

The usual scheme of changes in the development flows and intersector relations appears roughly as follows. Capital concentration is necessary for the construction of new industries. Domestically capital could be derived first from a poor agricultural sector, which results in depressed prices for agricultural products over a longer period, which in turn discourages the development and modernization of the agricultural sector. Foreign capital is available in the form of credits and joint ventures with foreign partners. In either case foreign partners try to derive maximum profits on employed capital. Even in the case of long-term credits, the burden of repayment begins relatively soon, after four to five years at best, which means that the balance-of-payments must provide the necessary room for external debt service early enough. On the other hand, more rapid development of new industries absorbs agricultural surpluses that otherwise could be exported. Similarly, a sharp rise in the standard of living produces higher consumption not only of basic foodstuffs but also of other goods and services not present in previous consumption patterns. This produces two shocks to the balance of payments, which immediately enters a chronic deficit. The new industries require foreign equipment, technology, know-how, means of transportation, construction equipment, etc. The higher price levels at which capital equipment exporters sell equipment to developing countries further aggravate the balance-of-payments positions of the latter. At the same time, new industries require increasing imports of raw materials and semifinished products, since in general they are not available in the country in sufficient quantities. Soon enough there is a conflict between the relatively limited purchasing power of the domestic markets and the productive capacity of modern industrial plants, which should operate on a large-scale basis in order to ensure appropriate returns on capital and to avoid the negative effects of economic autarchy.

Exportation of new products to other markets faces various obstacles which the other countries raise in the form of customs and other protection barriers, as well as those created by the powerful multinationals, cartels, etc.

This necessarily leads to a drop in export prices or to strong export subsidies by developing countries, with a negative impact on their balance of payments and the consequent outflow of a part of their national income to their foreign partners.

The Yugoslav case was aggravated by the existence of another serious problem — the need to construct a modern social and economic infrastructure. As early as in the First Five-Year Plan of 1947-51, we started very ambitious programs to electrify the country, to build a railway and road network, etc., which further continued on a large scale and even expanded to include construction of ports, airports, telecommunication systems, etc. A social infrastructure had to follow due to the extremely backward and poor condition of various objects of social welfare, health protection, education, culture, etc.

Around 1950, at the start of a thirty-year period of accelerated development, Yugoslavia had $339 of social product per capita, i.e., only a third of the European average and nine times less than North America. The portion of the population engaged in agriculture amounted to over 70%. Over a thirty-year period of development, the social product per capita rose seven times, and the agricultural population fell to around 30%.

Two questions can be asked. First, how long the present phase, characterized by the adverse effects of the overall accelerated growth on the country's balance-of-payments, might last. Second, whether the effects inherent in the phase should be so strong, or whether the magnitude of the balance-of-payments deficit should be so large.

To answer the first question, various elements should be taken into account. One is closely related to the present demographic and socioeconomic structure. With a 30% agricultural population, Yugoslavia cannot achieve the level of productive forces characteristic of developed countries. So large a proportion of agricultural population also means that the country's overall productivity is on a relatively low level; but even with 30% of the population producing food and agricultural products, Yugoslav agriculture does not represent a significant sector on the export side. Over the years the annual transfer of agricultural population into nonagricultural sectors amounted on average to 1% or more of total population. The transfer may also slow down due to balance-of-payments difficulties. If we assume that the total agricultural population declines to 15%, as in those industrialized countries which have significant agricultural production, then, based on previous experience, such a development phase should take another fifteen to twenty years.

A few other specific aspects should be taken into account. First, at the moment we have around four million people employed in nonagricultural sectors who continue to live in nonurban areas. We would normally expect that so large a share of population would naturally try to settle in urban areas, thus maintaining urban development at intensive levels, as well as new housing construction in cities, etc., with all the attendant consequences for inflation and the balance of payments. Second, there is a relatively large number of people registered as unemployed. In 1979 an average of 762,000 people were looking for jobs, of which 450,000 were unskilled and 410,000 were women. They are primarily workers who intend to leave the agricultural sector and therefore register with employment agencies. Years will pass until new investments in fixed and working assets can solve this problem. Third, even now there are several hundred thousand Yugoslavs working temporarily abroad. Their return would be useful and purposeful in any respect, but it depends on new jobs opening up in both the social and private sectors, which also means long-term programs for intensive capital spending, which in turn will produce new inflationary pressures and balance-of-payments disturbances.

If for the moment we put aside the above demographic and socioeconomic fundamentals, we encounter problems relating to the national scientific and research potential. The level from which Yugoslavia started its accelerated industrialization after World War II was in this respect *tabula rasa*. At the end of 1978, however, there were around 800 scientific and research development institutions employing more than 55,000 people, of which almost 22,000 were highly skilled research specialists.

During the school year 1978/79 we had about 350 university institutions (colleges and faculties) producing about 28,000 graduates, 1,600 masters, and 850 doctorates. It goes without saying that this potential will in the future be able to make its initial contribution to further promotion of organization and technology, to technical and scientific innovations, to further improvements in productivity, etc. For the time being, however, the Yugoslav scientific and research potential has not reached a level that will release the country from scientific and technological dependence on foreign achievements.

Of course, there are some exceptions. For example, Yugoslav achievements in the field of agriculture — selection and breeding of new kinds of corn and wheat, and so on, are well known. Still, we can expect that scientific and technological dependence on foreign achievements will continue for some time, resulting on the one hand in higher expenditures for imported technology licenses and know-how, and on the other in an inadequate assortment of imported equipment, production processes, and know-how. To overcome the present phase and to achieve a level that would allow for larger exportation of technology and know-how to other countries, we would need a decade or more, provided that development policy for the scientific and research sector was consistently conducted in order to concentrate national intellectual and financial resources along lines that suit Yugoslav development targets rather than to continue the current dispersion of staffs and programs and parallelism in the establishment of scientific and research institutions.

We might need less time, but not much less, to construct, on the basis of self-management, an efficient financial mechanism capable of assuring mobility of capital resources toward major investment projects, with intensive orientation toward exports or import substitution, better participation in international labor distribution in specific sectors, higher returns on capital, and higher foreign-exchange earnings and savings.

To answer the second question, i.e., the size of the balance-of-payments deficit, we should try to examine the efficiency of the present economic model in terms of its impact on the balance of payments — undoubtedly a very sensitive task. There may be dilemmas concerning the priorities established by the economic policy for each development phase.

More rapid growth of social product and employment is a priority target of each developing country. It is necessary only to define them appropriately in terms of volume and period involved. After a longer period of paying relatively less attention to balance-of-payments aspects of the development process, they have now become very acute, and they are classified among the major problems of the country.

The problem is twofold: on the one hand, it will be necessary to remove temporary difficulties in balance-of-payments deficit and external liquidity, and on the other to cope with the fact that the Yugoslav economy has grown accustomed for thirty years to higher rates of growth and employment, accompanied by chronic deficits. Any sudden changes in existing patterns of growth and employment will not be that easy to make because they may cause serious problems in the sphere of production, employment, commodity supply, standard of living, to say nothing for the moment about questions of a social and political nature.

Capital spending undoubtedly has a major influence on the Yugoslav balance of payments. Its volume has been exceptionally large, particularly recently, when capital spending ranged between 39 and 40% of the total social product. Such spending patterns are direct reasons for major disturbances in all the three main accounts: physical, financial, and foreign exchange. Current economic policy anticipates a considerable slowdown in capital investment programs to adjust them to the time frames defined by the financial potential of the country and to cut down heavy borrowing abroad. This appears to be a necessary step toward a gradual easing of balance-of-payments difficulties.

However, capital inefficiency is even more serious a problem. It has characterized the extensive development of the country during all these years. The 1965-66 economic reform had announced that one of its objectives was a rise in productivity, particularly in capital efficiency. In this respect only some modest and sporadic successes have been achieved. Return on capital (the ratio between capital invested in fixed assets and the increase in social product) varied widely over the period 1967-76, remaining on the whole substantially unfavorable if compared with the developed countries. The capital coefficient (showing the capital spending needed for a unit increase in social product) was 4.5 in 1977, and was among the best achieved in the postreform period. Then it deteriorated to 5.4 in 1978, 6.3 in 1979, while in 1980 we expected to spend roughly between 7 and 8 dinars to achieve a one-dinar increase in social product.

Similarly, capital spent for housing construction is also inefficient. As in other economic sectors, construction time is very long. The ratio between unfinished and finished construction is unfavorable. Recently, for each completed building we had 2.5 unfinished. Consequently the sector needs an overall reorganization which should involve changes in construction, financing, maintenance, new acquisition patterns, new rentals policy, etc. So far only some partial solutions have been proposed.

The reasons for capital inefficiency are very complex. Some relate to various weaknesses evident in the area of planning and social compacts. We will have to eliminate some major problems in our economy to permit planning of capital investments on rational and realistic principles. Among the most serious problems, perhaps, will be elimination of the price imparity existing among sectors which favors some sectors, giving them benefits of higher capital efficiency, and disfavors others, keeping them on the edge of capital inefficiency and losses.

Regional control of development trends, which are under the strong influence of local, regional, or republic authorities, is another problem. So far economic policy has not appropriately used the interest rate as an active instrument in capital allocation. However, this problem is now being approached with the aim of strengthening the role of the interest rate as a factor of behavior of economic entities with regard to their current operations and capital-spending alternatives. In this way we can expect better solutions and more appropriate concentration of financial resources from both domestic and foreign sources for those capital projects which have been given priority in economic plans and social compacts.

For the time being, credit is a major form of capital concentration, the attractiveness of which for the economic entities and investors is understandable in view of the policy of cheap money that has been carried on for years.

The pooling of financial resources, which would represent a more progressive form of capital concentration, is for the time being faced with the problems of price imparity, regional control of development, low interest rates, etc.

Public placements of bonds, as a method of acquiring available funds, has not been used to a larger extent, although there exist legal possibilities and economic justification for such a form of capital concentration.

Inefficiency of capital investments has several consequences for the balance-of-payments situation. We may, for example, point to a high volume of imported equipment which is, in terms of its technical capacity and performance, used on considerably lower levels than in the developed countries. Extensive capital project construction also causes high importation of raw materials and energy. The weak places are particularly evident in the field of energy. National programs for saving energy and substituting domestic for imported energy have been delayed.

In the absence of domestic capital and foreign exchange sources, external borrowing for financing the construction of capital projects is proportionately very extensive, causing high expenditures in current accounts for repayment of principal and payment of interest. Due to all this, producers' prices are set at higher levels, reducing Yugoslav competitiveness in foreign markets and in turn adversely affecting the country's balance-of-payments position.

From examining the present status of Yugoslavia's social and economic development, we can conclude that balance-of-payments difficulties and tensions will continue, probably until the end of this century, and also that necessary changes and improvements in our development pattern should lead to better ratios between capital investment spending and performance, reducing the balance-of-payments deficit. Experience from the period from 1972 to 1976, when the balance-of-payments situation improved, shows that an active economic policy can in a relatively short time achieve considerable improvements in the balance of payments.

The other group of factors that define the Yugoslav balance-of-payments position relates to those emerging from the international environment: prevailing conditions in international trade, price movements, competition, the behavior of certain countries and international economic groups, etc. It is not necessary to further discuss the Yugoslav position in the prevailing pattern of terms of trade. It should, however, be emphasized here that Yugoslavia, as a developing country, although already making progress along the path of accelerated economic and social development, is in a so-called sandwich position. On the one hand its balance of payments is strongly affected by rising prices for imported energy and, on the other, by sharp increases in prices for capital equipment, which Yugoslavia largely imports, as well as by the rising interest it pays on the foreign credits by means of which it finances equipment purchases.

Consequently, it is obvious that the volume and pattern of Yugoslav development programs should undergo some major changes. The new system of planning should consistently insist that further development of productive forces and further promotion of the standard of living should mainly rely, much more than in the past, on those domestic sources which in the long run can promote an improvement in the Yugoslav balance-of-payments position. Obviously, such sources are, in the first place, agriculture, tourism, nonferrous metals, coal, etc.

This question is very important, the more so because our country does not belong to any international political or economic bloc, with nonalignment being the fundamental principle on which its international policy and position are based. Specific arrangements concluded with important international economic groups yield some results, but they do not offer a sufficient guarantee against the open or tacit protection or the reluctance with which some developed countries greet Yugoslav efforts on the export side. The struggle for a new international economic order is not for Yugoslavia merely a question of international solidarity or a philosophic perception of the world rearranged on the principles of economic justice; it is also inherent in its fundamental national interests. Due to the economic nonalignment of the country, changes in capital-spending and development patterns are even more imperative.

The third group of factors that can define the balance of payments relates to the foreign-exchange system. Various solutions incorporated in the institutional components of the foreign-exchange system may consequently encourage or discourage economic entities toward more rational behavior with regard to the country's balance of payments from the point of view of major national interests.

It is difficult to consider the foreign-exchange system in the framework of a single definition, and no efforts will be made to this end. However, there exist certain elements and categories which undoubtedly define the character of the system, and some of them will be considered here. Since the history of the Yugoslav foreign-exchange system may be of no specific interest here, and in view of limited space, we will focus only on the presently prevailing aspects of the foreign-exchange system.

The basic principles of the current law on foreign exchange and credit relations reflect the substantial changes that were inaugurated six years ago by the new Yugoslav Constitution. They meant further democratization of decision-making in economic life in line with the main principles of vesting basic responsibilities and rights in the basic organizations of associated labor, since such organizations form the basis for combining labor and resources and, accordingly, for planning and implementing the foreign-exchange system.

At the same time, decentralization of federal competency in the area of the foreign-exchange system and policy, through a transfer of a considerable share of responsibility from federal to republic and provincial institutions, finds its equilibrium in the joint foreign-exchange policy of the country instituted by the law as an important principle in the country's economic policy. Consequently, the country's economic policy should have been implemented within the framework of a joint foreign-exchange system and joint Yugoslav market.

The organizations of associated labor may freely dispose of their earned foreign exchange. They may hold it in accounts with Yugoslav banks authorized to deal abroad, or they may use it to satisfy their foreign-exchange requirements or pool these funds with those of other organizations of associated labor. On the republic or provincial level, the plans for the economic relations with abroad are adjusted in the self-management communities of interests of a republic or a province. On the federal level, in the community for international economic relations, republic or provincial communities review and agree on joint principles and objectives defined in respective plans of international economic or credit relations, the latter being of considerable importance for the overall balance of payments of the country and the unity of the Yugoslav market.

So far no systematic study has been made of the effects of the foreign-exchange system. Roughly speaking, one might conclude that it was responsible for the large balance-of-payments deficits recorded from 1977 to 1979, and also in 1980, because of their coincidence with the actual period of the operation of the system. However, only careful examination and analyses would show which failures should be attributed to the foreign-exchange system and which to the actual performance of the current economic policy. The most obvious problems that have already been identified as badly aggravating the Yugoslav balance-of-payments situation and the country's economic position in the international framework should be closely studied. Such studies were started by the middle of 1980, and consequently, significant changes in the law of foreign exchange and credit relations should follow.

One question that has already been mentioned relates to the consistency of the link existing between the quality of the national currency and rights and responsibilities for the disposal of available foreign exchange. It is almost certain that the current liberal regulations governing exports and imports, or a free disposal of available foreign exchange by basic organizations of associated labor, or by republic or provincial communities for international economic relations, would not have been questioned at all had the Yugoslav currency been convertible. However, under the circumstances the conflict could have been resolved only by large-scale mechanisms of synchronized self-management agreements or social compacts, providing that great disparities in prices and capital efficiency by individual sectors had also been removed and that the factors causing the regional control of social and economic development had been further suppressed.

In the meantime, we face larger oscillations in dinar parity, utilization of available foreign exchange to purchase reprocessing material abroad for those producing capacities which show an artifically high capital efficiency level, lack of foreign exchange for those basic organizations of associated labor that import some basic raw material and energy, negative foreign-exchange rate differentials in banks dealing abroad, strong interventions of republic and provincial self-management communities in the allocation of foreign exchange, etc.

The obligatory assignment of some portion of available foreign exchange earned by ultimate exporters of goods and services to permit the importation of needed raw materials and energy, mainly crude oil, appears to be the most practical solution. Foreign exchange should be assigned to republic and provincial self-management communities, which would be, by all means, equally responsible for the importation of the commodities needed by the Yugoslav markets taken as a whole. The assignment might also be given to the National Bank of Yugoslavia, enabling it to rehabilitate the domestic foreign-exchange market, at least to the extent of the foreign exchange assigned. Among other positive effects, this would lead to better utilization of available foreign-exchange potential and would eliminate, to some extent, disturbances in the domestic foreign-exchange market and reduce the balance-of-payments deficit.

For some time after the economic reform of 1965-66, Yugoslavia consistently made considerable efforts to terminate bilateral economic agreements and international barter, clearing, or similar arrangements. Such efforts were understandable from the point of view of the country's clear and homogenous foreign-exchange system as well as with respect to the adopted target of achieving external convertibility of the national currency. As a member of the International Monetary Fund since its inception, Yugoslavia endeavored to adjust its foreign-exchange system to the former's statutory rules. Later, when due to international economic and financial disturbances the fundamental principles of the International Monetary Fund underwent significant changes, and when due to the international energy crisis and the weaknesses of the national economy the convertibility of the national currency was postponed, this question did not receive appropriate attention. With disturbed and disrupted international trade relations, with a relative worsening of the economic position of the developing countries, many of which experienced economic stagnation, so that trade relations could continue only with reliance on intergovernmental or other similar arrangements, the problem grew in importance.

There are no reasons why the developing countries should not organize among themselves certain forms of cooperation and self-assistance and thus face the severe protectionism of the developed countries. Consequently, the inadequate attention paid to specific intergovernmental arrangements contributed in part to the stagnation and even decline in Yugoslav trade with certain countries, particularly the developing countries, so that their share in total Yugoslav trade usually lagged behind the adopted objectives.

External accounts of private persons represent a special feature of the Yugoslav foreign-exchange system. At the end of 1979 Yugoslav citizens, residing in the country or abroad, held around $7 billion on deposit in about three million external savings accounts opened with Yugoslav banks. The federation guarantees the foreign-exchange savings deposits.

The motives for the development of a system of foreign-exchange savings deposits were rather clear, and they basically had to provide strong stimulation to foreign-exchange savings by private persons, particularly by those temporarily working abroad. Undoubtedly this had a favorable effect on the country's balance-of-payments position, counteracting the large trade deficit.

This problem appeared at a moment when the whole strategy had received new dimensions. It is estimated that about two thirds of the foreign-exchange savings deposits now belong to permanent residents of Yugoslavia. They acquire foreign exchange partly from their relatives permanently or temporarily residing abroad and partly by means of invisible flows from social sectors (tourism, trade over a frontier, etc.) toward private individuals who now hold more than 50% of total national savings in currencies other than the dinar, with a tendency to faster growth compared to dinar savings. The importation of goods and services to which the holders of external accounts are entitled by using the funds available in their accounts has grown enormously. In 1979, for example, the total remittances from Yugoslav emigrants and workers temporarily residing abroad amounted to around $3.4 billion, while in the same period the expenditures by foreign-exchange savings deposits holders amounted to around $1.7 billion.

Another problem should be taken into account. The banks pay interest on these deposits in foreign exchange, even on those held by Yugoslav residents. Despite the Yugoslav deficit at the end of 1979, interest totaling around $0.5 billion was paid to holders of foreign-exchange savings deposits, thus improving their external purchasing power, which in turn created additional pressures on the country's balance of payments.

Without focusing on the social, psychological, or political aspects of this issue, it is clear that in further reforms of the national foreign-exchange system, it will be necessary to institute new solutions in order to permit the rational functioning of the system from the point of view of both the social economy and the joint and common domestic market. At the same time, any new solutions based on reasonable economic principles in a situation of nonconvertible national currency should provide full protection to the genuine foreign-exchange savings of individuals.

The foreign-exchange system anticipates that the balance-of-payments deficit be covered in two ways: by means of borrowing abroad (financial and commercial loans) and by joint venture investments in Yugoslavia.

Borrowing abroad is almost exclusively done for the account of basic organizations of associated labor, as basic nuclei of the whole country's economic structure in accordance with the principle of their basic responsibility for the total performance of the national economy. The provisions of the law, which prohibit borrowing by banks for their own accounts (banks are otherwise responsible for handling all operations relating to borrowing abroad), are not appropriate. The problem arises around the formal interpretation of the expression "for one's account." According to Yugoslav regulations, the bank's founders and members decide on the disposal of the total income earned during a year; the banks may not create their own independent funds, since there is a joint and unlimited secondary responsibility of the bank's members and economic and other organizations of associated labor for the bank's operations. Consequently, if the banks were in a position to conclude large foreign loans at more advantageous times and under more favorable terms and conditions, they would assign such funds to those members who were entitled by law to foreign borrowing, which would decrease the cost of foreign borrowing and improve the financial standing of the Yugoslav economy and Yugoslav banks abroad.

Legal regulations permit Yugoslav basic organizations of associated labor to obtain financial resources abroad by selling their bonds, denominated in foreign currency, in the international capital markets. However, there have been no attempts to do this. It would be useful to analyze the reasons why this type of access to foreign capital markets was not used in the past and also to find ways to encourage it.

The second vehicle for offsetting the balance-of-payments deficit is by means of foreign capital investments in joint ventures in Yugoslavia together with domestic organizations of associated labor. In this regard the Yugoslav foreign exchange system has a positive approach and several motives: first, to provide for the importation and incorporation in the Yugoslav economy of the most modern foreign equipment and technology; second, the advantage of penetrating foreign commodity markets with the assistance of their strong foreign partners; third, to increase available capital resources by attracting capital from foreign sources; and there is also a fourth group of motives that relate to balance-of-payments considerations.

After the introduction of the first regulations on joint ventures in 1967, practical experience showed that certain solutions proposed by the regulations were not attractive enough to foreign partners. Therefore initial results were rather modest. The recently amended law on joint venture operations has resolved many of these issues, and even the most critical approach may be hard pressed to find its weak points.

There remain, however, other factors which may adversely affect joint venture operations, such as high domestic inflation, frequent changes in regulations that do not permit long-term forecasts, substantial regional control of development plans, the large influence of local and regional sociopolitical communities on the overall functioning of the basic organization of associated labor, etc. Improvements in this respect will encourage the potential foreign partners to undertake joint venture operations in Yugoslavia.

Finally, the fourth group of factors which define the balance-of-payments position relates to current economic policy. In rough terms, the current economic policy for 1980, in the national institutional framework and under the conditions existing in the international environment, makes considerable efforts to gradually eliminate and overcome the problems emerging from the enormous balance-of-payments deficit. It is evident that the policy is now much more active than during the period from 1977 to 1979; it attempts to take advantage of the lessons learned during the first and second international energy crisis and also of a rather widespread stagnation and recession in the major industrial countries, on the one hand, and to eliminate more promptly the obvious domestic weaknesses in the area of the foreign-exchange system, planning, social compacts, and self-management agreements on economic movements and flows, on the other. The obvious results recently achieved in restraining personal consumption and imports, as well as major efforts to cool off capital spending, with results yet to be achieved, should be stressed. Export earnings increased considerably in 1980, and the deficit will undoubtedly decrease by more than one third of the 1979 figure. A major problem in this respect remains strong inflation, which will be considerably higher than in 1979, when it amounted to 24% on an annual basis. However, considerations relating to this issue are beyond our topic here.

Although the present economic policy applies virtually all the measures and instruments institutionally available, there are some additional measures that may seem appropriate. A recent devaluation of the national currency, though implemented with considerable delay, did yield some results that could have been even greater if other measures directly influencing the balance of payments had also been introduced. We should mention a timely provision of funds for fiscal support to exports of goods and services. There are at least three unresolved points in this regard. First, there is uncertainty about the volume of support to be given to specific commodities and services due to insufficient readiness to give up certain inherited privileges. The second open question relates to timely provision of funds for fiscal support; it is attributable to insufficient readiness to adopt fiscal support of exports as a top priority of the country's economic policy. Third, the most important problem relates to the inadequate mechanism of federal, republic, and municipal fiscal systems, which are unable to efficiently provide equal and synchronized support for Yugoslav exports. A decentralized fiscal mechanism, organized on the municipal, provincial, and republic levels, is not yet capable of providing sufficient support for the export of goods and services, which is one of the country's most important tasks.

The link between the self-management communities (in the area of health protection, education, social benefits, sports, science, roads, etc.) and the country's general endeavors to promote exports as inadequate. Legal contributions to their funds by all users of social resources (basic and other organizations of associated labor) establish their purchasing power irrespective of the country's balance-of-payments position.

The Yugoslav Bank for International Economic Cooperation is an important institution that supports Yugoslav exports of capital goods (equipment, vessels, construction of capital projects abroad, etc.). Chronic insufficiency of the bank's capital is not a minor handicap in stimulating larger exports of machinery, equipment, means of transportation, processing equipment, etc., or concurrently those sectors which on the one hand are not fully employed and on the other are able to provide good quality and a satisfactory assortment of commodities. This is a crucial point for further development of economic relations between Yugoslavia and developing countries. Economic policy remains responsible for providing full financial support to these activities.

Likewise, the current credit-monetary policy is to some extent irrational from the point of view of the need to improve the balance-of-payments position. The Yugoslav commercial banking community is, by prevailing regulations, bound to certain limits in its lending activities. These limits also apply to loans extended to Yugoslav enterprises to finance their exports of goods and services; but on the other hand, they do not apply to loans for housing construction, although the latter strongly influences domestic demand and, indirectly, the balance-of-payments deficit. However, all these points do not represent major obstacles, and their solution might be achieved relatively easily through improvements in current measures and mechanisms.

It has been rather difficult for me to present all the complexity of the Yugoslav balance-of-payments policy in the space available here: problems deriving from ideological and political fundamentals, institutional framework defined by the national Constitution, and the international environment in terms of actual movements and influences and the ability of the current economic policy to cope with them. It is always easier to critically examine and gauge results after the fact than to define the contents of a practical program in advance. However, problems must be identified first in order to be solved; there remains the question of whether we have identified the problems, whether we have identified all of them, and whether we have done so clearly enough.

From the balance-of-payments point of view, we will have to closely examine the trends and prospects of the international economic situation to be better able to adjust our policy. International crises like those in the area of energy and the international monetary system, exceptional disturbances in international financial markets, and the obvious resistance of the developed countries to changes in the present economic order have given us some clear experience which should undoubtedly be taken into account.

The control of domestic inflation, which cannot be eliminated but should be kept at least at moderate levels, is a necessary condition for improving the country's balance-of-payments situation.

If we have to maintain further higher rates of economic growth and social development along with the principles of self-management socialism, it will be necessary in the coming years to pay much more attention to balance-of-payments policy. We will probably have to take into account various parameters deriving from the country's foreign-exchange position in order to determine the pattern and rates of growth which would best suit our overall economic position, assuming that we have to make our best efforts to achieve the targets set. The debt service ratio should perhaps be taken into consideration, or the annual amount of the country's foreign-exchange liabilities resulting from foreign borrowing, which undoubtedly should be done at the right moment; then we would have to define the requisite volume of exports of goods and services and other foreign exchange revenues, on the one hand, and the volume of expenditures for goods and services to be imported, on the other.

Such a methodology will clearly indicate those sectors which should be given priority to permit their active contribution to further development (agriculture, nonferrous metals, tourism, etc.) or to substantial import substitution (coal, forestry, etc.).

In settling the new five-year plan for the period 1981-85, all these questions should certainly receive our attention.

8 THE FOREIGN TRADE SYSTEM OF YUGOSLAVIA

Ljubiša S. Adamović

The foreign trade system of Yugoslavia is increasingly becoming an integral part of the overall economic system, sharing the process of evolution of the economic system as a whole. At the same time, due to the special role of foreign trade and economic relations with the rest of the world in general, the Yugoslav foreign trade system has various specific features that merit special attention.

The foreign trade system is based on several principles formulated in the Constitution of the Socialist Federal Republic of Yugoslavia of 1974, Part II. Some of these principles are:

— peaceful coexistence and active cooperation among equal states and nations, regardless of their respective internal socioeconomic system, represents the *conditio sine qua non* for maintaining world peace;

— Yugoslavia participates in international relations and respects the national sovereignty of other states and nations;

— Yugoslavia is against interference in the internal affairs of other states;

— all international problems should be settled peacefully;

— in international relations Yugoslavia respects the rules and principles laid down in the United Nations Charter, fulfilling her international obligations in general and in particular within the international organizations in which she functions as an active member.

In order to implement the basic principles on international cooperation, Yugoslavia is developing her activities along the following lines:

– the freest possible international exchange of both material and cultural values;

– development of a liberalized international information system;

– development of international economic relations based on equal rights of all the participants in order to realize the common economic, cultural, and other interests of states, nations, and peoples;

– development of forms of international cooperation that would provide the possibility for sovereign control over national natural resources;

– development of international relations that would create favorable conditions for the more rapid development of the less developed countries;

– as a socialist country, Yugoslavia stands for the development of political, economic, and scientific cooperation that contributes to democratic types of cooperation among states, nations, and peoples. In this respect Yugoslavia represents an open community.

As a result of this general platform, it is of utmost importance to point out Yugoslavia's unique position as a socialist state developing toward an open society. In the area of foreign economic relations, this engenders our special concern to provide conditions for an open economy whenever and wherever it is possible. Limitations in this respect are present mainly in two basic cases:

a) national defense and security;

b) protection of the domestic market on the basis of the infant industry argument.

The positive attitude toward openness of the Yugoslav society is of vital importance and is one of the most important features of contemporary Yugoslavia. It has been a very healthy resource and one of the key reasons explaining our social and economic progress. In the area of foreign trade this means that Yugoslavia is trying to apply an institutional setup that will stimulate a free exchange of goods and services among various countries on the principles of nondiscrimination and mutual benefit. Various laws and regulations in the area of foreign trade and economic cooperation with other countries in general have been inspired by these principles. It is important, however, to take into account the fact that the reality of international economic conditions, as well as the achieved level of economic development in Yugoslavia, in some cases represents a limiting factor in applying those principles. This is why the foreign trade system has to reflect dynamic changes both in the process of the internal development of the economy and in the dynamics of the international economy. It has to reflect the policy and rules of various international institutions to which Yugoslavia belongs, such as the IMF, IBRD, GATT, UNCTAD, etc., as well as the specific economic conditions of a labor-managed economy like our own.

The Importance of External Economic Factors

Since the end of World War II, the foreign trade system has been developed under conditions of heavy pressures from abroad. These pressures were expressed mainly in the form of a permanent lack of foreign exchange. During this whole period the foreign trade deficit, as well as the deficit in the balance of payments, has been the most important reason for introducing various forms of restrictions. The balance-of-payments deficit has been one of the most important limiting factors in the process of economic development, and it certainly has influenced the foreign trade system as a whole. Since the country has a typical developmental balance-of-payments deficit, it is to be expected that various forms of restrictions will persist in the future, despite the fact that these restrictions are in conflict with the principles established in the Constitution. In this respect Yugoslavia's position is in many ways, as are the stances of the many more developed economies, based on the principles of trade liberalization, but at the same time with a need for (temporary) restrictions of various kinds.

The deficit in the balance of trade and balance of payments has been used from time to time as an argument to support certain autarchic tendencies. From time to time these tendencies have influenced the formation of the Yugoslav foreign trade system; but considering the whole period after World War II, they have been overcome by tendencies toward liberalization. Autarchic tendencies conflict not only with the intentions of the foreign trade system but with the overall socioeconomic development of the country. Therefore one of the important features of the foreign trade system is to improve the position of the Yugoslav economy in the international division of labor. The less the presure of the foreign trade deficit, the more the openness of the foreign trade system will come to the fore.

The Evolution of the Foreign Trade System

The foreign trade system could be analyzed from various standpoints; but in order to follow its evolution, one of the best ways to studying it is to consider it as an integral part of the economic system and to follow the stages of development of the economic system as a whole and the foreign trade system as a segment of it. Changes in the foreign trade system reflected changes in the development of productive forces of the whole economy as well as the ways and means which could have been used to connect the economy with the rest of the world. That is why we feel a historical approach is the most relevant in explaining the evolution of the foreign trade system. Therefore, in our further analysis the main stages in that evolution will be explained.

The state monopoly on foreign trade was the most important characteristic of the foreign trade system from 1946 to 1952. This institutional arrangement was in perfect accord with the system of central planning and administrative control and management in the Yugoslav economy as a whole. Within the framework of administrative management, in which government in general and the federal government in particular was omnipotent, foreign trade had to be organized on the basis of a state monopoly. The federal government was the only seller and the only buyer in all deals between Yugoslavia and the rest of the world. The well-known advantages and disadvantages of a state monopoly on foreign trade did not reveal in Yugoslav practice any particular deviation from the general rule. The state trading system was accompanied by very strict foreign exchange control. The Ministry of Foreign Trade was the main administrative organ in charge of carrying out the foreign trade plan, both in the area of exports and imports as well as in implementing intergovernmental trade and payments treaties. Actual foreign trade transactions were executed by the eleven large state firms that were in charge of particular branches and sectors of the economy in the area of exports and imports. Every foreign trade transaction had to be previously "covered" by a special foreign trade license issued by the Ministry of Foreign Trade.

Export earnings were concentrated in the central foreign exchange fund, and from that fund payments were provided according to the planners' priorities. As for the exchange rate for the dinar, it was established at fifty dinars for one dollar. This rate was used for dealing in effective currency as well as for invisibles. For payments in goods exchange, various parities were established due to the existence of the Equalization Fund. The Equalization Fund covered the difference between internal (planned) prices and external (market) prices for enterprises producing for export and/or importing goods from abroad. Differences between internal and foreign prices were significant due to the fact that within the system of central economic planning, internal prices served as a means to collect important governmental income as well as the instrument for capital accumulation (savings). Generally speaking, industrial items had higher prices to foster industrialization, while agricultural prices were considerably lower. Among the prices of industrial products, highly manufactured goods were particularly privileged. Foreign markets, however, did not accept the very subjective pricing policy of the centrally planned Yugoslav economy, and therefore the Equalization Fund played a very important role in bridging the gap between internal and external prices in export and import transactions. The functioning of the Equalization Fund was based on the existence of a variety of exchange rates for various products and various sectors and economic branches. Automatic intervention from the fund was important so that export and import flows were smoothly executed. For all practical purposes, it is safe to say that exporting firms could be subsidized from the Equalization Fund, while importing firms (or import transactions) had to pay the fund. At the same time, even for a single type of goods, the real exchange rate applied by the Equalization Fund could have been different for each transaction, depending on the price paid by the importer or on the exporter earnings from abroad. This is how the system of state trading created and applied a large variety of exchange rates for both export and import transactions. This type of multiple exchange rate system, however, emerged as a result of the central planning system and its effects on internal prices and discrepancies between the internal pricing system and the prices on foreign markets.

Due to the existence of the Equalization Fund, Yugoslav exporters and importers were able to remain indifferent to the type of their export or import items, or to the prices they paid for imports or got on the world markets for their exports. These effects were absorbed by the Equalization Fund, while exporters and importers operated internally on the basis of internal prices. These prices were planned in such a way that some profit for the firms producing the items or commissions for the exporting and importing firms were administratively provided for. One of the most important consequences of this arrangement was the lack of real criteria for comparing the productivity and efficiency of Yugoslav enterprises to foreign firms.

The Period of Decentralization in Foreign Trade: 1952-61

The most important legal and institutional step toward decentralization of the Yugoslav economic system as a whole and toward the introduction of workers' self-management happened in the middle of 1950, when the Law on the Establishment of Workers' Management over Enterprises and Higher Economic Associations was introduced. The law is considered the basic legal act on the labor-managed economy. It was difficult, however, to deal immediately with all sectors of the national economy. Therefore, the Law on Labor Management was applied first to the productive sector of the economy, and it took some time to spread to other areas.

Economic relations with other countries — of which foreign trade is still the most important part, while in the midfifties it was practically the alpha and omega — was one of the last sectors where decentralization took place. This can be explained by the fact that the productive sector of the economy had to apply the law first, so that performances in the most tangible and visible areas could be checked and analyzed. Second, various restraints in foreign economic relations represented a more complex barrier to decentralization. There were justified doubts that a quick dismantling of the state monopoly of foreign trade might provoke various difficulties. Considering both the political environment, the economic, military, and political blockade of Yugoslavia by the USSR and the satellite countries, as well as internal economic difficulties, this hesitation and relatively slower pace in introducing decentralized and self-managed foreign trade seemed appropriate.

For the reasons mentioned above, the process of decentralization and the gradual introduction of the self-management system in the foreign trade sector began in 1952, almost two years later than in the productive sector of the Yugoslav economy.

The existence of the Equalization Fund did not have any justification within the system of decentralization, and it was replaced on June 1, 1952, by the so-called system of export and import coefficients, which could be compared to a multiple exchange rate system. Foreign trade enterprises, which until 1952 functioned as an extension of the Ministry of Foreign Trade and its General Divisions (*Generalne direkcije*) were for the first time given opportunities to behave like real enterprises. In other words, due to the decentralization of the planning and management system, foreign trade firms had to be controlled and managed by the employees and to operate on a profit-making basis. The role of prices changed, and prices began to be treated as one of the most important criteria of profitability. As for foreign trade planning, the centralized system of planning in detail was replaced by planning in global frameworks of exports and imports. By the same token, export and import licensing and licensing for foreign trade payments automatically lost their importance.

Between 1952 and 1961 the foreign trade system underwent several changes, more often than creators of the system had expected. The main reason for this was the weakness of the internal market and the difficult time the domestic market had in adjusting to such deep changes in the foreign trade system. The mechanism needed to absorb and cushion shocks from the external and internal markets had to be revised several times. One of the most important visible causes of difficulties could be found in disparities between external and internal prices. The role of the export and import coefficients was to bridge prices between internal and external markets, but not automatically for each individual transaction. Instead, price floors and ceilings for various products were established in advance. The range of coefficients was from 0.80 to 4.00, with a total of eighteen steps between the two limits. Each step represented a space, or value, between the two coefficients, e.g., 0.80 to 0.90, 0.90 to 1.00, etc. In fact, the 1.00 coefficient meant the official exchange rate, which since June 1, 1952, had been 300 dinars for one dollar. Differences between various coefficients were not equal, however. They grew as the coefficients grew (2.25, 2.50, 2.70, 3.00, 3.50, 4.00).

The export coefficient meant that the exporter was entitled to receive from the National Bank a counterpart sum in national currency at the official rate plus an addition based on the coefficient he was entitled to receive. Selling abroad goods entitled to an export coefficient of 1.20 meant that for each dollar earned, the exporter received 360 dinars (with 300 dinars the official exchange rate for one dollar, and 60 dinars the result of application of the 1.20 coefficient).

In the case of imports the mechanism worked in the opposite direction. When the import coefficient was above 1.00, the importer had to pay the bank accordingly; and when the coefficient was below 1.00, the bank had to pay the importer. The former case, however, was much more typical than the latter one.

The mechanism of coefficients had above all the task of serving as a bridge between the Yugoslav internal pricing system and the prices quoted and respected on world markets. Both exporters and importers were given the opportunity to compare internal to external prices. After the introduction of the coefficient system, participants in foreign trade operations received incentives to become price conscious and to monitor their own profitability when dealing abroad. Yugoslav society did not accept any price of foreign trade transaction, as had been the case during the existence of the Equalization Fund. Therefore, after the middle of 1952, Yugoslav producers, exporters, and importers began to behave in accordance with certain basic rules of a market-type economy: they sold abroad only when it was more profitable than to sell internally, and they bought abroad when it was more profitable to do so than to buy internally. Despite the fact that such behavior was not always possible, particularly in the case of imports due to the lack of foreign exchange, the basic attitudes of market-type behavior had been introduced into the foreign trade sector of the Yugoslav economy.

For all practical purposes, it could be said that the foreign trade coefficients acted as a mechanism to correct the official exchange rate as well as the most important incentive for exporters. As for importers, in practice coefficients acted as a specific form of tariff. A high import coefficient meant that it was more profitable to buy internally than to import.

Changes in the foreign trade system in 1952 also included the opportunity for foreign trade firms to retain at their own disposal 45% of foreign exchange earnings; but before the end of the year, this amount (the retention quota) had been reduced to 20% of foreign exchange earnings. At the same time, a new institution was introduced to act as a replacement for the foreign exchange market. This was the Foreign Exchange Settlement Center, or DOM (*Devizno obračunsko mesto*). This foreign exchange market was meant to serve as a buying and selling center for the foreign exchange at the disposal of enterprises based on the legal retention quota. Foreign exchange rates established at DOM could be compared with the fluctuating exchange rates based on demand and supply, at least for the smaller amount of the total foreign exchange at the disposal of the Yugoslav economy. Due to the fact that demand was always much higher than supply, exchange rates established at DOM were too high, and this is why in 1956 only the

National Bank was entitled to sell foreign exchange at DOM. The foreign exchange market had to be organized and controlled mainly because of the main constraint in the Yugoslav foreign trade sector: foreign exchange starvation.

The Foreign Trade Reform of 1961

Further changes in the foreign trade system were necessary for several reasons:

a) the decentralized, self-managed Yugoslav economy, which already had various features of a socialist-market economy, needed a foreign trade sector that could act accordingly as a more integrated part of the national economy than had been the case;

b) the foreign trade sector as such was handicapped in measuring its own profitability and efficiency both internally and internationally because of the large fan of multiple foreign exchange rates (the system of foreign trade coefficients, for practical purposes, could be called a system of multiple exchange rates);

c) Yugoslavia had developed intensive international activity within the United Nations and among the newly developed countries, both in political and other fields (economic, scientific, technical, cultural, etc.). As a founding member of the United Nations and as an active member of practically all specialized agencies of the UN, Yugoslavia had to adjust to the rules of the games applied in the international community, in accordance with the level of economic development of the country and the growing need to become more integrated into the world economy and international economic relations.

The most important change introduced by the foreign exchange reform of 1961 was a new commercial exchange rate (the official exchange rate remained the same) of 750 dinars for one dollar (the official exchange rate of 300 dinars plus 150%). At the same time, since the newly established unified commercial exchange rate was not sufficient to replace a variety of formerly used coefficients, a system of export premiums was established, amounting to 10, 22, and 32% of the achieved foreign market price, for exports of goods and services. In practice this meant that exporters of particular goods and services (officially listed) could price their foreign exchange earnings at a rate of 825, 915, or 1,040 dinars per dollar. This change meant that the dinar had been devaluated from an average level of 600 per dollar to 750 dinars per dollar.

The new exchange rate was not good enough to adequately replace the system of coefficients, and this is why premiums for exports were introduced; but at the same time, additional protective measures were needed (in order to make up for the lack of high import coefficients). In the middle of March 1961, the Decree on Temporary General Custom Tariff was introduced. A protective function of tariffs for a developing economy like Yugoslavia's was, and still is, given serious consideration. According to the Temporary General Custom Tariff, all goods imported into Yugoslavia were subject to custom duties from 0 to 60% *ad valorem*.

Additional forms of foreign exchange control were needed for the same reason: lack of an adequate foreign exchange reserve, lack of gold reserves, and heavy pressure to import foreign goods and services to cover the needs of a growing economy. As the main additional forms of foreign exchange control, various kinds of foreign exchange quotas were introduced, such as: a general license for payments abroad for particular imports; a foreign exchange quota for imports of mass consumption goods; a foreign exchange quota for imports of capital equipment.

As for the trade restriction mechanism, the use of a quota system with imports and exports licensing was introduced.

One of the most important features of the foreign trade system established in 1961 was that the principle of nondiscrimination was preserved. All rules and procedures had to be applied equally in trading with convertible currency areas as well as in trading with the so-called clearing currencies or with countries with nonconvertible currencies. But it should be noted that dealing with a very heterogeneous world on the principle of nondiscrimination has been a risky experiment. Lower prices on markets with convertible currencies were more attractive to Yugoslav importers, while higher prices in countries with nonconvertible currencies were attractive to Yugoslav exporters. This was one of the main reasons for the discrepancy in Yugoslav foreign exchange balances with the convertible currency area and the clearing currency area. Since most Yugoslav foreign trade is with European countries (and the more one goes into the past, the more obvious is the preponderant role of Europe in Yugoslav foreign trade), such a discrepancy meant that the Yugoslav deficit was growing with Western Europe, while surpluses were growing in trade with Eastern Europe. Yet the need for Yugoslav imports and payments for imported goods and services were much more concentrated in Western European countries.

External Aspects of the Economic Reform of 1965

The process of the development and growth of the Yugoslav economy and the openness of that economy and society to impulses from abroad, in both economic and noneconomic areas, has contributed greatly to an increase in the general understanding among all strata of Yugoslav society that the Yugoslav internal economic system, being unique and sui generis as compared with societies in the West and in the East, has to become a more integrated part of the world economy. It has to have internal and external mechanisms that will assure the preservation of the self-managed socialist system, and at the same time it must provide a broad enough framework for economic cooperation with the rest of the world. Such a social and political climate was not possible under the conditions of extreme poverty experienced immediately after World War II, and it was not possible unless some experience had been accumulated within the Yugoslav nation, experience marked by a positive attitude toward growing economic and other forms of cooperation with the rest of the world.

This is why external factors were a very important component of the social and economic reform of 1965. For the purpose of the further evolution of the foreign trade system, it is important to mention that internal prices were increased for many agricultural products and raw materials. Many prices, particularly in the service sector, were freed and deregulated, which meant a new input into the foreign trade sector. The main objective of this price policy was to reduce the disparity between internal and world prices, so that more realistic comparisons could be made between the performance of the Yugoslav economy and the economies of her main foreign partners. At the same time, under these conditions a realistically defined, unique foreign exchange rate could serve as the best and simplest instrument guiding the foreign trade sector and the behavior of Yugoslav participants in foreign economic transactions.

In order to establish conditions for the stable and more balanced growth of the Yugoslav economy, the economic reform of 1965 also dealt with the problems of taxation and primary and secondary distribution of national income; the role of enterprises was increased in various areas like investments, self-financing, science, education, etc.

In the area of foreign economic relations, the main objective of the economic reform was to expose Yugoslav economic performance to the more direct influence and direct impulses from the world market. In other words, this was the first time since World War II that the role of the foreign sector in the national economy, both in theory and practice, was not considered a necessary evil but one of the most important factors in further economic growth. At the same time, 1965 was also when the convertibility of the dinar began to be seriously considered as one of the goals of the internal and external economic activity of the Yugoslav economy. In order to achieve convertibility of the national currency, it became of utmost importance to introduce measures that might permit the dinar to have the same or similar purchasing power both internally and abroad.

The economic reform of 1965 contributed to the further liberalization of Yugoslav foreign economic relations. One of the first measures introduced by the reform was further devaluation of the dinar, which in 1965 had a parity of 12.50 dinars per dollar (after July 25, 1965). Since the end of June 1980, the exchange rate for the dinar has been 27.00 per dollar.

Another important component of the Economic Reform of 1965, but one that pertained to the foreign trade system as well, was the enactment of the Law on Permanent Custom Duties. Newly introduced duties were 50% smaller than the existing ones, so that the average tariff applied for imports according to the Law on Permanent Custom Duties of 1965 was about 11%.

The newly established foreign exchange rate meant at the same time higher incentives for exporters and higher limitations on importers. One group of exporters was privileged, however, because within the Economic Reform, exporters enjoyed liberalized imports of primary commodities and raw materials, provided that they used their own foreign exchange resources to buy the above-mentioned items. The process of liberalization of dealings in the area of foreign trade and foreign exchange can be illustrated by the following components of the foreign trade system:

The free disposal of foreign exchange earned by the enterprise, provided that the foreign exchange is used in accordance with regulations dealing with imports of goods and services. In other words, the enterprise is not forced to sell foreign exchange to the National Bank but can keep it on its own account and use it according to its own needs within the framework of the law. At the same time, as a general rule, foreign exchange earnings have to be repatriated (deposited in a Yugoslav bank) ninety days after they have been earned.

Foreign exchange accounts of enterprises and other persons can be established in Yugoslav banks, and foreign exchange can be used for payments abroad for various business transactions. Payments in foreign exchange between domestic firms and persons for internal business transactions are not permitted. But if Yugoslav enterprises have mutual contractual relationships on long-term business and technical cooperation or cooperation in production, they can have common foreign exchange accounts and can settle their mutual obligations using foreign exchange.

A prevailing exporter institution was introduced to provide incentives to those firms exporting more than 50% of their production. These enterprises were given the right to use freely their foreign exchange (earned by their exports) to import raw materials and semifinished goods they needed for their own production process.

The retention foreign exchange quota was used in order to stimulate exports. Enterprises could keep for themselves about 20% of their foreign exchange earnings as their retention quota and use it for practically any purpose, from importation of necessary raw materials and finished products to payment of their various contractual obligations, including patent rights, general debts, etc. This is why the retention quota could be treated both as an export promotion instrument and an instrument for the further liberalization of Yugoslav foreign trade.

Foreign exchange self-financing was introduced in order to enable Yugoslav enterprises to enter various forms of credit arrangements with foreign firms, banks, etc., whenever they have an interesting project, mutually acceptable for the domestic and the foreign partner.

The interbanking foreign exchange market was introduced to provide a more flexible mechanism for adjusting the Yugoslav economy to changes on world markets. Both commercial banks and the National Bank of Yugoslavia participate as members of this market both to make the adjustments described and to coordinate the introduction of the dinar into the international system of payments.

At the same time, the regulation of the flow of goods and services, both exported and imported, complements foreign exchange regulation. These two areas are two sides of the same coin in all economies which do not have convertible currency, as is the case with Yugoslavia.

It is important to recognize the logical connection between foreign exchange and foreign trade regulations. By regulating the foreign exchange flows, some influence is exerted on flows of goods and services. By regulating the flow of goods and services, it is possible to indirectly regulate the flow of the means of payments, in other words, the flow of foreign exchange. These are monetary and material aspects of the same process.

As far as the regulations dealing with exports are concerned, it could be said that exports from Yugoslavia are deregulated and free from restrictions. They depend on Yugoslav enterprises (basic organizations of associated labor) in productive or trading sector deciding about their preference to sell their goods and services internally or abroad. There are, however, two exceptions to the rule under which exports could be restricted:

— an export license is necessary when there is a shortage of certain goods on the domestic market, when national health could be endangered, or when national security is at stake;

— export permission is necessary when free flows of exports could endanger the regional balance of Yugoslav foreign trade. This situation develops from time to time due to the fact that Yugoslavia, more than any other country, has to maintain balanced flows of trade between the convertible currency areas and the clearing currency areas (the important role of the USSR and Eastern Europe) in Yugoslav foreign trade.

Export regulations are thus relatively unimportant. Far more important are regulations of imports. The system of import regulations includes eight institutional arrangements dealing with particular categories of imports:

1) Free imports, or so-called "LB" imports, meaning liberalized imports. For all the goods assigned to the LB category, authorized banks have to provide the requisite amount of foreign exchange so that an importer can complete and pay for a particular import transaction. Enterprises have to report earlier about their intentions to import larger amounts of particular goods and services. At the same time, thirty days before the transaction, an importing enterprise might have to deposit funds in dinars equivalent to the foreign exchange needed. These two constraints were introduced to create more favorable conditions for the foreign exchange liquidity of banks as well as to increase the level of responsibility of potential importers, both in terms of planning in advance and in terms of financial responsibility. Inasmuch as some Yugoslav imports belong to the "LB" category, one could speak of the beginning of convertibility of the dinar, since the bank has to provide convertible currency for dinars deposited by the enterprises.

2) The conditionally free import, or "LBO," has been introduced

so the government can intervene and regulate flows of imports when serious regional disequilibria might appear. This means that an enterprise first has to consider importing particular goods and services from the clearing currency areas, so that obligations in bilateral trade agreements can be fulfilled. When this source is exhausted, or when there are no opportunities to import from the nonconvertible currency region, the importer can apply for foreign currency under the conditions of "LB" import.

3) The global foreign exchange quota is an instrument restricting imports on the basis of the total value of the previously achieved level of import transactions. It is required by the fact that the amount of available foreign exchange is limited and must be distributed on the basis of common participation of various groups of producers and importers. In other words, representatives of particular branches have to decide about the distribution of the foreign exchange quota (in organizations and under the auspices of the Federal Chamber of the Economy). If the representatives of the business enterprises are not able to reach an agreement, the Federal Secretariat for Foreign Trade steps in and assumes the position of decision-maker in the matter.

4) The goods contingent (quota) covers a relatively small category of goods used to improve regional balances in flows of goods. It is also used to provide a minimum supply of those goods not being imported by enterprises. In other words, for various reasons enterprises might not import certain goods which are important for the general level of supply in Yugoslavia. Distribution of the goods contingent is settled in the same way as the distribution of the global foreign exchange quota. The Federal Executive Council (federal government) determines the amount of the goods contingent, consulting the Federal Chamber of the Economy and the Federal Secretariat for Foreign Trade.

5) An import license "D" is issued by the Federal Secretariat for Foreign Trade for specific types of imports, like drugs, armaments, etc. To import arms, a license has to be issued by the Federal Secretariat for National Defense. Having received this import license, the importing enterprise is not provided with foreign exchange. Payments have to be made from the importer's own sources.

6) Imports based on export earnings is a category of imports that could be considered a part of the old system transferred into the new foreign trade system after the introduction of the economic reform of 1965. Enterprises that have earned foreign exchange

income can use part of it to pay for imports of raw materials or semifinished products for their own needs. Due to the foreign exchange problems of the late seventies, this category of imports is a very important part of the current foreign trade system.

7) The import of capital equipment is subject to a specific procedure. The global foreign exchange quota for the import of capital equipment is distributed among the six republics and two provinces, which decide the type of capital equipment to be imported. Enterprises are able to pay for the importation of capital equipment from their own sources as well as to use a certain part of their depreciation allowances to buy capital equipment.

8) The import of personal consumption goods does not represent a specific category of imports as far as the foreign trade system is concerned. Personal consumption items are imported on the basis of liberalized imports ("LB") or on the basis of the global foreign exchange quota. From time to time, however, certain items for personal consumption are imported by the Food Product Reserves Administration (*Direkcija za rezerve prehranbenih proizvoda*) and by the Material Reserves Administration (*Direkcija za materijalne rezerve*). These two agencies are in charge of intervening by importing products and placing them on the Yugoslav market to stabilize the market or to reduce pressure for price increases. They use the services of the most favorable supplier among the Yugoslav import enterprises that serve as agents importing the types and amounts of goods decided by the two federal agencies.

Joint Business Ventures

Yugoslavia was the first socialist country to permit the establishment of joint business ventures between domestic and foreign firms. Legal acts dealing with these activities were proclaimed in 1967. Since then, on various occasions some technical and legal details have been changed and adjusted according to the needs of the time and real life, but the basic reasons and motivations for this form of foreign economic cooperation remain the same.

Yugoslav experience has shown that basic trends in the world economy, and in world trade in particular, affect every single country in the world, regardless of its socioeconomic system. One of these relatively new features is that trade tends to grow more quickly among nations that are cooperating in the area of capital flows and joint organization of production. Another world trend: the international division of labor is based not only on specialization in products but more and more on specialization in making certain stages of the product, while the other stages are completed in other countries.

These and other basic changes in world production and world trade have been important in the light of certain specific needs of the Yugoslav economy:

a) as a small and underdeveloped country, Yugoslavia has difficulties in importing new technology and know-how;

b) with a small internal market, Yugoslavia cannot be a competitive producer in many lines of production. Therefore it has to produce for foreign markets in order to achieve certain economies of scale;

c) even if it were able to produce at competitive prices, Yugoslavia faces difficulties (as do many other less developed nations) in placing its products on world markets;

d) Yugoslavia's intensive process of industrialization has been financed both internally and externally. Its level of indebtedness is increasing; instead of using foreign capital in the form of credits, it may be more efficient and cheaper to attract foreign capital in the form of joint business ventures. Therefore joint business ventures could serve as a new source of capital financing;

e) through joint business ventures Yugoslavia could create conditions for more efficient use of foreign capital. A foreign partner would invest only in those Yugoslav enterprises which, in the investor's opinion, could provide a certain rate of profit. The foreign investor is not limited by various constraints present when Yugoslavia imports foreign capital in the form of credits and when political criteria, regional distribution, etc., are at least as important as economic criteria in the allocation of investment funds. Therefore, through joint business ventures the Yugoslav economy might introduce another objective criterion when measuring the efficiency of capital, or when decisions on investment allocation have to be made.

According to legislation in this area, the foreign partner cannot have more than 49% of the total value of joint investments. Foreign capital can be invested in the form of joint business ventures in various branches, such as: production (manufacturing), transportation, tourism, and scientific and technical research. But it is not permitted in trade, banking, and other services. All aspects of management, control, profit, and risk sharing, etc., are left to the partners. These issues are regulated on a contractual basis. As for repatriation of capital, taxation of profits, and profit transfers, Yugoslav legal stipulations are more or less adjusted to international practice. The net profit of the foreign partner is taxed at a rate of 35%, but this tax can be progressively smaller provided that the foreign partner decides to reinvest his profits within the same or in some other Yugoslav business firm. It is also stipulated that a business committee (poslovni odbor) must be established and be based on the investment shares of the partners. The workers' council of the Yugoslav business firm has to transfer some of its power to the business committee.

The foreign investor can place his capital in various forms of investments: foreign exchange, capital equipment, patents, and licenses. The contract on a joint business venture between a Yugoslav and foreign partner becomes legally valid after it has been confirmed by the Federal Committee for Energy and Technology.

Export Promotion

Increasing competition on world markets creates additional difficulties in placing goods from Yugoslavia, as from many other developing countries that do not have any particular natural monopoly (oil, etc.). Therefore certain measures for import promotion are more justified as part of Yugoslav foreign trade practice than the same or similar measures used by industrial powers. But even export-promoting measures applied in the Yugoslav foreign trade system reflect the relatively low level of economic development of the country and the lack of powerful means to boost exports. These measures are:

1) a 3% tax benefit for goods exported to overseas countries, provided that convertible currency has been earned;

2) a 5% tariff compensation on imported inputs used in the production of goods to be exported to countries with convertible currencies;

3) preferential treatment for credit discounts for capital equipment and ship exports, as well as for investment activities abroad (construction and others);

4) some aid could come from the fund for credits and insurance of export activities;

5) special funds have been established to promote exports of cattle, and processed meat, tobacco, fish and canned fish;

6) under the auspices of the Federal Chamber of the Economy, a special Fund for the Promotion of Economic Publicity Abroad has been created.

Basic Considerations in Import Regulations

Relatively liberalized imports under conditions of high internal pressures and increasing demand for foreign goods, as well as internal inflation developing at higher rates than inflation in the main partner countries, resulted in heavy pressure on the balance of trade. This is why the trade deficit is still the main reason for the Yugoslav balance-of-payments deficit.

Since the domestic currency has been overvalued and foreign currencies seem to be "cheaper," there has been long-term high demand for importation of semifinished products and parts to be assembled in Yugoslav "factories," which in many cases were nothing more than assembly plants. Therefore various measures of shorter or longer duration were undertaken in order to regulate imports:

1) preferential treatment of imports from developing countries in the form of easier credit conditions – the interest rate is 3% instead of 6%;

2) lowering of custom duties for imports of specific types of capital equipment and some steel products;

3) instead of conditionally free imports ("LBO"), certain new categories have been introduced, like the "global license" and the "global permission."

It is to be expected that the import regulation features of the Yugoslav foreign trade system will from time to time be diversified and "enriched" in order to provide some administratively determined framework for the balance-of-trade deficit. Increased prices of oil since 1973 have had a detrimental effect on the Yugoslav economy, which was on an excellent road toward achieving equilibrium in its balance of payments by the middle seventies. As a relatively rapidly developing underdeveloped country, Yugoslavia gets the worst of both worlds when it comes to the effects of the oil price hike:

a) as a relatively heavy importer of oil (domestic production does not cover more than 20% of consumption), Yugoslavia has a substantial outflow of foreign exchange earnings to pay for its oil;

b) at the same time, the Yugoslav economy is not developed

enough to be able to compensate for high oil prices by increasing prices for capital equipment, technology, and know-how, as all the highly industrialized countries are doing. In fact, Yugoslavia is paying increased prices for capital equipment, technology, and know-how as if it were an oil exporter!

Finally, despite the fact that Yugoslav enterprises are independent in dealing with the rest of the world and in choosing partners and areas of business activities, in order to adjust foreign trade activities to the other sectors of the economy, certain institutions are constantly in charge of regulating foreign trade activities and therefore contributing to the development of and necessary changes in the foreign trade system. These institutions are:

— the Federal Secretariat for Foreign Trade;

— the Federal Secretariat for Finance;

— the National Bank of Yugoslavia, with its arrangement of national banks for six republics and two provinces;

— the commercial banks;

— the Federal Chamber of the Economy.

According to the constitutional transformation in the early seventies and the new elements introduced into the Yugoslav economic system, the area of foreign trade has also been complemented by the establishment of several new institutions. All these new elements are based on Article 43 of the Constitution adopted in 1974. These new institutions are:

— self-managed communities of interest for economic relations abroad (samoupravna interesna zajednica za ekonomske odnose sa inostranstvom). This institution is established at the state and provincial levels as well as at the federal level. Each community of interest for economic relations abroad plans the foreign exchange balance of the republic and autonomous province as well as the federal foreign exchange balance;

— coordination committees at the state, provincial, and federal levels coordinate foreign trade activities and the application of legal acts in the area of foreign trade;

— common economic representations abroad (zajednička privredna pretstavništva u inostranstvu) coordinate the activities of Yugoslav production and trading firms abroad. They are formed for an individual country, and their offices are established in that country; but it is also possible to organize one common economic representation abroad for several countries.

The main features of the newest constitutional transformations and their effects on the Yugoslav foreign trade system can be summarized as the intention to develop more intensive cooperation between the productive and trading enterprises (organizations of associated labor), cooperation which makes both types of organization share the risks and benefits of production and trade. The second feature is the intention to put republics and autonomous provinces more directly in charge of foreign economic relations, so that they share with the federal government responsibility for the foreign trade balance and the balance of payments. It is to be expected that after some time, the whole nation is going to become "export conscious." This is a precondition for the external economic factor to become an integral part of internal development policy.

Since most of the current permanent or temporary foreign trade restrictions are the result of the presently heavy pressure on foreign exchange reserves, the only safe way to decrease the role of foreign trade regulations is to improve the balance of trade on the basis of more rational investment allocation, increased productivity, and the efficiency of the Yugoslav economy.

BIBLIOGRAPHY

1. Adamović, Ljubiša. Teorija medjunarodne trgovine, Belgrade, "Savremena administracija," 1978.

2. Adamović, Ljubiša. Medjunarodni ekonomski odnosi, Belgrade, "Savremena administracija i Institut za ekonomska istraživanja," 1979.

3. Aleksić, Milan, and Unković, Milorad. Medjunarodna trgovinska politika — spoljnotrgovinski sistem Jugoslavije, Belgrade, Savremena administracija, 1978.

4. Institut za spoljnu trgovinu. Analiza devizne reforme iz 1961, Belgrade, 1964.

5. Savezna skupština. Devizni i spoljnotrgovinski režim, Belgrade, 1966.

6. Fabinc, Ivo. "Elementi programa zastite jugoslovenske privrede," Ekonomist, 1968, no. 1.

7. Macesich, G. Yugoslavia: The Theory and Practice of Development Planning, Charlottesville, University of Virginia Press, 1964.

8. Mrkušić, Žarko. Problemi prilagodjavanja deviznog kursa?, Belgrade, Ekonomska misao, 1969, pp. 133-41.

9. Pertot, Vladimir. Ekonomika medjuna rodne razmjene Jugoslavije, Zagreb, Informator, 1971.

10. Vlaškalić, Milena, and Zeković, Velimir. Ekonomika Yugoslavije, Belgrade, Privredni pregled, 1979.

11. Čobeljić, Nikola. Privreda Yugoslavije, book 2, Belgrade, Savremena administracija i Institut za ekonomska istraživanja, 1976.

12. Službeni list SFRJ no. 17, September 30, 1966.

13. Constitution of the SFR of Yugoslavia, Belgrade, 1974.

14. *Zakon o deviznom poslovanju i kreditnim odnosima sa inostranstvom*, Službeni list SFRJ no. 15, March 1, 1977.

15. *Zakon o prometu robe i usluga sa inostranstvom*, Službeni list SFRJ no. 15, March 1, 1977.

16. *Zakon o obavljanju privrednih delatnosti u inostranstvu*, Službeni list SFRJ no. 15, March 1, 1977.

17. *Law on Long-term Industrial Coproduction, Business and Technical Cooperation and Acquisition and Granting of Industrial Property between Organizations of Associated Labour and Foreign Partners*, Belgrade, Jugoslovenski pregled, 1979.

18. *The Law on the Yugoslav Bank for International Economic Cooperation and on Joint Financial Organizations*, Belgrade, Jugoslovenski pregled, 1978.

19. Balog, Nikola, and Varady, Tibor. *Joint Ventures and Long-term Economic Cooperation with Foreign Firms*, Belgrade, Jugoslovenski pregled, 1979.

9

THE DEVELOPMENT OF THE PEASANT ECONOMY IN SOCIALIST YUGOSLAVIA

Vladimir Stipetić

The development of the peasant economy can be properly analyzed only within the broader context of the socioeconomic development of socialist Yugoslavia over the last three decades and against the background of the economy and social conditions inherited from the pre-World War II period.

1. The Development of Yugoslav Agriculture

The economy of prewar Yugoslavia reflected its predominantly agrarian structure. Agriculture was the main branch of the economy, and transport, trade, and other activities were heavily dependent on its prosperity. In years in which good weather was combined with a satisfactory sale of farm produce, the economic situation was generally favorable. And conversely, consecutive bad years, combined with unfavorable market conditions, usually deadened the country's whole economy.

Yugoslavia's postwar economic development has negated so large a role for agriculture in the country's economy. Through an extraordinary effort and an adequate economic policy, Yugoslavia has contrived to emerge from the backwardness for which the agrarian structure of her economy had been responsible. The deep changes effected in the structure of the economy resulted in a gradual but steady decline in the importance of agriculture in the national economy.

The Yugoslav economy between the two world wars was characterized by slow economic and social development. During the fourteen-year period from 1926 to 1939, national income increased at an annual rate of 2.14%, which (after allowing for a rather high rate of population increase of 1.4% annually) resulted in a very low rate of increase of per capita income of only 0.64% per year. This permitted only minor changes in the predominantly agrarian structure of the national economy. Between 1923-25 and 1938, the share of industry and mining in total national income increased from 20.5 to 25.7%, while the share of agriculture and forestry decreased from 58.1 to 52.6%.[1] This slow process of industrialization was accompanied by an equally slow process of change in the socioeconomic composition of the population, so that while the total population increased over the two decades 1921-41 by four million, the share of agricultural population in the total population declined by only 5%, from 78.8 to 73.9%. This meant that the absolute number of the agricultural population had increased.

On the eve of World War II, per capita national income was about $115, ranking Yugoslavia among the least developed countries in Europe. However, the capitalist system of production and socioeconomic relations produced a highly uneven distribution of an otherwise low income. Thus 4.5% of the population belonging to the upper stratum of the capitalist class of rentiers and landowners received almost 22% of total national income. Within the nonagricultural population, the upper 10%, consisting of prosperous capitalists, appropriated 30% of the total income generated in nonagricultural activities, while the working class, representing 34% of the nonagricultural population, received only 12% of that income.[2] According to the 1931 census, about 1.4 million, or more than two thirds, of all agricultural individual holdings belonged to low-income holdings up to five hectares in size, accounting for 28% of the total agricultural area; 3.1% of the prosperous landowners, with holdings over twenty hectares in size, owned 23% of the total agricultural area of the country. This, together with the fact that the average size of all holdings was only four hectares, shows the magnitude of social tensions in the rural areas caused by the extremely uneven distribution of landownership.

The share of the agricultural population in total population is the most general indicator of the importance of agriculture in the Yugoslav economy (and of the country's economic development in general). The basic data are presented in Table 1.

In the interwar period the agricultural population made up be-

Table 1

Total and Agricultural Population on the Territory of Present-Day Yugoslavia, 1910-77

Year	Population (in thousands) total	Population (in thousands) agricultural	Increase (+), decrease (-) in agricultural population	Share of agricultural population in total (in %)
1910[1]	12,936	10,494	...	81.0
1921	12,545	9,885	-510	78.8
1931	14,534	11,132	+1,247	76.6
1941[2]	16,650	12,300	+1,168	73.9
1945[2]	15,100	11,100	-1,200	73.3
1948	15,842	10,606	-694	67.2
1953	16,991	10,316	-290	60.9
1961	18,549	9,198	-1,118	50.5
1971	20,523	7,884	-1,354	38.2
1977[3]	21,775	6,790	-1,094	31.2

[1]According to population censuses in individual parts of Yugoslavia's territory.

[2]Author's estimates for March 31, 1941, and for June 30, 1945. Other data are based on population censuses.

[3]Official estimate — given in Statistical Yearbook of Yugoslavia, 1979.

tween four fifths (1921) and three quarters (1941) of the total population. The 1961 census showed the agricultural population to be only half of the total; in 1971 only 38.2% of the population was engaged in agriculture; and in 1977 it was officially estimated at less than one third. Thus a steady and a marked fall in the share of the agricultural population has occurred, suggesting an essential change in the socioeconomic structure of the population.

Note should be taken of certain tendencies manifested within the scope of this general trend. During the interwar period from 1921 to 1941, there was some decrease in the relative size of the farming population; the decline amounted to only 4.9% in the twenty years surveyed. In absolute terms, however, the farming population continued to increase during this period, its numbers rising by 2.4 million people. About three fifths (60%) of the total natural population increment during this period remained on the land. In the period since the war, a qualitative change has occurred in this respect. Not only has the relative share of the farming population declined much faster during this period, but the absolute number of farmers has also been on the decrease. In the thirty-two postwar years from 1945 to 1977, the proportion of the agricultural population has dropped by as much as 42% (from 73% to 31%)[3] and in absolute terms by about 4.3 million people. Expressed in annual rates, total population growth averaged 1.4%, and the increase in the agricultural population averaged 1.13% during the interwar period. In the postwar period from 1948 to 1977, the annual population growth rate decreased to 1.08%, while the agricultural population declined at an average annual rate of 1.43%. Thus, a fact long since established by economists, i.e., that rapid economic development is inseparably tied to a change in the population structure, has also been confirmed in the case of Yugoslavia. The slow change in the socioeconomic structure of the population during the interwar period, distinguished by a negligible decline in the share of the farming population in total population, was closely connected with the slow economic growth in prewar Yugoslavia. And conversely, the marked changes in the postwar population makeup, most apparent in the decrease in the farming population, have been prompted by rapid economic growth.

Similar conclusions will be arrived at if the share of farmers in the structure of the labor force is taken as an indicator of the importance of agriculture. In 1931, 75.8% of the 6.98 million economically active persons in Yugoslavia were engaged in farming. In 1953, 68.3% of all economically active persons were engaged in agriculture, while the 1971 population census showed a further decrease in this figure to 43.9%. The importance of agriculture is thus shown to be greater when determined according to "share of active persons" than according to "percentage of the farming population." The principal reason for this is that during population censuses, many housewives in agricultural households are entered in the category of "active persons" (because they do sporadic work in the fields and stables during the season), whereas this is not the case with urban housewives.

The most widely applied and economically most relevant indicator of the importance of agriculture in the economy is the contribution of agriculture to national income. In the five years before World War II (1935-39), agriculture accounted for about 40% of Yugoslavia's national income. With the rapid expansion of nonagricultural activities after the war, the importance of agriculture declined in its contribution to national income, having been 34% in 1947-51, 27% in 1957-61, 23.7% in 1966-70, and only 16.3% in 1975-77.

The contribution of agriculture to the national income declined in relative terms despite a steady growth in the total income generated in agriculture.

2. The Labor Force in Agriculture

The most mobile component of the declining agricultural population during the postwar period has been the labor force. Apparently, the tendency has been for agriculture to be abandoned gradually, in phases. Usually one active member of a family has found himself a second job to provide the family with an additional source of income, which might help it build a new home or overcome momentary financial difficulties. Gradually, however, such extra earnings become ever more significant, until they come to be regarded as essential. As time goes by, the idea of going back to the old way of peasant life becomes less attractive, so that eventually the farm is abandoned — left in the hands of the other members of the family. When conditions are ripe, the others, too, move out and settle in town; the land is sold plot by plot, until the link with agriculture is completely severed. A quantification of the thousands and millions of versions of this typical "story" of how a peasant household is relinquished, with slight variations, is presented in Table 2, which shows the dynamics of the movement of manpower in Yugoslavia's agriculture.

Although a slightly different methodology was applied in each new population census, particularly in the case of female labor (which affects the comparability of the data), it is nevertheless possible to draw some important conclusions from this table concerning the dynamics and structure of the labor force in Yugoslavia's agriculture.

The foremost and most important trend has been the steady decline over the postwar period in the number of people active in agriculture, a process which has accelerated in recent years. Between 1948 and 1953 the number of active farmers decreased by about 1% annually, and between 1953 and 1971 by 1.4% annually. The tendency has also been for more men to abandon agriculture than women. Thus the number of men active in agriculture dropped between 1948 and 1971 by 36%, and that of women by only 26%. As a result, the importance of women in the agricultural labor force has increased. While in 1931 women made up 36.9% of the entire labor force in agriculture, their share rose to 43% in 1961, to

Table 2

The Dynamics of the Movement of the Labor Force in Agriculture, 1921-77

Year	Agricultural population	Active farmers male	female (in thousands)	total	Percentage active in farming population
1921	9,885	3,027	2,091	5,118	51.8
1931	11,132	3,339	1,955	5,294	47.6
1948	10,606	3,357	2,270	5,827	52.7
1953	10,315	3,198	2,162	5,360	51.8
1961	9,198	2,676	2,016	4,692	51.1
1971	7,884	2,149	1,671	3,820	48.5
1977	6,790	1,750	1,510	3,300	48.6

Sources: Population censuses; for 1977, official estimate.

43.7% in 1971, and to 45.8% in 1977.

An ever-increasing number of farms is being managed by elderly people with no heirs or young people to help them. From the census data it follows that the proportion of active farmers aged sixty-five and upward is steadily increasing. In 1948 men of that age group accounted for 7.2% of all active farmers; in 1971 — for 15.4%. The share of women of the same age group in the total number of active farmers rose from 3% in 1953 to 8.4% in 1971. By contrast, the number of active farmers below thirty-four years of age steadily declined. In the case of men the share of this category dropped from 48.5% in 1948 to 33.4% in 1971; and in the case of women the drop was even sharper — from 69% in 1953 to 42% in 1971.

This "aging" of the labor force in agriculture has had a deleterious influence on agricultural production. Many farms have been left without any heirs who would stay on the land. Old people are unwilling to invest in any improvements on such farms, on which production is therefore stagnating or increasing very slowly. Moreover, many of the elderly people left to run the farms are illiterate (in 1948 one third of all active farmers were illiterate, and in 1971 there was still an estimated 20% without any schooling at all) and are therefore more conservative than the traditionally conservative peasant. This characteristic becomes a particularly serious impediment under conditions of a dynamic technological revolution in agriculture that requires the permanent supplementary training of farmers.

3. Long-term Tendencies in the Development of Production

We would like to begin this analysis of the economics of Yugoslavia's peasant agriculture by looking into the dynamics of the development of production. The many epiphenomena which we observe in this sphere can only be explained through a historical analysis which reveals the inherent laws of growth of this sector of production, determining in many ways the path and level of social development. If we analyze the growth rate of agricultural production in present-day Yugoslavia over the past sixty years, we get the results shown in Table 3.

What are the fundamental conclusions to be drawn from the figures in Table 3?

Table 3

Growth Rate of Agricultural Production in Yugoslavia, 1920-78

Production branch	Annual growth rate for period (in %)	
	1920-40	1946-78
Crop growing	2.7	3.2
Fruit growing	0.6	4.0
Viticulture	0.8	3.1
Animal production	3.0	3.6
Agriculture, total	2.3	3.31
Population growth	1.4	1.08
Agricultural production per capita	0.9	2.2
Agricultural population	1.1	-1.4
Productivity in agriculture	2.2	4.7

The first and most important is that despite a reduction in the labor force of the farming population, the postwar period brought about a considerable expansion of agricultural production, so that the average annual growth rate was almost 50% higher than before the war.

An annual 3.3% increase in production, maintained over a period of over thirty years, marks a major increase in production, measured by the results achieved in the agriculture of other countries. Pronounced progress was especially recorded in increasing available supplies per capita: between the two wars available supplies increased by only 0.9% per annum, but after the war this figure almost tripled, reaching 2.2% annually.

With a 3.3% growth rate of production per annum, Yugoslavia ranks among the countries with very high growth of production. Only a few countries top this figure over a longer span of time, a figure which exceeds those achieved by the world's developed agricultures. Only Greece, Bulgaria, Mexico, and Israel have achieved growth rates equivalent to or higher than Yugoslavia's in postwar development. It is universally agreed that after the war Yugoslavia scored outstanding results in its agriculture, results which are almost unparalleled in the world.[4]

And yet it would not do to be overly self-satisfied with this growth rate. There are still untapped potentials for increasing production even further, as can best be seen by an analysis of the development of production by five-year periods (as shown in Table 4). All data have been grouped in five-year averages so as to eliminate the influence of climatic oscillations; it is on this basis that the annual growth of production has been calculated.

The table draws its own conclusions. Throughout the entire postwar period, agriculture recorded a 3.3% annual growth rate, which (in a comparative analysis of agricultures) represents a high growth rate of production.

A closer analysis of this average high growth rate shows that it is extremely uneven: in the first ten years after the war (1946-55), the growth rate (1.7%) just exceeded the population increment (which was 1.4% a year), thereby causing an increasing deficit in foodstuffs, which was covered by imports.

The picture began to change in 1956-60, when production expanded, meeting the rapidly rising demand for foodstuffs on the domestic and foreign markets. The rising income of farmers (about 55% of the population at the time) enlarged the domestic market, permitting the expansion of industrial production as well.

Table 4

The Development of Agricultural Production in Yugoslavia, 1946-78

Period	Physical volume of production		Index (previous period = 100)
	1954-63=100	1955=100	
1946-50	63.8	75.4	..
1951-55	72.6	84.6	113.8
1956-60	98.2	116.4	135.3
1961-65	113.8	132.6	115.9
1966-70	132.6	153.2	116.5
1971-75	148.2	170.4	111.7
1976-78*	166.3	191.6	112.2

Period	Annual rates of growth (in %) of agricultural production	population	production per capita
1948-77	3.31	1.08	2.2
1953-77	3.49	1.02	2.4
1958-77	2.72	1.00	1.7
1963-77	2.70	0.96	1.7
1968-77	2.54	0.93	1.6
1973-77	2.95	0.95	2.0

*Three years.

This led to more rapid economic development together with stable market conditions.

4. The Strategy of Agricultural Development

The conception and strategy of an agrarian policy took time to be formulated; we have learned from our successes and from our mistakes. But as our knowledge of the relevant technical, economic, and sociological factors grew, today's concept of development began to take shape and confirmed its effectiveness and driving force by achieving a high rate of production growth.

In the period between 1947 and 1952, agrarian policy aimed at collectivizing Yugoslav agriculture. The intent of the agrarian policy of the day was to bring about the socialization of agriculture through socially owned agricultural estates and, especially, through peasant producers' cooperatives, which would lead (it was believed) to a considerable increase in agricultural production and would solve the existing difficulties of insufficient production and food in towns and villages.

The experiences of the USSR and the positive results achieved in the first peasant producers' cooperatives influenced the creation of this concept of agrarian policy. Thus immediately after the liberation, and particularly after settlement was carried out (1945-46), numerous cooperatives were set up as a form of association of agricultural producers meant to increase production. The first cooperatives were created on a voluntary basis and were composed of people of the same (social and economic) status; they proved to be extraordinarily vital in their initial stage. Some of them, formed in those first years of socialist Yugoslavia, are even today considered to be among the best agricultural working organizations.

In the years that followed, from 1947 to 1951 in particular, agrarian policy advocated the creation of producers' cooperatives by economic and other means. Thus the cooperative members had fewer obligations (with regard to state purchases and taxation), while political and other pressures were exerted on the peasants to join the cooperatives. Cooperatives were formed both in areas where suitable conditions existed as well as in those where they did not. The acceleration of this process after 1948, during the arduous times of an economic blockade and a strained political situation, led to many of the newly formed organizations failing to receive new, modern means of production; they were "reduced to a primitive form of simple labor cooperation, which was destined under our conditions to yield a negative result."[5]

This kind of simple aggregation of agricultural land reached a peak in 1951, so that in the same year almost one fifth of the arable land had been incorporated into producers' cooperatives. The simple integration of labor along these lines failed, however, to yield the anticipated results. The individual producers lost material incentives which could not be compensated for by the advantages of land unification and simple distribution of labor. Or, as E. Kardelj stated:[6] "We consider the character of production to be determined by the character of the basic means of production, the tools of labor. It influences both the degree of the social character of labor as well as the form of property relations in socio-economic relations. Land ownership in this context is only one material factor, the role of which, moreover, under the conditions of socialism, is diminished in proportion to the increase in the scope of modern social agricultural techniques in the process of production. And conversely, if modern techniques do not exist, or are insufficient, the question remains: which is more productive, individual landholdings or production organization based on simple labor cooperation which the state must necessarily maintain."

From an economic standpoint collectivization was not a success,[7] with the result that the peasant producers' cooperatives were reorganized in 1953 and were gradually dissolved.

A resolution of the Federal National Assembly on the promotion of agriculture and the system of cooperatives laconically states that "the attempt to develop a large scale of social and modern production on previously conceived principles by organizing peasant producers' cooperatives had failed to yield positive results under our conditions. The producers' cooperatives in practice proved, over a short period of time, to have a negative effect in our country — the producers' loss of interest and the degradation of production."[8] Dr. Slavko Komar, Secretary for Agriculture, therefore observed that "no one today or in the future counts on a solution in that form."[9]

Since the situation after 1952 meant the rejection of the previous concept of development, there was no clearly defined concept of a developmental policy until 1956. It was in fact defined only in 1957 on the basis of an analysis of the experiences gained from 1953 to 1956.

The slow development of the productive forces in agriculture during the first ten years after the war (the growth rate between 1946 and 1955 amounted to a mere 1.67% per annum),[10] which caused difficulties in food supply and the balance of payments and became a serious obstacle to the further development of the economy, called for an examination of ways and means to achieve more rapid development in agricultural production. During 1956 and 1957 an in-depth analysis was carried out of domestic and foreign experiences in the development of agricultural production, on the basis of which, in the course of 1957, the Federal National Assembly brought in a resolution on the prospective development of agriculture and the system of cooperatives. This document became a basis for the creation of a new concept of agrarian policy, which was later elaborated and supplemented by various program documents (Program of the LCY, Conclusions of the LCY Congresses, and the Ninth Plenum of the Socialist Alliance of the Working People of Yugoslavia, the Resolution on the Development of Agriculture of the Federal National Assembly in 1964).

The foundations of the new agrarian policy can be summarized as follows:

1. A speedier advancement in agricultural production than that achieved in the past was called for; the advancement was "necessary in order to obtain a more equally balanced development of the productive forces and to meet the ever growing needs of the working people, as well as to create favorable conditions for the socialist transformation of villages and overall social development."[11] This was to be accomplished through greater investment in agriculture, changing the conditions of production in agriculture, and a series of other technical and systematic solutions.

In essence, the same attitude was to be found in the League of Communists (Communist Party) program, adopted at the Seventh Congress of the LCY (1957), in the Conclusions of the Fourth Plenum of the Central Committee of the LCY (1964), and in the Conclusions of the Executive Committee of the Central Committee of the LCY on current socioeconomic and political questions related to the development of agriculture and the villages (1966), all of them stressing the need for a broader engagement of the financial resources of individual producers for investment in agriculture.

2. The basic factors and methods of accelerating the development of agriculture are also indicated. Taking as a point of departure the historical experience (our own or foreign) that it is impossible to step up agricultural production under conditions of the continued prevalance of small holdings, the new agrarian policy called for the introduction of ever new means of production and techniques (a new technology of production) into agriculture and a simultaneous gradual transformation of the prevailing socioeconomic relations in agriculture.

The basic principles of the new agrarian policy are laid down in the relevant Resolution of the Seventh Congress of the League of Communists of Yugoslavia, which states:

> The modernization of agriculture and its socialist transformation represent one of the most important tasks in the struggle for the country's further socialist construction.
>
> It is therefore necessary:
>
> — to pursue a more resolute policy of applying contemporary technological processes and promoting

> production in all spheres of agriculture while simultaneously reinforcing socialist relations in the countryside;
>
> — to expand the material basis of agricultural estates and work cooperatives so that they might become modern, large-scale socialist producers and the main protagonists in the struggle for advancing agriculture and promoting its socialist transformation as quickly as possible;
>
> — to encourage and intensify the development of cooperatives, notably production cooperatives and individual producers, such cooperation being instrumental in stepping up large-scale socialist agricultural production.

The Statute of the LCY, adopted at the Seventh Congress, specified that the socialist agricultural organizations were the main vehicles of expanded production. At the same time, several documents point to the need of mobilizing the financial resources of individual producers for investments in agriculture.

The new concept of bimodal agrarian policy was tested in practice, and its results were evaluated at the First Conference of the LCY (held in 1970 in Belgrade). There the validity of the basic course taken in the transformation of our agriculture was confirmed, as were the methods by which to promote the development of agricultural production. An identical appraisal was also given by the Tenth Congress of the LCY (1974).

We shall now deal more fully with the results of the policy laid down in this way for the advancement of Yugoslav agriculture through socially and individually owned holdings (peasants' farms).

The socialist agricultural organizations — the socially owned agricultural holdings — deserve a position of prime importance in the transformation of Yugoslavia's once backward agriculture into a thriving and highly productive agriculture. It is clear that an approach of this kind calls for an examination of only the essential economic indices common to all the organizations without entering into a discussion of the differences in organizations, their individual efficiency, and any other aspects having to do with them.

The results of this policy can be seen in Figure 1, which shows global production and its development broken down between the private and the socialist sectors. The figures indicate that agricultural production between 1954 and 1979 rose by 7% in the so-

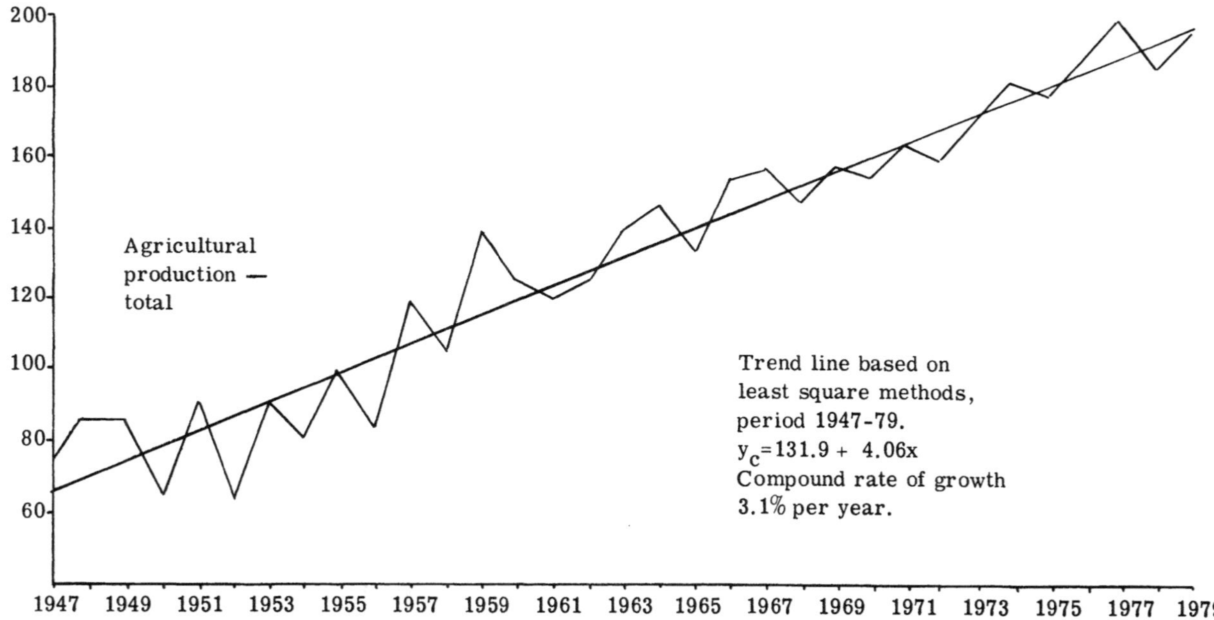
200
180
160
140
120
100
80
60
Agricultural production — total
Trend line based on least square methods, period 1947-79.
y_c=131.9 + 4.06x
Compound rate of growth 3.1% per year.
1947 1949 1951 1953 1955 1957 1959 1961 1963 1965 1967 1969 1971 1973 1975 1977 1979

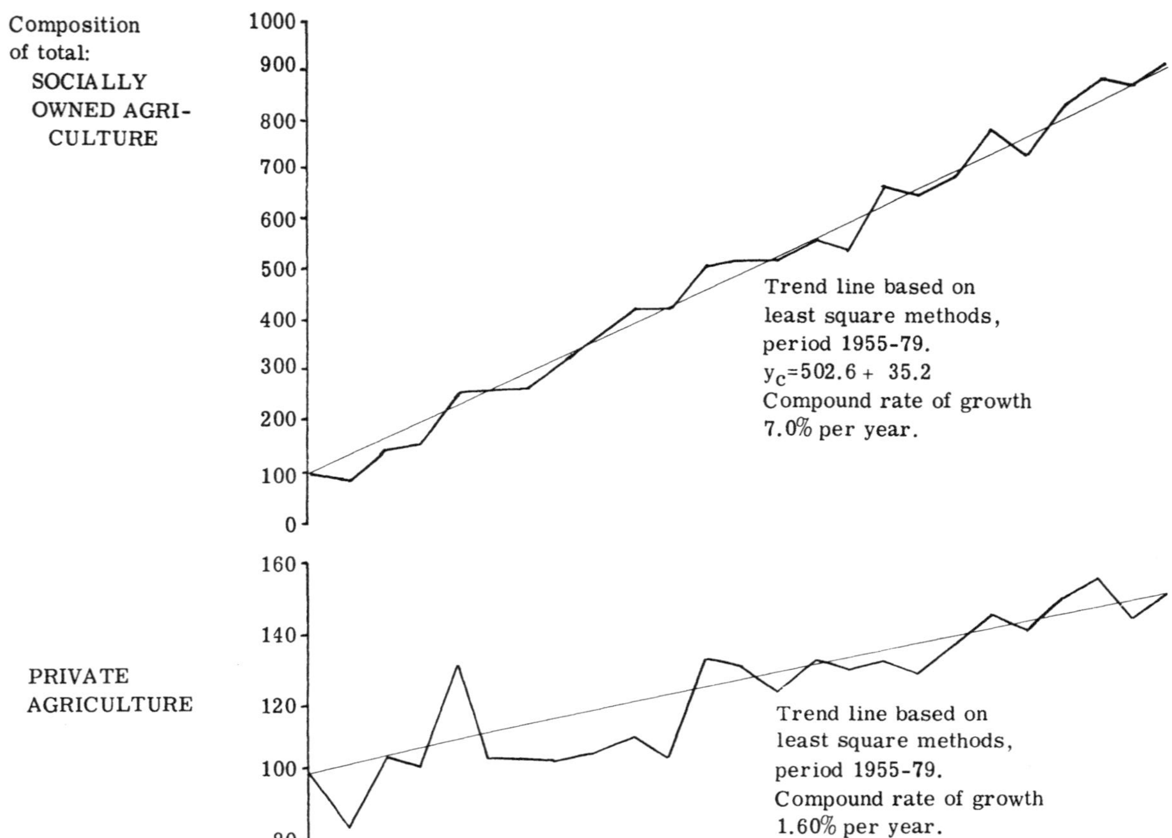

Figure 1. The Development of Agricultural Production in Yugoslavia, 1947-79 (Index of Production, 1955=100).

cialized sector as against some 2% in the private sector. This led to an increase in the share of the socialist sector in overall production: from only 8% in 1957 to 29% in 1968 and as much as 32% in 1978.

Peasants' (privately owned) agricultural holdings are still the most important category in Yugoslavia's agriculture. In 1978, 84% of the arable land and around 88% of the livestock belonged to this type of holding. About 68% of the overall value of agricultural production was produced on individually owned holdings, as well as almost three fifths of all market supplies and approximately 54% of all purchases through the social trade networks (the difference between the data on purchase and market supplies results from the existence of "peasant markets").[12]

The high percentages clearly indicate the significance that trends and processes in this type of holding can have for overall agricultural production and agrarian policy. Any possible neglect of agricultural production on the land of individual producers, or conversely, an all-out adoption of new agricultural technology, can have a profound impact not only on the quantity and structure of their own production but also on agricultural production as a whole. We shall now deal with some of the basic trends indicated by our private farms as well as the role of measures of agrarian policy in those processes.

5. The Peasant Economy

The number of individually owned holdings in Yugoslav agriculture is extremely high. According to the last agricultural census (taken in 1969) there are 2.6 million individually owned holdings. That means that there are approximately 20% more farms in Yugoslavia than in the whole United States. They encompass a little over 10 million hectares of agricultural land, so that the average size of the peasant holding amounts to only 3.9 hectares. Although the number of rural inhabitants is falling, the land has nonetheless continued to be fragmented. This is due both to the inheritance laws (according to the old Slavonic laws, all children get equal share in the property of parents) and the fact that very few people from an agricultural background will sell land which has been in the hands of their forefathers for centuries.

According to the structure of farms, peasants tend to be small holders. The 1969 agricultural census indicated that 1.01 million holdings (or 39% of the total number) had under 2 hectares of arable land, accounting for only 10% of the land. On the other hand, there were 276,000 larger holdings with over 8 hectares (or 10.6%) that held 35% of the land in the private sector. Therefore the majority of farms fall into the category of small holdings without resources to fully employ existing manpower. It is thus not surprising that the labor force in many cases has left the smallest farms to seek employment elsewhere in the country or abroad.

Worker-peasant holdings. Socioeconomic development put an end to the old form of autarkic villages and led to the birth of specific socioeconomic categories, which by becoming incorporated into an ever stronger social distribution of labor, moved and developed in a specific way. The rapid changes in the postwar social and economic structure of the population did not parallel changes in the level of urbanization and the town-country ratio.[13] Thus in Yugoslavia the social distribution of labor ran largely within the framework of rural settlements; and the labor force, finding insufficient employment on the agricultural holdings, sought employment in nonagricultural economic activities but remained resident on agricultural holdings. Only a minor portion of these new workers made up what was called an "urban element," while the remainder formed a new socioeconomic category in our villages known as the worker-peasant holdings. This social category grew rapidly in the period after the war and introduced new elements to agricultural production and rural relations. This can be seen in the data shown in Table 5.

The phenomenon of increasing numbers of agricultural workers leaving agriculture as their main occupation but retaining agricultural holdings gave rise to a series of difficulties in the development of agricultural production. The basic factor with regard to raising the living standard of persons living on holdings ceased to be higher agricultural production and became income earned outside agriculture. Persons employed in factories or elsewhere were no longer able to spend as much time in the fields as had once been the case. They tended to have all the heavier work done by their own machines or by others (the cooperative or their neighbor-agricultural workers). Yields on their land did not follow the same rising pattern as did those on the holdings of "pure" peasants. If they had a considerable amount of land, more often than not they leased it to cooperatives or privately, retaining only their house and a yard for themselves. Accordingly, a substantial portion of Yugoslav land (more than 20% of arable land according to 1969

Table 5

Number of Individually Owned Holdings with Persons Permanently Employed outside Agriculture, 1931-69

Census	Agricultural holdings	Holdings with one or more persons permanently employed outside agriculture	% of holdings with persons employed outside agriculture
	in thousands		
1931	2,069	185	9
1949	2,607	500	19
1955	2,563	814	32
1960	2,618	1,018	39
1969	2,600	1,118	43
1975	2,550	1,250	49

Sources: 1931 population census; 1960 and 1969 agriculture censuses; 1949 and 1955 livestock censuses; for 1975, estimated.

data) acquired a specific status which was by no means favorable for promoting crop production, which grew more slowly in those areas than elsewhere.

Some of these problems were offset by cooperation in agriculture. The concept of socialist cooperation designates all forms of cooperation mainly in production between socialist economic organizations (socially owned agricultural estates, producers' cooperatives and cooperative farmland, and in some cases, industrial and trade organizations) and individually owned peasant holdings. This cooperation prepares, establishes, and develops elements of the social process of production founded on social organization and the preparation of land for the process of production so as to enable socialist organizations, based on social investment and socially owned means of production, to become the protagonists of expanded reproduction.[14]

Various forms of cooperation have been developed in recent years. In order to have a clear overview, we might group them into three categories: services, contract farming, and joint production and distribution.

Each of the three categories had their own specific forms and variations, but we will describe only the most characteristic in each category.

Services were the initial form of cooperation and are still the most common form today. This category includes each and every individual service that the cooperative offers the peasant farmer. There are countless services of this kind, ranging from the selling of seeds and artificial fertilizers to lending tractors. The possibilities are endless and varied.

Contract farming represents a more complex relationship between socialist organizations and individual producers. The organizer of the process of production is still the individual producer, and the peasant can take advantage of several of the services offered by the cooperative in the process of production (mostly on the basis of loans and usually crediting the purchase of seeds and artificial fertilizers and the sale of products through the cooperative, etc.). Accounts are settled after delivery, and the cooperative charges interest on loans and retains a percentage for its own funds. Cooperation of this kind differs from one region to another, and variations exist depending on the product. Nevertheless, all forms of cooperation have one characteristic in common: through social investment the technology of peasant production alters and becomes substantially more productive.

Cooperation based on joint production and distribution is generally based on the long-term lease, in which the peasant-owner of the land gets rent defined by contract. This sum is regarded as his share in the total costs of production, bringing him an additional sum in the case of profitable production. This category is characterized by the fact that property relations are formally defined by contract and not by the degree of socialization in the process of production and true economic content.

Furthermore, another characteristic feature is that joint production is not based on credit relations but on joint participation in production. The cooperative and the peasant farmer are both owners of the product in question; they share the risks involved and distribute the benefits of production in proportion to their share in the costs of production. Efforts are made to ensure that the operations of the peasant farmer meet the demands of contemporary production. The distribution of products is usually proportionate to the costs that have to be met by each partner, which are fixed by contract. In some cases after the costs have been paid, surplus income is distributed. Accounts can be squared through money payments or in kind.

These changes in structure of farms, with peasants relying more and more on nonfarm incomes, brought about a considerable change in <u>farmers' receipts</u>. Since 1952-53 the Federal Bureau of

Statistics has conducted a sample of rural households through which receipts and expenses, as an indication of the income position of peasants, might be observed. This study is carried out regularly on an annual basis, with the number of farms analyzed and the quality of data growing each year. The main findings are presented in Table 6.

During the twenty years observed, receipts of agricultural holdings have increased 25 times, which was mostly due to inflation. When deflated (by the index of retail prices), the increase in real receipts of agricultural households in this period more than doubled (which means that the annual increase in real receipts of households was about 4.8% yearly; but considering the decrease in the number of members of the household, the increase per member of the household amounts to a little bit over 5% annually).

Basic changes occurred in the receipt structure. While toward the end of the '50s natural consumption (a term that describes peasant production, primarily of food, in self-owned households for the family's own consumption, without entering the market) accounted for almost half of total agricultural holding receipts, this share toward the end of the '70s had decreased to only 25%. And conversely, receipts from off-farm jobs, as well as from agricultural output, increased (relatively and absolutely).

The increase in the real receipts of the agricultural population led to considerable changes in consumption. Peasants set more and more aside for household investments (the share of these expenses more than doubled in the structure of expenditure, while in real terms they quadrupled), while the share of current operating expenses in the expenditure structure was stagnating (actually slowly decreasing), primarily because of the decrease in taxation of agricultural households. In the expenditure structure the share of personal consumption was decreasing; however, due to the greater volume of total expenses, it increased in real terms.

Two tendencies are evident here: One is the peasant's constant desire for improved housing conditions, to build himself a house more comfortable than those in towns, which he was now so frequently visiting. The electrification of the villages (which in the '70s had reached even the most remote villages), the installation of running water systems in villages, and sometimes the building of sewer systems significantly increased the rural housing standard, gradually equalizing housing conditions in urban and rural areas. This is obvious from the data in Table 7.

It turns out that in 1951, the average urban inhabitant had at his

Table 6

Receipts and Expenses of Peasants' Households in Yugoslavia, Selected Years, 1959-78

Indicator	Average per household					
	1959	1964	1969	1972	1975	1978
A. Receipts, total (in new dinars)	4,070	8,544	16,329	34,393	60,962	102,608
agricultural estate (in cash)	1,191	2,738	4,453	9,475	15,602	30,778
employment outside agriculture[1]	1,008	2,307	6,763	16,658	30,145	46,427
household in kind (natural consumption)[2]	1,871	3,499	5,113	8,261	15,215	25,403
B. Structure of receipts (total = 100)						
agricultural estate	29	32	27	28	26	30
employment outside agriculture	25	27	41	48	49	45
in kind (natural consumption)	46	41	31	24	25	25
C. Expenses, total (in new dinars)	4,070	8,544	16,329	34,393	60,962	102,608
for personal consumption	2,825	6,509	9,739	19,627	36,499	57,162
current operating expenses[3]	605	872	2,147	4,387	6,991	13,110
investments on farm[4]	640	1,163	4,443	10,378	17,471	32,335
D. Structure of expenses (total = 100)						
personal consumption	69	76	60	57	60	56
current operating expenses	15	10	13	13	11	13
investments on farms	16	14	27	30	29	31

Sources: Statistical Yearbook of Yugoslavia, various issues; statistical bulletins of Federal Bureau of Statistics.

[1]Including credits, sales of machinery, etc.

[2]Including changes in agricultural inventories and livestock.

[3]Taxes, investments for seed, lubricants, fertilizers, etc.

[4]Including investment for dwellings and equipment on farms, investments in livestock, and repayments of debts and savings.

Table 7

Housing Conditions in Towns and Rural Areas of Yugoslavia, 1951-79

Indicator	1951	1961	1971	1979
A. Number of inhabitants (in thousands):				
total	16,588	18,612	20,574	22,159
town	3,490	5,267	7,942	10,282
village	13,098	13,345	12,632	11,877
B. Total housing stock (in million m^2):				
total	144.2	182.7	249.9	322.5
town	42.9	54.2	107.1	147.2
village	101.3	128.6	142.8	178.3
C. Average area of useful floor space in dwellings per person (in m^2):				
total	8.7	10.0	12.2	14.7
town	11.5	10.3	13.8	14.3
village	8.3	9.8	11.2	15.0

Sources: 1979 population census; Statistical Yearbook of Yugoslavia, 1980, p. 288; for rural and urban population, Statistical Yearbook of Yugoslavia, 1980, p. 416.

disposal more dwelling space than the rural inhabitant. But the following three decades brought radical changes both to town and village. In 1979 the citizens of Yugoslavia had 70% more dwelling space than in 1951; whereas the dwelling space of the average urban inhabitant had increased only 25%, that of the average rural inhabitant rose over 80%.

The peasant diet. Beside significant improvement in the housing standard, the second tendency saw basic improvements in the peasant diet. The diet of the Yugoslav peasant before World War II was overloaded with carbohydrates, coming mainly from cereals, or more precisely, from corn (maize). It was usually consumed in the form of bread or as cornmeal mush. It has been estimated that almost half of the total calories consumed by the peasant derived from this source. On the other hand, extremely low consumption was common for sugar and honey (less than 4 kg per year for the peasant population) and, especially, for livestock products. Meat and poultry consumption in the village was as low as 14 kg per person yearly; only about 30 eggs were eaten yearly per "average" peasant, and only about 5 kg of fats and oils per person. Expressed in terms of calories, the average peasant's diet was relatively good (around 2,600 calories per person per day), but it was not well balanced. The peasantry in large portions of the so-called "passive regions" suffered from malnutrition and, particularly during poor harvest seasons, even from undernourishment.[15] So despite the relatively good daily caloric intake, the diet of the Yugoslav peasant was far from satisfactory. The improvement in the standard of living made it possible for the village to change its diet considerably after World War II.

The farmers spent a considerable portion of their growing income on improving their diet. The Federal Bureau of Statistics has continually observed the changes in patterns of food consumption among the rural population.[16]

The consumption of foodstuffs among this portion of the population (as presented in Table 8) provides a typical example of improvement in diet due to the increase in real income.

Table 8

Consumption of Foodstuffs in Agricultural Households, 1952-53 to 1977-78

Foodstuffs	Annual intake per household member (kg/year)			
	1952-53	1959-60	1969-70	1977-78
Cereals, total[1]	201.5	190	173	156
Corn	65.6	50	26	13
Potatoes	45.7	46	46	42
Beans	5.2	8.5	9.5	8.5
Other fresh vegetables	26.0	43.5	51	49
Fresh fruit[2]	18.3	23	32	35
Meat[3]	18.8	21.5	28.5	39
Fats	8.5	11.5	17	16
Oil	1.5	2.5	5	7
Milk (liters)	74.1	80	83	107.5
Cheese	3.2	6	9	12
Eggs (number)	47	72	104	158
Sugar and honey	5.9	7.0	12.5	15

Source: Annual Survey of Rural Households; see Statistical Yearbook of Yugoslavia, various issues.

[1]Flour equivalent.

[2]Processed fruit expressed in fresh fruit equivalent.

[3]Processed meat expressed in fresh meat equivalent.

Consumption of all cereals (expressed in flour equivalent) had a downward tendency, reaching a level of 156 kg per person in 1977-78, 45 kg lower than in 1952-53. However, there has been a marked change in the pattern of cereal consumption. Corn, a traditional food for a majority of prewar peasants, has been replaced by wheat. The whole decline in cereal consumption is therefore due to the decline in corn consumption, partly compensated by an increase in wheat consumption. A similar trend could be observed with potatoes, where consumption stagnated in the first two decades of the observed period and has only recently declined in consumption per person.

Beans have played a traditional role in the peasants' diet: they were regarded as essential for many occasions. For that reason there was an increase in bean consumption until 1970, after which a gradual decline in per person consumption can be observed.

As representative of the changes in the diet, we should note a considerable increase — a doubling — in per capita consumption of fresh vegetables and fruits, showing a considerable change in the attitude of peasants toward these formerly rarely accepted food.

The most important changes have occurred, however, in the pattern of meat and livestock consumption as a whole.

In the period of twenty-five years for which the figures are available, meat consumption has doubled, reaching 39 kg per person in 1977-78; the consumption of eggs per person of the rural population increased more than threefold; the fresh milk consumption rose 45%, but cheese consumption went up fourfold, which brings the total milk consumption in 1977-78 (expressed in fresh milk equivalent) to the level of 205 liters per member of a rural household.

Consumption of fats and sugar increased over the whole twenty-five-year period. Per capita consumption of all fats increased by almost 90%; as a result of nutritional education there was a marked tendency to replace lard with vegetable oil. Sugar consumption increased by 2.5 times in this period, starting from a very low level in the fifties.

All these changes have led to a considerable improvement in the diet of the agricultural population. Total calories consumed per person rose from 2,750 in the early fifties to 3,027 (in 1963) and 3,551 per day (in 1978). Total protein consumption in the seventies reached 110 grams per day, of which 32.3% were of animal origin.

This represents a considerable improvement in the diet of the formerly poor peasants of Yugoslavia, who, historically speaking, were hungry until quite recently.

Investment on peasants' farms. The new policy toward peasant agriculture, created in 1957 and given additional impetus in 1967 (when special measures were taken encouraging peasants to buy agricultural machinery and subsidizing the introduction of new agricultural inputs), has had a favorable effect on peasants' attitudes toward investment on their own land. More and more of them found that agriculture is still a good occupation capable of supporting a decent life under the favorable conditions in which their forefathers had lived for centuries. Price incentives, created by additional demand for food products on local, domestic, and international markets, coupled with deep and sudden changes in the rural environment (where good roads, electricity, better housing, schools, and other facilities were built), have been mainly responsible for these alterations.

More and more of the peasant's receipts were earmarked for fixed capital: in the last ten years, two thirds of them went for the purchase of machinery and equipment.

A picture of fixed capital investment in Yugoslav agriculture is given in Table 9. In this table only investments in agriculture are given, not counting spending for dwellings and other nonproductive uses. Investments are given in current prices, and for that reason (under the inflationary conditions which prevailed in Yugoslavia in the sixties and seventies) the figures inflate real progress. However, even such figures provide some insight into the mechanism of agricultural growth.

Let us start by analyzing investment in agriculture in relation to the gross national product of agriculture. The socially owned sector experienced extraordinary capital growth in the fifties, when state policies provided special treatment for credits in agriculture, thus enabling the social sector to annually invest more than the previous GNP in this sector. This was the beginning of the creation of capital-intensive agriculture in the socialist sector, with high yields and productivity. This tendency was much less marked in the sixties and seventies (when only a third of GNP was reinvested in agriculture).

On the other hand, the peasant economy invested far less in the fifties and early sixties — under 5% of their GNP. The aforementioned measures caused changes under which the rate of investment by peasant households went up from 4.9% of GNP (for the period 1967-71) to 7.9% (five-year average, 1972-76) and 12.5%

Table 9

Fixed Capital Investment in Yugoslav Agriculture, by Sectors, 1952-78

	Yearly averages for the period:					
	1952-56	1957-61	1962-66	1967-71	1972-76	1977-78
A. Fixed capital investment in agriculture (in millions of current dinars)						
Total	423	1,280	2,090	2,988	8,264	18,808
social	205	900	1,539	1,965	4,263	9,273
private	218	380	551	1,023	4,001	9,535
B. Investment in agriculture (as % of GNP of agriculture)						
Total	12.1	19.1	13.4	11.1	12.3	18.7
social	68.1	129.0	50.3	33.1	25.9	38.5
private	6.9	3.6	4.4	4.9	7.9	12.5
C. Investment in agriculture (as % of total national investment)						
Total	11.1	14.9	10.2	6.7	6.4	6.0
social	5.4	10.5	7.5	4.4	3.3	3.0
private	5.7	4.4	2.7	2.3	3.1	3.0
D. Structure of agricultural investment (total = 100)						
social	48	70	74	66	52	49
private	52	30	26	34	48	51

Sources for fixed capital investment in agriculture: For the period 1952-73: Institute for Investment Economics, Investment in Yugoslavia 1947-1966, Belgrade, 1968, and Investment in Yugoslavia 1947-1973, Belgrade, 1976; statistical yearbooks, various issues, 1975-80, Belgrade, 1976-80.

of GNP (in 1977-78). This was a result of measures by which banks and other financial sources were obliged to finance their capital requirements (two World Bank loans were also used for this purpose). These encouraging tendencies, however, should not be exaggerated. In 1977-78 private farming investments were still relatively low: their share in total investments in fixed capital amounted to only 3%, whereas their contribution to gross social product was 9.4%. Although precise figures are lacking, it can be said that by far the larger part of all capital expenditure by private farmers was self-financed, credit playing only a marginal role.

With these capital outlays private farmers have considerably improved their productive capacity. The number of tractors in private hands was only 901 in 1948, 4,963 in 1959, and 30,090 in 1969; but it was 316,000 in 1979 and as many as 360,000 on January 1, 1980. The same huge increase occurred on private farms with trucks, combine-harvesters, and other machines, making the farmer less and less dependent on the machinery of cooperatives and socially owned farms.

An important instrument for stimulating the private sector of production was the provision of production and marketing credit for farm products. In the framework of a selective credit policy, the National Bank of Yugoslavia, together with the national banks of the republics and provinces, was prepared to rediscount a portion of the current production and marketing loans granted by commercial banks. Commercial credits were available to private farmers, with priority given to those who were engaged in cooperation with the social sector.

Rediscount facilities are available on loans for production and marketing of major products: on December 31, 1978 (for example), outstanding operating capital loans to agriculture amounted to 27,108 million dinars, or 13% of such loans in Yugoslavia in total.

This created an opportunity to introduce into agriculture many innovative practices in farming methods more rapidly than would have been possible without such credits. For example, the consumption of fertilizers on private land rose sevenfold in twenty years: from 369,000 tons in 1957 (with 82,000 tons of plant nutrient content), to 859,000 tons in 1969 (with 275,000 tons of plant nutrient content), to 1,382,000 tons in 1979 (with 545,000 tons of plant nutrient content). The use of hybrid corn seed was limited to less than 1% of private land in 1958; today it is estimated that less than 10% does not use this high-yielding variety; the same is true for high-yielding wheat varieties, hybrid sunflower seed with high oil content, and many other innovations introduced to peasants.

In the livestock sector the process was even more rapid. Significant contributions to higher production and productivity have been made by Yugoslav research institutes, which have developed methods of improving domestic cattle and pig breeds, mainly through crossbreeding with high-yield animals. Modern feedlots have been set up on numerous peasant farms for fattening young cattle and pigs. Broiler and egg units were established in the past fifteen years, mainly on the basis of vertically integrated production patterns. Concentration of production in livestock was easier, owing to the fact that there was no ceiling for it.

Yields on peasants' farms. Increasing investments in fixed capital coupled with changes in inputs and modernization of production processes have led to a break with the legacy of the peasants' past: low yields per unit of land and per head of livestock.

In overpopulated pre-World War II Yugoslav agriculture, yields were low, among the lowest in Europe.[17] Industrialization in the postwar period lowered the population pressure on land, enabling peasants to considerably increase yields. Socially owned holdings were usually the vanguard of progress, showing in practice how to obtain higher yields: peasants usually followed with a time lag that gradually lessened.

In a sense we can say that the level of yields obtained and the dynamics of their development measure the progress of peasant communities. The reasons for this are simple: the level of yields depends on the national framework, on complex and synchronized work, on improving the biological properties of seeds, on preparation of the soil, the use of manure and mineral fertilizers, the knowledge of the farmer and his efficiency, and on many other factors. Judging by this criterion, we can say that the performance of Yugoslav peasants was excellent, since they were able to increase the average yields on their land two to three times over twenty-five years (see Table 10 and Figures 2 and 3).

All this was done under prevailing conditions of dry farming, without irrigation. Wheat yields have risen almost four times, corn and sugar beet yields three times, and sunflower yields almost doubled during the twenty-five years.[18] Since the land in Yugoslavia intended for agriculture is limited (even shrinking owing to urbanization, road and airport building, and similar ventures), raising yields per unit of land area was the most important factor in increasing the production on peasant farms.

Table 10

Yields of Main Crops in Peasant Households in Yugoslavia, 1954-80

Year	Yields (in metric tons per hectare)			
	wheat	corn	sunflower	sugar beet
1954	0.75	1.22	1.00	15.9
1959	1.94	2.58	1.32	29.7
1964	1.76	2.86	1.78	32.0
1969	2.42	3.26	1.78	38.1
1974	3.41	3.56	1.49	41.2
1978	3.13	3.56	2.16	40.8
1979	2.96	4.48	2.04	42.3
1980	3.35	4.13*	1.69*	42.2*

*Preliminary

With such progress in yields, Yugoslav agriculture is gradually catching up with the level of yields obtained in Western European agriculture, narrowing the huge gap which existed forty years ago.[19]

Next in importance was the more efficient use of feed in livestock production. Following modern feeding practices and with improvement in breeds, Yugoslav peasants were able to lower the feed consumption per unit of livestock production by almost one third (in the period 1956-78). This improvement in feed conversion rates very considerably stimulated a shift in the pattern of production favoring livestock.

Finally, an additional source of larger peasant receipts was the tendency to increase production of competitively better priced agricultural goods, for which demand by far outstripped supply. Peasants produced more fresh vegetables and fruits, rapidly adapting to changes in customers' preferences and market conditions. The peasant farmers lost no time in adopting new types of production when they saw profitability in them.

Specialization has also gained ground among formerly mixed peasant farms. There are more and more farms producing several thousand pigs annually in feedlot units; others specialize in broiler or egg production; specialization in gardening is also popular, and we have many farmers producing hundreds of tons of vegetables or fruits. This is especially the case with farmers living

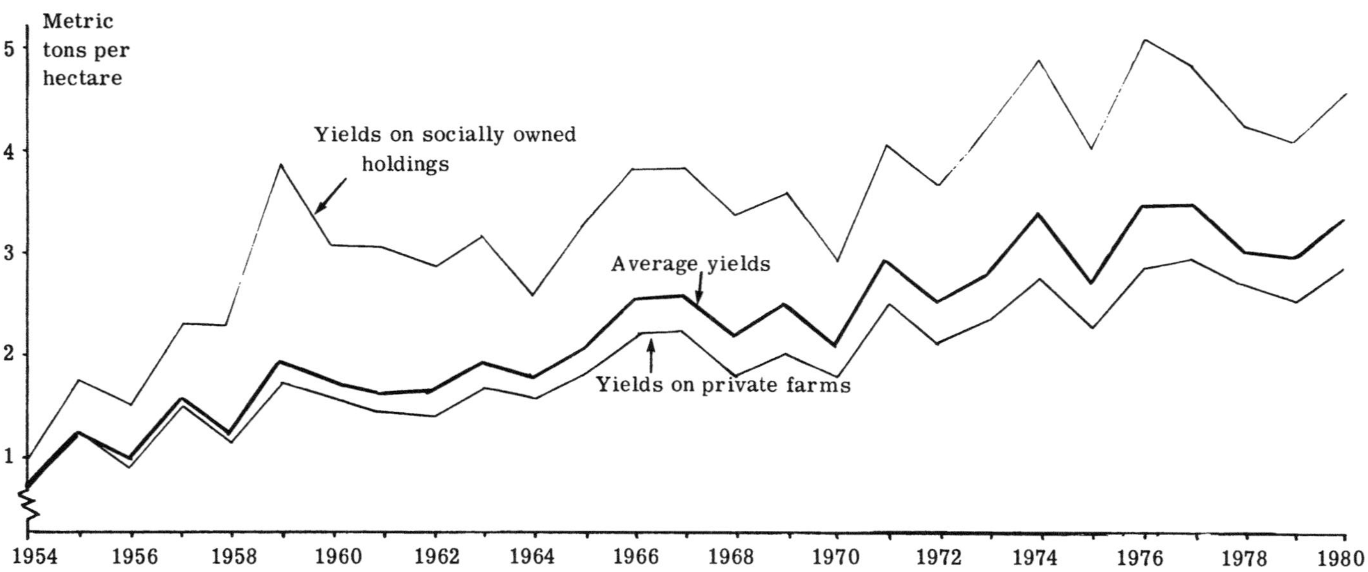

Figure 2. Wheat Yields in Yugoslavia, 1954-80.

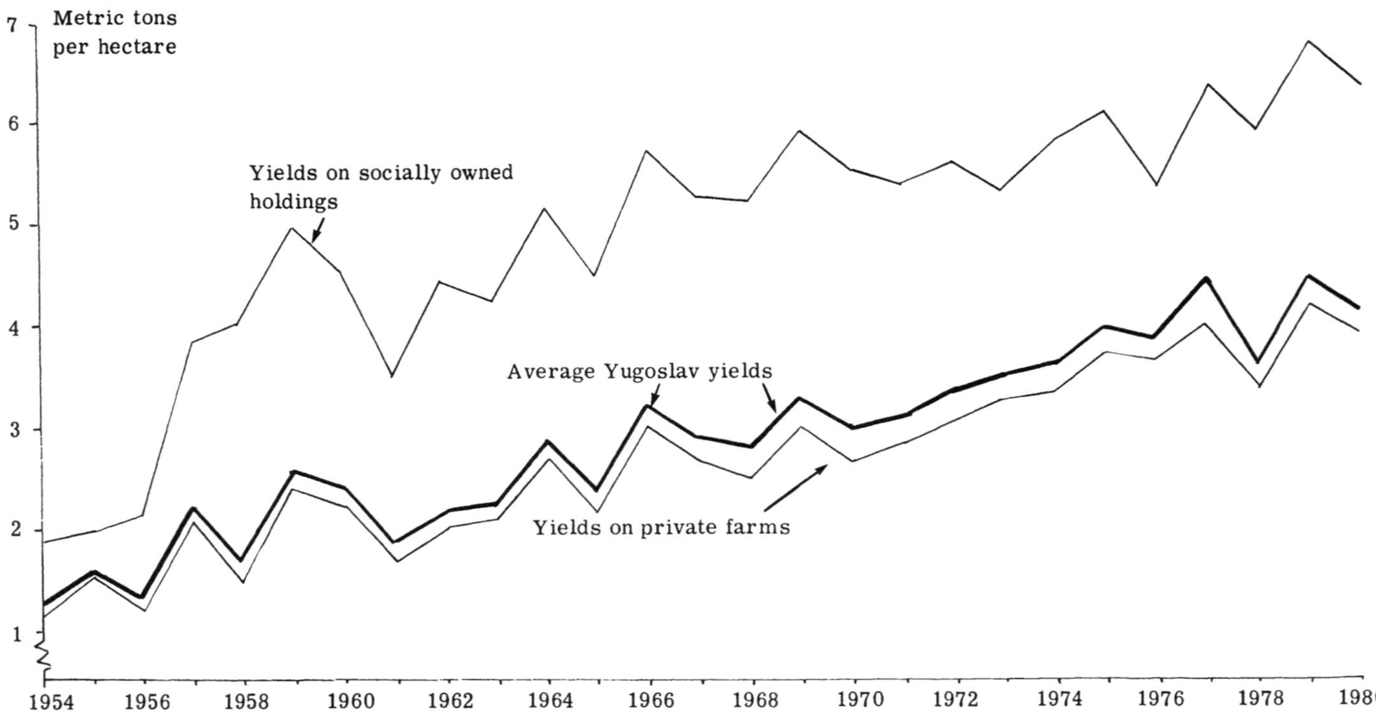

Figure 3. Corn Yields in Yugoslavia, 1954-80.

near large consumer centers, where islands of prosperous farmers are growing in size and strength (for example, the region of Grocka Village near Belgrade, Tetovo in Macedonia, Podstrana near Split, and others).

Specialization, with mechanized farming practices and modern methods of production, has considerably increased the productivity of the peasant economy: the annual rate of growth of labor productivity has surpassed 4% annually. This is the rate of growth of productivity obtained by the national economy as a whole, a clear sign of how vigorous the peasant economy is under market conditions.

NOTES

[1]S. Stajić, Real National Income in Yugoslavia in the Periods 1926-39 and 1947-56, Economic Institute FPRY, 1957 (in Serbo-Croatian).

[2]Dr. Ivo Vinski, The Class Division of the Population and National per Capita Income in Yugoslavia in 1939, Zagreb, 1970 (in Serbo-Croatian).

[3]To illustrate the meaning of this fact more vividly, note that other countries have taken from seventy to ninety years to cover the same path of development. For example, Sweden required ninety years to reduce the proportion of its farming population from 71 to 31% (between 1840 and 1930); it took the United States ninety years to effect a similar change in its socioeconomic structure (to reduce its farming population from 72% in 1820 to 32% in 1910); Japan, a country noted for its rapid economic growth, had in 1887 a farming population amounting to 78% of the total population and managed to bring it down to 33% only in 1960 (i.e., after seventy-three years). The cited figures (taken from S. Kuznets, "The Quantitative Aspects of Economic Growth of Nations," Economic Development and Cultural Change, and Modern Economic Growth, New Haven, 1967, pp. 106-7) show that Yugoslavia has achieved its growth in the postwar period in less than half the time it had taken many economically developed countries.

[4]It might be appropriate at this point to cite three such opinions as a counterweight to the popular Yugoslav view, which often places the "main" blame for inflation, the balance-of-payments deficit, and other difficulties on agriculture. The FAO Yearbook (The State of Food and Agriculture, 1960, p. 15) states that of forty-eight analyzed countries, only in Greece, Israel, Japan, Yugoslavia, and Mexico did the growth of production top the population increment by 4 to 6% (for the 1952-57 period). The FAO report comments that "the growth rate in these countries was so stable that it may be worth studying how these countries stimulated and advanced their production." Five years later the FAO again stressed that out of fifty-five analyzed countries (in the second postwar decade), only three developing countries achieved a growth rate of agricultural production which enabled per capita production to increase by more than 3% a year. The three countries were Israel, Greece, and Yugoslavia (FAO, The State of Food and Agriculture, 1965, "Review of the Second Post-war Decade," Rome, 1965, p. 16). The U.S. Department of Agriculture issued a publication which offers a similar assessment of Yugoslavia's growth rate ("Changes in Agriculture in 26

Developing Nations, 1948-1963," Washington, D.C., 1965). Studying the development of plant production in the developing countries, this report ranks Yugoslavia among six countries with the most rapid development of this kind of production, noting that it is recording a rise in yields per unit of land areas (others achieve this increase in production by expanding cultivated areas). Ibid., pp. 15 and 19.

[5]E. Kardelj, Problemi socijalističke politike na selu, Belgrade, 1959, p. 16.

[6]E. Kardelj, ibid., p. 14.

[7]E. Kardelj, ibid., p. 19.

[8]The Federal National Assembly, Stanje poljoprivrede i zadrugarstva i perspektive njihovog razvoja, Belgrade, "Kultura," 1957, p. 136.

[9]Ibid., p. 122.

[10]See V. Stipetić, "Poljoprivredna proizvodnja na današnjem području FNR Jugoslavije 1929-1955," in Ekonomski problemi, Belgrade, 1957, p. 97.

[11]Federal National Assembly, Stanje poljoprivrede i zadrugarstva, Belgrade, 1957, p. 135.

[12]V. Stipetić, Jugoslavensko tržište poljoprivrednih proizvoda, Belgrade, 1964, and SGY, 1980.

[13]A correlation exists between the level of economic development and urbanization, but it is possible to slow urbanization noticeably in the process of rapid economic advancement. This was, in fact, what Yugoslav economic policy undertook to do: in order to increase the volume of investment in production, it slowed investment in construction and the organization of towns and cities. For more detailed information, see D. Vogelnik, Urbanization as a Reflection of the Economic Development of the SFRY, Belgrade, 1960, and V. Stipetić, "Some Questions Related to Changes in the Socioeconomic Structure of the Population," Ekonomist, Belgrade, 1961, no. 3.

[14]See E. Kardelj, op. cit., p. 151.

[15]For a more detailed and comprehensive view on food in rural areas, see J. Tomasevich, Peasants, Politics and Economic Change in Yugoslavia, Stanford University Press-Oxford University Press, 1955, pp. 540-69.

[16]The first survey covered only 615 agricultural households; since that time the number of observed households has constantly grown, reaching 3,174 households in 1977-78.

[17]According to the FAO, the five-year average wheat yields for 1934-38 were (in hundreds of kilograms per hectare): Austria 16.7; Belgium 26.9; Czechoslovakia 17.1; France 15.6; Germany 22.9; Hungary 14.0; Italy 14.4; Netherlands 30.3; Poland 14.6; UK 23.1, and Yugoslavia 11.4; for corn — the main Yugoslav crop — for the same period, the yields were as follows: France 15.8; Germany 28.4; Hungary 19.9; Italy 20.6; Yugoslavia 17.6; United States 14.0; Argentina 18.1.

[18]Analyzing Yugoslav yields by linear regression, I have concluded that corn yields in Yugoslavia have risen (between 1950-54 and 1970-74) 102 kilograms per hectare annually (compared to the same period in Italy, where the increase was 84 kg/ha; India 15.5; South Africa 28; Argentina 43; Mexico 25; USSR 80; Brazil 11; USA 144; France 158); for wheat the annual increase in yields was: Australia 6; Argentina 11; Canada 22; India 27; USSR 31; Italy 37; USA 44; Netherlands 60; Yugoslavia 71; UK 72; Germany 76; Hungary 80; Bulgaria 88; and France 91 (all figures represent the annual increase in yields and are expressed in kilograms per hectare). For details, see my article, "Pedeset godina povećanja prinosa pšenice i kukuruza — komparativna analiza," in Economic Institute of Zagreb,

<u>Problemi privrednog razvoja i privrednog sistema Jugoslavije</u>, Zagreb, "Informator" Publishers, 1977, pp. 486-506.

[19] In 1978 wheat yields in the main wheat producing countries (expressed in hundreds of kilograms per hectare) were: Austria 31.2; Czechoslovakia 42.7; France 47.7; Greece 25.1; Italy 26.0; Yugoslavia 29.6; Poland 27.8; UK 51.4; India 15.7; USA 23.0; Argentina 15.3; Australia 13.4; USSR 14.5; as far as corn is concerned, the appropriate figures for the main producing countries are: France 51.0; Yugoslavia 45.0; Romania 35.7; USSR 22.9; China 25.9; USA 68.7; Argentina 31.1; Brazil 14.6 (according to FAO preliminary figures).

10

SOME ASPECTS OF TECHNOLOGICAL INNOVATION POLICY

Milosav Drulović

Technological Development Indicators and Policy

Yugoslavia belongs to the group of countries that sustained a relatively high rate of growth of GNP throughout the thirty-five-year postwar period. Unquestionably, such progress is to be attributed to a process of rapid industrialization.

To achieve more rapid development of both industry and other branches of the economy — such as agriculture, housing, hydropower, forestry, and communications — Yugoslavia has invested a significant portion of its GNP.

In the period between 1959 and 1978, investments amounted to between 28.4 and 35.4% of GNP. This trend continued, so that in 1979 a full 40% of the GNP was spent on investments. Technology — know-how and equipment — made up 40-50% of total investments. With the exception of the first ten to fifteen years following World War II, new investment projects predominantly meant adopting imported technology and importing equipment. Thus, having achieved a rapid rate of development of technology, Yugoslavia found great support for its own technological development through the export of know-how.

Difficulties originating from a low level of initial accumulation and the extensive use of foreign loans to import equipment contributed to a major lag in the development of Yugoslavia's own technology. Consequently, equipment imports grew significantly, the main portion of which can be attributed to the metalworking industry (SITC Section 7; see Tables 1 and 2).

Table 1

Metal Industry Products in the Imbalance of Yugoslav Exports and Imports

Products	1975	1976	1977	1978	1979
1. Total — growth	100	68.7	120.7	119	119
rate of balance*	100	100	100	100	100
2. Total capital equipment	32.9	37.5	31.0	33.1	33.4
3. Machine-building industry products	30.3	45.0	31.0	33.5	30.8
4. Machinery and transport equipment** (SITC Division 71, 72 and 73)**	40.6	45.0	39.2	42.4	41.8
5. (Nonelectric) machinery (SITC 71)	35.4	43.7	32.4	38.2	33.3

*Value of exports minus value of imports = imbalance in trade.
**Standard International Trade Classification — SITC.

This has all resulted in substantial export-import imbalances. During the period 1975-79 capital equipment was responsible for 31-37.5%, machinery for 30.3-45%, nonelectric machinery for 32.4-43.7%, and products of SITC Section 7 for 39.2-45% respectively of the imbalance.

Here is the first real sign of a genuine lag in technological development which, in the last two years, has shown a tendency to become critical, to the extent that the gap, coupled with a high trade deficit resulting from substantial imports of know-how and equipment (and meager exports), has created a serious obstacle to overall economic development. In the past few years the growth rate of GNP has been falling. For 1981 it was planned at 4.5 to 5%.

Significant attention has been paid to the development of science and research as well as to the training of highly skilled scientific personnel. A marked acceleration of the development of science and the system of higher education in general took place after

Table 2

The Share of Machinery and Transportation Equipment (SITC Section 7) in Total Imports and Exports

Imports	1975	1976	1977	1978	1979
Total	100	100	100	100	100
Machinery and transportation equipment (SITC Section 7)	34.0	33.7	35.2	36.4	35.9
Nonelectric machinery (SITC 71)	20.2	20.3	20.5	22.0	22.3
Exports					
Total	100	100	100	100	100
Machinery and transportation equipment	28.0	28.0	31.9	31.7	29.6
Nonelectric machinery	6.6	8.1	10.5	9.6	10.5

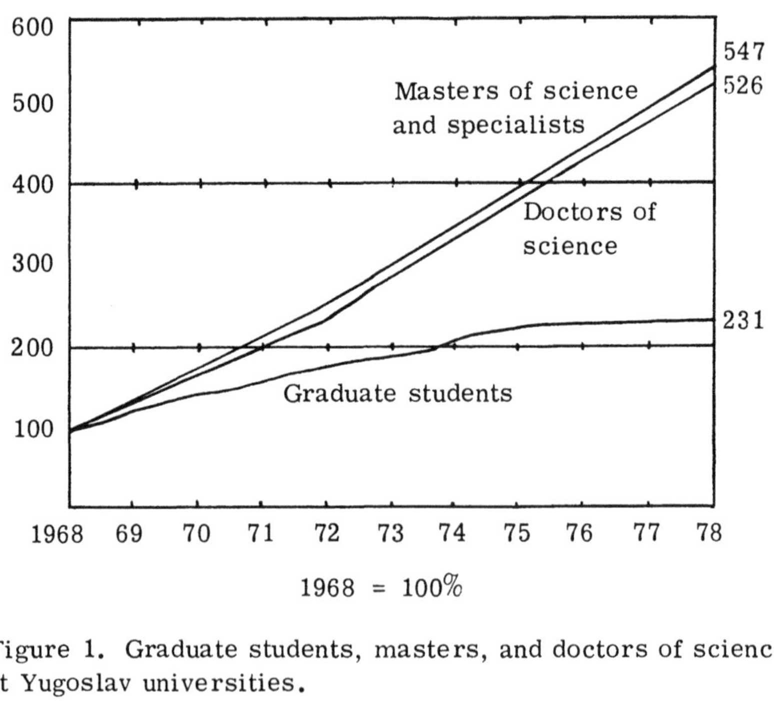

Figure 1. Graduate students, masters, and doctors of science at Yugoslav universities.

1960, when organizational efforts and financing were directed toward putting research and scientific activities to work on developing domestic know-how and technology. This policy resulted in a major increase in the number of scientists employed by nonuniversity scientific institutions, which were set up throughout the country. At the same time, teaching staffs grew at universities. Less progress was made in increasing funds for science and research.

Nevertheless, under the conditions in which industrial development has taken place and investment policy has been forged, the policy changes aimed at fostering science and research have produced results that fall far short of the needs of domestic technological development.

There are 22,000 researchers in Yugoslavia — approximately one for every 1,000 citizens. Costs of research and development have risen each year, despite the stagnation besetting both re-

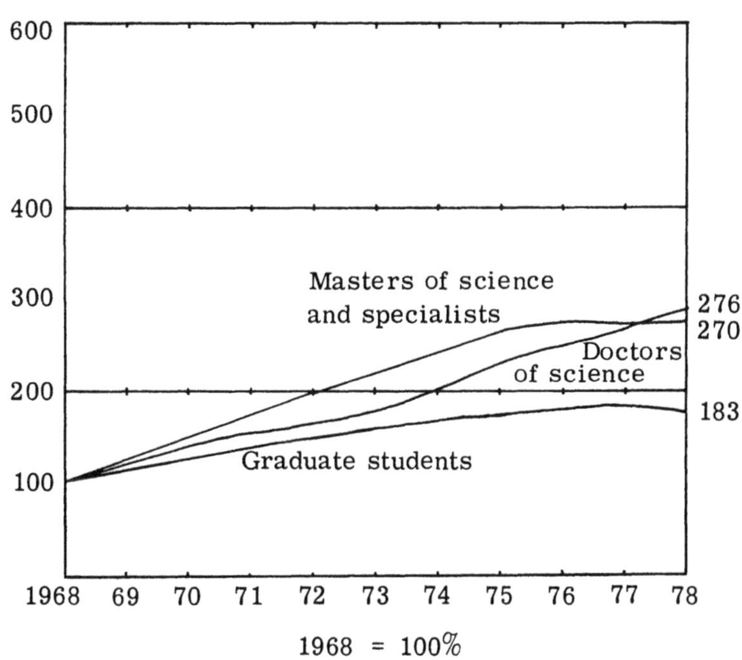

Figure 2. Graduate students, masters, and doctors of science in natural sciences.

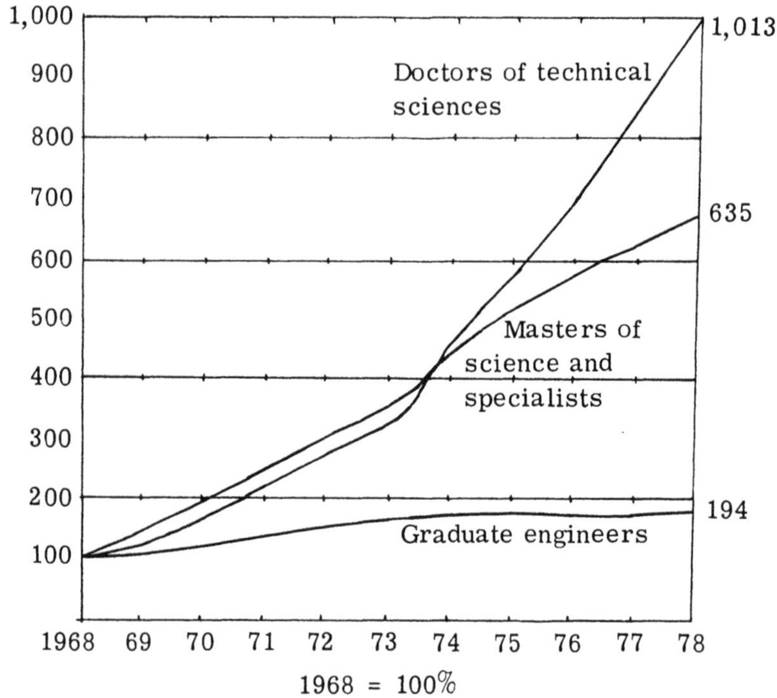

Figure 3. Graduate students, masters, and doctors in technical sciences.

search activities and real funds for research and development in the period between 1970 and 1976. Since 1977 there has been an upsurge in research activity, resulting in an increase in the number of researchers.

The underutilization of scientific potential at universities is evident. Thus between 1973 and 1975 only 25-28% of the total number of researchers were employed by universities. During the same period, however, universities accounted for no more than 8-10% of the total costs of research and development. Since 1977 this share has been increasing.

Only one fifth of the total cost of research and development is financed by republic and provincial science associations. The rest of the cost is covered by enterprises as well as from abroad.

Through the implementation of technological development policy, significant results were achieved in the education and specialization of highly skilled personnel. This will be a great asset in future efforts, i.e., attempts, to make science a contributing factor to further technological development in Yugoslavia.

The Influence of Equipment Imports on Technological Development

Certain weaknesses displayed in formulating technological policy encouraged excessive reliance on imports of know-how and technology, thus obstructing the creation of domestic technologies. In the postwar period Yugoslavia underwent rapid industrialization, which logically led to an increase in imports of foreign technology. At the same time, in view of the country's high-skill labor endowments, relatively few domestic patents and innovations have been registered. This can be explained, possibly, by a lack of incentive resulting from excessive importation of foreign technologies. Symptomatically, no significant improvements in acquired technologies have been noted, as was often the case in many other countries. Also, in some instances excessive reliance on imports of equipment made trade relations between Yugoslavia and foreign countries more developed than trade relations among enterprises within Yugoslavia itself. A slowdown in integral industrial growth in the country ensued, coupled with a weakening of the multiplier effect.

For some time, imports of capital equipment, used to build industrial capacities and develop certain other branches of the economy, resulted in more complex forms of economic cooperation with foreign partners, such as long-term cooperation, joint ventures in building production capacities in Yugoslavia, etc. — all forms that would produce stability in Yugoslavia's foreign economic relations, i.e., a greater equilibrium in the international balance of payments.

The existing flows of equipment imports also fall under the influence of some other factors, such as more favorable credit conditions for foreign suppliers of equipment; the fact that use of equipment in Yugoslavia does not require the foreign operator to further develop the techniques applied; overestimation of the value of imports, etc. Also, there are numerous cases of equipment production potential not being fully utilized so as to replace imports, partially or fully. Therefore substitution for imported equipment, as well as the replacement of foreign technologies with domestic ones, positively affect the country's balance of payments, at the same time forming a fundamental part of the country's technological innovation policy. Thus the basic prerequisites are achieved for reaching a position that is economically and politically equal to that of other countries in international relations.

The last decade has brought about significant changes in self-management relations under the conditions of socialist commodity production. These changes have led to decentralization of decision-making in which organizations of associated labor (enterprises) formulate their own technological development policies, thus achieving goals specified in self-management agreements and social negotiations. These changes, stimulated by the Association of Labor and Planning Acts, have spurred the processes of technological innovation and substitution for imports.

Furthermore, improvements in the quality of management were initiated in complex systems based on production linkages. More attention has been accorded to solving problems of structure and the selection of criteria for determining research programs.

Organizing Complex Systems Based on Production Chains

The abandonment of organization conducive to sectoral growth or growth of individual enterprises, in favor of establishing industrial systems based on production chains, signifies a new phase in organizing the machine-building industry. Thus an enterprise that requires the process of pooling labor and resources to be done in such a way as to close an entire production cycle — and to include research, development, planning, investment, production, and other components — attains strategic importance. Thus a new level of management is being introduced, as are solutions for strategic issues of better planning and management that facilitate choosing priorities and selecting investment programs, as well as more efficiently implementating development policy.

In view of the limitations inherent in the market, long-term negotiations appear crucial, first, in assigning special weight to development priorities (securing a greater rate of accumulation and productivity in priority sectors). Results expected of the medium-term plan at the complex systems level include: (a) rationalization of investments to be achieved through the division of labor (specialization) and pooling of labor and resources (concentration and effective allocation of resources) within a production chain; (b) more rapid technological progress and productivity growth due to increased research and development effects; and (c) promotion of new products and new sales methods for the domestic and world markets.

Problems of securing loans for equipment and of developing technology within the system underlie the organizational characteristics cited above.

For management of the whole economic system to be improved, development of complex systems and their structural expansion are needed. Thus in international exchange flows of intellectual services exceed flows of material goods. The level of development attained by Yugoslavia demands a strong link between science and the production process. Science is accorded an especially important role in overcoming weaknesses in the structural competitiveness of our exports.

Maintaining a position in international relations which is on a par with other nations requires much research and development. Also, the more complex the issue of export strategy, the more cooperation among enterprises becomes decisive in effecting those structural changes initiated and defined by that same export strategy. The assertion of Yugoslavia's position on the world market also requires that significant attention be accorded to engineering and consulting activities, which are positively correlated to changes in equipment exports.

Planning-business unions, which operate within technological groupings that cover production linkages, determine the respective socioeconomic positions of project, engineering, and consulting organizations in the marketing of industrial technologies. Results achieved in the development of project and engineering activities strengthen feedback links between equipment producers and project organizations developing new equipment. This strengthens the respective positions of project and engineering organizations whose productive capacities, although substantial, were largely underutilized in the past due to lack of cooperation with producers.

Problems of Structure and Criteria Involved in Formulating Research Programs

Existing scientific and research potentials (bearing in mind the significant results achieved in higher education) offer a sound basis for even greater accomplishments in the field of science and their immediate application in the development of domestic technologies (provided that financing is secured and organizational and management aspects of research are improved). Currently, expenditures for research and development in Yugoslavia range from 0.8 to 1.0% of GNP (data for 1978). Twenty percent of these funds was spent by republic, provincial, and regional associations for science and research.

The fact that investments in science and research have not yielded correspondingly high results — expressed in the production of new products based on newly acquired know-how — can be explained by weaknesses primarily in the systems of programming and management of science and research.

Within the scope of this discussion lies one of the most essential problems — that of structuring and ranking criteria entailed in the determination and selection of the specific research and development programs that most effectively contribute to the development of Yugoslavia's own technology. Accordingly, the basic issues these criteria ought to be concerned with are:

— establishing a direct quantitative relation between programs and specific research projects, on the one hand, and selection of goals and fields of technological development on the basis of domestic know-how, on the other;

— establishing quantitative relations between the needs and dynamics of investments in research and development and their effects, expressed through an increase in income resulting from new production, i.e., from marketing technology domestically and abroad;

— adjusting the structure of research and development programs to priority needs in development, as well as an increase in the importance of research and development in industry itself;

— achieving rationality in the utilization of disposable and limited resources of capital and labor, employing them most effectively, and thus securing higher income and greater accumulation, which in turn are prerequisites for the development of science and research;

— coordinating scientific and research efforts with the processes of international exchange of know-how and utilizing the transfer of technology to achieve more rapid economic growth and growth of domestic technological development — a prerequisite for attaining the desired position in international exchange.

It is clear that current economic development policy, together with science and research policies, follows criteria based on projected goals and the priorities of socioeconomic development. Nevertheless, significant efforts are being made to implement a self-management mechanism of decision-making. In the complex area of science and research, the role of the system of management is to activate all scientific potential in order to accelerate the rate of socioeconomic development.

Long-term Planning and Education under the Conditions of Technological Change

Satisfactory social efficiency of productive resources depends heavily on the system of education and the utilization of its benefits in the process of production. Since the desired structural changes cannot be adequately effected through the market mechanism, planning becomes a significant component of development policy.

But compared to economic and technological processes, democratization and decentralization of decision-making require a sharp and far-sighted view of the future. However, short-term planning relies heavily on the role of the state and favors centralized planning, which is incompatible with the nature of the system of self-management. A long-term development plan, on the other hand, requires information and coordination, which are problems all self-management structures are concerned with because adequate information permits a certain degree of autonomy among economic actors — within the scope of accepted criteria arrived at through social negotiations and self-management agreements. Hence it becomes evident that only through the possession of information regarding long-term planning prospects can the participation of labor in decision-making be genuine.

Weaknesses in formulating long-term technological policy reduce planning to minor development projects, slow down integration processes in complex development projects, and lead to weak and inefficient efforts in research and development.

Crucial in implementing the policy of technological innovation are the changes made in the structure of the educational system. Recently, qualitative changes concerning production enterprises, science, and education have become more and more evident. The number of enterprises establishing long-term cooperation with educational and scientific institutions has constantly grown.

However, self-reliance based on the development of new technologies and marketing requires that enterprises train their own personnel capable of managing complex projects. In this respect priority is given to training experts for long-term planning and development strategy, for design and marketing, for the marketing of exports, for automatic management and regulation processes, for the development of construction and technologies, etc. Changes in required curriculums and methods of training personnel to adopt new technologies and solve the complex problems that arise in enterprises are among the issues dealt with in the medium-term plan.

Organizing Composite Organizations of Associated Labor — A New Quality in Managing Technological Innovations

In the period between 1970 and 1980, 338 composite organizations of associated labor were formed — according to the Pooling of Labor and Resources Act. These organizations played a significant role in the past decade in achieving a high level of accord between long-term economic objectives and research and development. In the pages that follow we will present the results of implementing technological innovation policy and its effects as they appeared at the level of a representative unit, the Composite Organization of Associated Labor Mašinogradnja-MAG.

Anticipated and achieved effects of technological innovations in C.O.A.L. Mašinogradnja-MAG

The period between 1976 and 1980 can be characterized as follows:

— average annual growth of output value:	23.9%
— average annual growth of physical output:	16.5%
— average annual growth of value added:*	58.4%
— average share of new production output in total output:	17.8%
— achieved maximum share of value added in total output:	23.2%

*The growth of value added was calculated only during the cited period, assuming that 1975 was the base year with an index = 0. This was necessary to obtain evidence of new output within the five-year plan.

— average share of exports in total output value: 16.8%

"Technological innovation" implies greater efficiency in production, yet it is largely based on new production. We will therefore analyze the structure of new production and its influence on the increase in output value and exports, as well as its effects on the further prosperity and expansion of MAG.

New production at MAG is achieved through:

a) MAG's own design and construction of machines and devices;

b) business and technical cooperation on projects or on specific technological lines;

c) long-term manufacturing cooperation, followed by a transfer of technology — and in certain cases through joint ventures with a foreign partner.

New production, i.e., change in production structure, permitted:

— the achievement of the planned value of output at the annual growth rate of 23.9%. The influence of new production on total output value was reflected in a relatively higher price per unit of weight;

— an increase in the share of exports in total output value of 16.8%. This is less than the planned 20% due to the appearance of competitive goods.

Structurally, new production was achieved in the preceding period through:

— MAG's own development, largely based on assembly-line machinery in the field of construction machinery and means of transportation, all of which contributed to 53.1% of total new production. The share of MAG's own development of energy and processing equipment in new production is 8.2%. This brings the share of MAG's own development (i.e., products resulting from its development) in its total new production to 61.3%;

— offers of business and technical cooperation or of component parts manufacturing, using foreign documentation, accounted for 27.3% of new production;

— long-term manufacturing cooperation through technology transfer, which is responsible for the remaining 11.4% of new production.

The basic strategic task of increasing exports, assigned to this composite organization from its first days, correlates positively with the process of introducing new products, i.e., with new production as a share of total production (total output). With a share of 55.5% of new production output in the preceding period, assembly-line machines have been the main items on MAG's export list. Exports of semifinished products and components, with a share of 26.9% of total exports, point to both the reliability of business and technical cooperation and the manufacturing potential of our industry.

On the basis of adopted long-term strategic goals and the experience of the preceding period, the next midterm period (1981-85), is best characterized by the following planned indicators:

— average annual growth of output value:	24% (22-26.5%)
— average annual growth of production in physical units:	12% (10-14%)
— average annual growth rate of new production output:	38% (35.9-41.4%)
— average share of new production output in total output:	27% (25.2-30.4%)
— achieved maximum share of new production output in total output (projection for 1985):	38.4% (36.6-40.3%)
— average share of exports in total output value:	30% (26.7-34.7%)

The relatively high planned annual growth of output value (based on 1980 prices) was set in spite of the relatively lower growth rate of production measured in physical units (per unit of weight). The results could be attributed to several factors:

1) a high share of new production output in total output;

2) high exports;

3) an increase in value added in marketing resulting from MAG's own designing and engineering in the field of energy and processing equipment.

New production output, based on MAG's own development and also on technology transfer, holds a relatively high share in total output value, due to:

- achieved development of construction machinery in the preceding period (a new series of construction machinery bulldozers TC-100, 140, 200, dumpers, etc.);
- investments made in a component plant that will start operating in 1981/82 (producing hydraulic gearboxes, drive axles, etc.);
- modernization undertaken in all MAG plants;
- contracts concluded on long-term business cooperation and

transfer of technology expected to be completed in 1981 (joint investments in an air-compressor plant, transfer for cranes, dumpers, etc.);
- negotiations and further actions on contracting additional long-term business cooperation and technology transfer with partners abroad;
- projects initiated for MAG's own development of machinery and components.

Data on shares held by main production lines in value of MAG's total new production output are:

— construction and mining machinery	34.9%
— machines and devices for railroad and highway traffic, including integral transportation:	28.4%
— components for assembly-line machinery:	17.4%

In addition, MAG's own development of assembly-line machinery produces 54.6% of total new production output value. Development of devices and components for processing and energy equipment has a share of 37.3% in production output value. Technology transfer, effected through long-term cooperation and joint ventures, now compensates, or will compensate, for the difference existing between actual and planned new production output value. Also, a relative increase in the importance of transfer of technology in achieving new production output has been noted. New production output secures horizontal and vertical ties within the composite system through:

- securing long-term supply for the composite system (semi-fabricated goods vary in assortment and quality and total about 260,000 kinds);
- existing production capacity and new investments in semi-finished product plants (castings, forgings, etc.) ought to secure and cover most of the needs of the system, as 27% of this production is exchanged within the system;
- by way of new production capacity, modular construction of assembly-line machinery will become feasible. Along with substitution of imports, this forms the basis for greater interdependence within the system. It is estimated that some 55% of this output will meet internal needs of the complex. Furthermore, the projected value of this output will make up 35% of the total new production output of the complex system.

The 1981-85 period will undoubtedly produce a strong correlation between exports and the introduction of new production lines. Exports of entire plants and technological lines will gain in importance as can be seen from the table below. Current export structure can be given in shares of the total value of exports:

- assembly-line machines (construction and mining machinery, traffic and transportation machinery): 48.1%
- components and semifabricated goods in long-term manufacturing cooperation: 32.3%
- complete technological lines and engineering services: 19.6%

Therefore, and in conclusion, one can say that the projected growth of MAG's exports is realistic but invariably linked to the realization of new production projects planned at the level of MAG's composite system.

11 THE DYNAMICS OF POPULATION IN YUGOSLAVIA

Dušan Breznik

The population of Yugoslavia has undergone great changes in the postwar period both with respect to the components of population movement (fertility, mortality, and migration) and in its structures. A decline in fertility and mortality, great spatial and socio-occupational mobility, and substantial shifts in age, socioeconomic, occupational, and other structures have been the primary features of its development. In spite of these changes, however, regional differences in many demographic characteristics have persisted to this day — although the extremes occur over ever diminishing areas. Arising with the shifts in demographic development are new problems to be solved which call for the institution of a consistent population policy. The principles, and even more so the measures of social, economic, health, educational, and other policies, should contribute to solving the problems that emerge in the course of demographic development.

While the recent trends in the development of the population of Yugoslavia most certainly have been greatly influenced by earlier trends and by the heavy human losses in World War II, since that time they have been determined preeminently by the rapid socioeconomic development, the socialist transformation, the development of the educational system, improved and more efficiently organized health services, etc. In addition to those already cited, major changes have taken place in family life and in households and in the part played by women in professional, cultural, political, and other activities, whereby they have become more equal to men in employment, schooling, and in decisions on all aspects of family life and child-rearing.

Just a few data will be enough to illustrate social and economic development since the war in comparison with the prewar situation. Between the wars the social product grew about 2% annually on average, and population growth was just a little lower (about 1.5%). Following World War II the average annual rate of growth of the social product in Yugoslavia was about 6% (in the period 1947-77), and the population growth rate was about 1.1% (same period). In 1939 about 300,000 people were employed in industry, whereas by 1979 this figure had reached about 2 million. Directly following the war the percentage of agricultural population in the total population was at a level of about 75%. In 1971 it was about 38% (census data), and in 1980 it is estimated to have dropped below 30%. Personal consumption has risen constantly since the war, and qualitative changes have also been evinced in its structure. As a percentage of total expenditures for personal consumption, expenditures for food declined from about 54% in 1947 to about 39% in 1976. Today more than 95% of school-age children attend eight-year elementary school, and more than 90% of those completing elementary school go on to secondary education. As far as the tertiary educational level is concerned, Yugoslavia ranks among countries with a very high number of students in relation to size of the corresponding age group. Furthermore, in 1952 there was still only one physician per 2,300 persons approximately, whereas by 1979 this coefficient had dropped to below 700. With respect to health insurance, today practically the entire population is covered by health services of general significance for society as a whole, safeguarding the health and working capacities of each person.

1. Natural Population Movement

The process of demographic transition came to full expression in the postwar period in Yugoslavia. There was a downtrend in the birth and death rate. There was a rise in the birth rate only in the brief postwar compensation period due to the considerably higher nuptiality (marriages had been postponed during the war) and other reasons (separation of spouses during the war; deliberate choices by spouses to postpone increasing their family in the face of wartime conditions, etc.). Natural increase is moderating, and in some regions it is already very low. Only the Kosovo population has maintained a very high level of natural increase.

In the less-developed regions (Bosnia and Herzegovina, Macedonia, Kosovo, and Montenegro) a secular decline in the birth rate was only mildly in evidence between the two world wars[1] but became considerably stronger following World War II, with the exception of Kosovo, where the birth rate has remained at a high level. In the other, more developed regions (Slovenia, Croatia, Serbia Proper, and Vojvodina) the process of decline began much earlier (at the end of the nineteenth century and the beginning of

Table 1

Components of Natural Movement in the Yugoslav Population, 1950-79 (annual averages)

	Period	Yugoslavia	Bosnia-Herzegovina	Montenegro	Croatia	Macedonia	Slovenia	Serbia			
								Total	Proper	Kosovo	Vojvodina
Live births per 1,000 population	1950-54	28.8	38.2	32.7	23.2	38.4	22.8	27.4	26.1	43.5	23.2
	1955-59	24.8	35.4	30.0	20.8	34.0	19.4	22.0	19.6	42.2	18.4
	1960-64	22.0	31.4	26.7	17.2	29.4	18.0	19.8	16.6	41.5	16.2
	1965-69	19.5	25.0	22.1	15.7	26.5	16.7	18.3	15.2	38.3	14.4
	1970-74	18.1	21.0	19.9	14.7	22.6	16.4	18.0	15.1	36.7	13.5
	1975-79	17.7	18.5	18.3	14.9	21.7	17.0	18.1	15.2	33.7	14.4
Deaths per 1,000 population	1950-54	11.6	12.0	10.0	11.7	14.5	10.9	12.4	11.4	18.0	12.4
	1955-59	10.4	11.6	8.5	10.1	11.7	9.7	10.2	9.3	15.7	10.3
	1960-64	9.4	9.0	7.3	9.7	9.8	9.6	9.5	8.7	13.0	9.7
	1965-69	8.7	7.0	6.3	9.7	8.2	10.1	8.8	8.5	9.4	9.5
	1970-74	8.8	6.6	6.2	10.2	7.4	10.1	9.1	8.9	8.3	10.4
	1975-79	8.6	6.2	6.1	10.2	7.0	10.1	9.0	8.9	6.6	10.4
Natural increase per 1,000 population	1950-54	17.2	26.2	22.7	11.5	23.9	11.9	15.0	14.7	25.5	10.8
	1955-59	14.4	23.8	21.5	10.7	22.3	9.7	11.8	10.3	26.5	8.1
	1960-64	12.6	22.4	19.4	7.5	19.6	8.4	10.3	7.9	28.5	6.5
	1965-69	10.8	18.0	15.8	6.0	18.3	6.6	9.5	6.7	28.9	4.9
	1970-74	9.3	14.4	13.7	4.5	15.2	6.3	8.9	6.2	28.4	3.1
	1975-79	9.1	12.3	12.2	4.7	14.7	6.9	9.1	6.3	27.1	4.0

Sources: Demografska statistika, 1970-1977; Savezni statistički godišnjak, 1980, Federal Institute of Statistics, Belgrade.

the twentieth)[2] and was also stronger in the interwar period. During the period of demographic compensation (1948-54) the birth rate rose somewhat but then resumed its downtrend until the seventies, when it stabilized at a low level.

Whereas the general death rate before the war was still strongly influenced by infant mortality as well as age-specific disparities, at the end of the period differences in the general rate were increasingly dependent on age structure. Regions with a younger age structure have lower general rates, while regions with an advanced process of aging have higher rates or rates with a mild uptrend.

Throughout the period following World War II, the natural increase in the population of Yugoslavia has had a downward trend. In regions with a young age structure, this decline has been lower than the drop in the birth rate because of a substantial downtrend in general mortality. Nevertheless, in Kosovo the increase has constantly been high — there has even been a mild rise — as the mortality rate has decreased more rapidly than the birth rate.

Female fertility and reproduction

In view of the wide regional differences in level and type of female fertility by age, Table 2 presents data on specific fertility rates by five-year age groups, the net reproduction rate of the female population (R_0), and data on total fertility rates (F_0) in Yugoslavia and the several republics and provinces.

Female fertility has fallen in all regions and in almost all age groups. Only among the youngest female age group has there been a rise in the specific fertility rate. Furthermore, in Slovenia there has been a significant increase in fertility in the 20-24-year age group. It is noteworthy that the fastest decline in fertility occurred in the oldest group of fertile-age women, and this in all regions. Maximum fertility rates occur in the 20-24-year group with the exception of Montenegro and Kosovo, where they appear in the 25-29 group. The general fertility rate (number of live births per 1,000 females aged 15-49 years) ranged from 55 (Serbia Proper) to 68 (Montenegro) in 1978. It was higher, and considerably higher, only in Macedonia (81) and Kosovo (142) respectively.

In the stage of fertility decline, birth control was first in evidence among women over 30, but it now encompasses the younger age groups as well, with the exception of the youngest (in all regions) and, in Slovenia, the 20-24-year group owing to a major shift in age at first marriage. Women bear children in the initial years of marriage, and when they achieve the desired number, they opt for birth control. In Yugoslavia birth control (by contraceptive methods or abortion) was accepted spontaneously without any special introductory programs, as was the case in most other European countries.

The net female reproduction rate is around one in the country as a whole and in Montenegro and Slovenia (simple reproduction of the population); below one in Croatia, Serbia Proper, Vojvodina, and Bosnia-Herzegovina (in the past two years); slightly above in Macedonia (1.08); and considerably above one in Kosovo (1.98). The total fertility rate[3] shows a similar pattern in view of the diminishing influence of mortality on the net reproduction rate. The decline in the net reproduction rate has been somewhat more gradual than the decline in the total fertility rate as a consequence of the rapid decrease in infant and young-child mortality.

Family planning

As already noted, birth control developed spontaneously in Yugoslavia. Today more than 75% of married couples consciously decide on the number of children they will have. From the legal and social standpoint, a broad concept of family planning has been adopted,[4] and a person's right to determine the number of his or her children and their timing and spacing is constitutionally guaranteed.[5] It is incumbent upon society and its services (health, education, etc.) to enable the exercise of this right (providing information and disseminating knowledge about ways and means of birth control, ensuring their availability). In addition, the concept of family planning adopted also entails provision of health, social welfare, and other services for the mother and child, intervention when child care and protection are not adequate, and furthermore, medical assistance for married couples and individuals who are unable to have children.

Legislation concerning abortions conducted in health institutions is liberal in Yugoslavia.[6] Abortion in an authorized health institution is freely available to women in the first 10 (or 12) weeks of pregnancy on request, insofar as there are no medical contraindications, in which case applications are considered by expert committees. These committees are also required to decide on applications by high-risk cases (advanced pregnancy, minors, etc.). The legislation does not consider induced abortion to be a desirable

Table 2

Age-specific Fertility Rates, Net Rates, and Total Fertility Rates

	Year	Live births per 1,000 women aged:								R_o	F_o
		15-49	15-19	20-24	25-29	30-34	35-39	40-44	45-49		
Yugoslavia	1950	111.7	38.7	198.4	201.2	160.4	92.3	46.1	10.8	1.47	3.74
	1960	91.9	51.8	178.4	155.8	94.2	51.8	26.4	4.4	1.19	2.81
	1970	66.4	51.4	161.8	124.6	71.9	34.0	10.8	1.5	0.98	2.28
	1977	67.1	50.3	159.3	122.0	66.1	29.0	8.4	1.0	1.01	2.18
	1978	66.3	49.7	158.1	121.3	64.5	27.2	7.8	0.9	0.98	2.15
Index: 1978/1950		59.4	128.4	79.7	60.3	40.2	29.5	16.9	8.3	66.7	57.5
Bosnia-Herzegovina	1950	149.2	30.4	223.3	263.7	227.0	165.1	92.7	23.0	1.90	5.13
	1960	133.0	49.3	203.7	208.1	160.7	109.9	52.6	8.6	1.63	3.96
	1970	80.3	43.6	173.7	142.2	90.1	54.5	20.6	2.3	1.12	2.64
	1977	67.0	40.9	146.7	121.3	70.8	34.8	10.5	1.1	0.97	2.13
	1978	66.9	39.3	139.6	116.2	65.0	31.3	9.5	0.9	0.92	2.01
Index: 1978/1950		44.8	129.3	62.5	44.1	28.6	19.0	10.4	3.9	48.4	39.2
Montenegro	1950	123.1	32.3	197.4	217.5	187.4	130.5	62.8	22.3	1.66	4.25
	1960	115.3	43.8	179.6	194.5	139.8	88.0	45.0	8.6	1.46	3.50
	1970	79.0	28.5	159.1	151.1	103.5	53.5	18.7	3.5	1.12	2.59
	1977	70.1	27.4	133.1	148.6	86.0	42.3	12.2	1.4	1.05	2.26
	1978	68.1	25.6	126.7	143.1	86.4	40.5	12.2	1.8	1.01	2.18
Index: 1978/1950		55.3	79.3	64.2	65.8	46.1	31.0	19.4	8.1	60.8	51.3
Croatia	1950	87.2	36.9	166.4	163.2	115.1	70.2	31.5	4.0	1.21	2.94
	1960	70.1	44.8	153.1	123.3	70.7	35.9	12.7	1.0	0.97	2.21
	1970	51.3	46.9	133.6	96.9	53.1	22.5	5.9	0.1	0.81	1.79
	1977	57.4	47.7	149.5	106.7	51.9	20.1	4.6	0.4	0.90	1.90
	1978	58.0	47.9	152.6	107.9	51.9	19.4	4.6	0.4	0.90	1.92
Index: 1978/1950		66.5	129.8	91.7	66.1	45.1	27.6	14.6	10.0	74.4	65.3
Macedonia	1950	168.1	29.6	237.0	302.7	278.7	167.3	93.9	31.4	2.08	5.70
	1960	133.9	41.0	218.9	247.5	162.4	95.0	48.0	10.8	1.64	4.12
	1970	90.4	41.1	194.4	182.2	103.7	49.0	15.6	3.2	1.21	2.95
	1977	82.4	49.9	180.2	151.7	79.2	35.5	10.5	1.5	1.11	2.54
	1978	80.9	49.5	177.6	150.6	77.8	31.7	9.0	1.0	1.08	2.49
Index: 1978/1950		48.1	167.2	74.9	49.8	27.9	18.9	9.6	3.2	65.9	43.7
Slovenia	1950	86.0	24.4	132.9	168.1	139.8	90.0	42.0	9.9	1.33	3.04
	1960	68.3	26.3	133.7	131.3	81.0	40.4	15.7	4.7	1.00	2.17
	1970	60.5	43.3	152.1	112.4	69.8	33.1	10.1	1.5	0.99	2.11
	1977	65.6	58.2	173.0	113.5	56.2	24.6	6.9	1.4	1.01	2.17
	1978	66.5	56.3	179.6	118.2	55.4	23.4	5.9	0.5	1.02	2.20
Index: 1978/1950		77.3	230.7	135.1	70.3	39.6	26.0	14.0	5.1	76.7	72.4
Serbia, Total	1950	108.4	48.4	213.7	191.4	142.2	68.2	33.8	9.9	1.39	3.54
	1960	83.1	65.7	180.2	137.3	70.2	34.3	22.6	4.7	1.08	2.58
	1970	64.4	63.0	165.2	119.8	63.9	28.4	8.9	1.5	0.97	2.25

Table 2 - continued

Serbia,	1977	69.1	58.4	165.8	123.4	69.3	29.7	9.1	1.1	1.04	2.28
Total	1978	68.4	58.0	165.2	123.2	68.2	28.4	8.5	1.1	1.02	2.26
Index:	1978/1950	63.1	119.8	77.3	64.4	48.0	41.6	25.1	11.1	73.4	63.8
Serbia	1950	100.7	46.1	207.4	185.5	121.8	51.0	22.9	5.7	1.31	3.20
Proper	1960	88.8	64.1	161.1	113.2	50.9	20.8	9.9	1.3	0.92	2.11
	1970	52.1	67.3	152.9	90.8	43.3	14.2	3.2	0.4	0.82	1.86
	1977	56.4	62.7	152.6	99.3	42.6	14.5	3.5	0.4	0.88	1.88
	1978	55.2	61.3	150.0	97.5	43.9	13.4	3.0	0.3	0.86	1.85
Index:	1978/1950	54.8	133.0	72.3	52.6	36.0	26.3	13.1	5.3	65.6	57.8
Kosovo	1950	214.4	46.1	329.8	342.7	348.5	250.8	158.3	66.9	2.37	7.72
	1960	205.7	78.4	288.8	330.0	267.6	195.3	132.4	42.1	2.40	6.67
	1970	165.4	58.2	270.0	287.6	218.8	158.9	70.3	16.4	2.02	5.40
	1977	149.0	53.1	239.4	269.2	215.3	137.9	56.8	12.0	2.09	4.92
	1978	142.1	52.0	230.9	258.3	202.6	127.9	51.8	8.9	1.98	4.66
Index:	1978/1950	66.3	112.8	70.0	75.4	58.1	51.0	32.7	13.3	83.5	60.4
Vojvodina	1950	90.9	56.2	193.3	161.7	100.0	48.7	19.3	2.2	1.20	2.91
	1960	68.7	61.9	176.6	121.4	52.7	22.0	6.3	0.5	0.97	2.21
	1970	47.5	53.9	137.5	88.6	40.6	12.8	3.4	0.2	0.75	1.69
	1977	53.8	52.3	146.4	101.5	44.0	13.5	3.1	0.2	0.85	1.81
	1978	57.0	55.5	153.9	110.9	46.2	13.5	3.2	0.1	0.90	1.92
Index:	1978/1950	62.7	98.8	79.6	68.6	46.2	27.7	16.6	4.5	75.0	66.0

Sources: Vitalna statistika, 1950; Demografska statistika, 1960, 1970, and 1977; and Statistički godišnjak 1980 (all published by the Federal Institute of Statistics, Belgrade).

mode of birth control, but a liberal stance has been adopted to assure women the exercise of their constitutional right regarding number of children once an unwanted pregnancy has occurred and to avert recourse to illegal (most often inexpert) abortion, which can have undesirable consequences for the health of the woman. Contraception is viewed as a more appropriate mode of birth control, and the legislation requires social, health, medical-research, and other services to channel their activities in this direction.

Table 3 presents data on knowledge about contraceptive methods among married women: (a) those who have heard of the methods; (b) those who know how they are applied. The methods are divided into the following four groups:

I. Personal methods (coitus interruptus, rhythm method, douching);

II. Local mechanical and chemical methods (condom, diaphragm, cervical cap, chemical preparations);

III. Intrauterine devices;

Table 3

Married Women Aged 15 to 49 and Their Knowledge about Contraceptives, in %

		Variable	Yugoslavia	Bosnia-Herzegovina	Montenegro	Croatia	Macedonia	Slovenia	Serbia			
									Total	Proper	Kosovo	Vojvodina
Total fertility rate												
		(x_1)	2.31	2.55	3.03	1.94	2.78	1.95	2.32	1.80	3.81	1.81
I	a	(x_2)	80.0	69.9	88.5	96.2	88.0	88.6	74.9	85.9	40.2	90.3
	b	(x_3)	78.4	68.7	88.5	95.4	81.4	85.4	72.6	84.2	37.8	85.4
II	a	(x_4)	57.8	55.0	41.0	78.0	47.7	73.8	50.2	55.5	23.4	74.8
	b	(x_5)	46.5	44.0	37.2	62.7	36.3	63.8	40.3	44.9	18.9	60.5
III	a	(x_6)	42.9	26.5	20.3	56.4	34.7	67.6	29.5	33.1	8.9	52.0
	b	(x_7)	21.9	14.1	15.5	34.0	20.4	50.9	17.1	18.9	6.8	28.8
IV	a	(x_8)	49.8	36.9	17.5	74.7	33.6	87.5	43.4	45.7	19.7	77.8
	b	(x_9)	33.8	26.0	12.5	45.0	19.5	71.8	30.4	31.2	15.4	55.0

Sources: Anketa 1976 (Documents of the Federal Institute of Statistics); Demografska statistika, 1976, published by the Federal Institute of Statistics, Belgrade.

Note: Total fertility rates are based on data for 1976.

IV. Hormonal preparations.

The correlation coefficient between fertility level (variable x_1) and knowledge about contraception (type a or b) ranges from −0.64 to −0.85, which indicates a considerable association between these two variables. Relatively scant knowledge about modern contraceptive methods (III and IV) underlies the significant recourse to abortion as a means of birth control, as may be seen from the data for 1971 and 1977 (Table 4).

Main features of mortality

Diminishing mortality is characteristic of all age groups in Yugoslavia (Table 5).

The downward trend in mortality has been most marked among

Table 4

Number of Live Births and Abortions per 1,000 Women Aged 15 to 49

	1971		1977	
	live births	abortions	live births	abortions
Yugoslavia	68.8	47.8	67.1	...
Bosnia-Herzegovina	83.9	29.1	67.0	37.8
Montenegro	80.5	34.0	70.1	43.4
Croatia	55.3	35.0	57.4	39.2
Macedonia	90.0	40.9	82.4	43.3
Slovenia	62.7	27.9	65.6	39.5
Serbia, Total	66.0	68.5	69.1	...
Proper	52.5	81.5	56.4	...
Kosovo	174.3	18.8	149.0	...
Vojvodina	48.9	57.6	53.8	73.9

Sources: For general fertility rates, Demografska statistika for 1971 and 1977; abortion rates, documentary materials of the Federal Institute for Health Protection, Belgrade.

infants, young children, youth, and the young middle-aged groups in Yugoslavia. It has been more gradual in the older middle-aged and edlerly age groups and has even shown a mild rise in the over-80 group. Female mortality has steadily fallen during the period under observation, while male mortality has showed a mild rise in the middle-aged group — particularly in the more developed regions — after 1960, and then a resumption of the downward trend after 1970, although to a lesser extent.[7]

Relatively higher mortality among males is increasingly becoming characteristic of the Yugoslav population, as in other populations with low mortality generally (Table 6).

In age groups with very low mortality and the widest sex disparities in mortality (15-49 years), to a great extent the higher male mortality is due to the frequency of unnatural deaths (accidents, suicides).[8] Besides this, other causes of higher male mortality stem from differences in occupational structure, higher frequency of hazardous habits (alcoholism, smoking, irregular life style, etc.) and partly lie in the biological sphere.

As can be seen from Table 7, regional differences in infant and small-child mortality (male and female) are still considerable. The mortality of males in the other age groups is higher in the

Table 5

Age and Sex-specific Mortality Rates in Yugoslavia, 1952-78

	Male					Female				
	1952-54	1960-62	1970-72	1974-76	1978	1952-54	1960-62	1970-72	1974-76	1978
Total	11.9	9.8	9.5	9.0	9.3	11.2	9.4	8.3	8.9	8.1
0	123.1	94.6	53.3	42.5	36.4	110.5	87.9	49.9	38.1	32.8
1-4	9.4	4.9	2.0	1.6	1.3	9.9	5.5	2.1	1.5	1.3
5-9	1.8	0.8	0.6	0.5	0.6	1.7	0.7	0.4	0.4	0.4
10-14	1.2	0.7	0.5	0.5	0.4	1.0	0.5	0.3	0.3	0.3
15-19	1.6	1.1	0.9	0.8	0.8	1.7	0.8	0.5	0.4	0.5
20-24	1.5	1.4	1.5	1.3	1.3	2.5	1.2	0.7	0.5	0.5
25-29	2.8	1.7	1.7	1.5	1.5	2.7	1.5	0.8	0.7	0.7
30-34	3.0	2.1	2.1	1.8	1.8	3.0	1.8	1.1	0.9	0.8
35-39	3.5	2.6	2.8	2.6	2.7	3.4	2.1	1.5	1.3	1.3
40-44	4.9	3.6	4.3	3.9	4.1	4.2	2.9	2.3	2.0	2.0
45-49	7.4	5.8	6.5	6.1	6.5	5.3	4.1	3.5	2.3	3.3
50-54	11.7	9.4	9.8	9.3	9.9	8.3	6.5	5.4	5.0	5.0
55-59	17.7	15.6	15.8	14.1	14.4	12.3	10.0	8.9	8.0	7.5
60-64	27.2	25.7	24.8	22.8	24.1	20.4	17.3	14.8	13.3	13.2
65-69	40.6	40.5	39.9	36.5	36.2	32.1	29.5	25.1	23.5	22.3
70-74	63.5	65.8	63.5	58.1	59.9	52.8	51.5	46.0	40.9	40.2
75-79	96.7	97.0	105.3	97.1	88.7	82.1	79.8	82.7	77.2	66.6
80-84	146.5	138.9	151.7	152.7	167.8	124.6	124.8	129.5	129.2	137.1
85 and over	209.0	188.8	217.0	216.5	233.1	184.6	162.4	194.0	202.3	204.2

Sources: Demografska statistika, 1960, 1971, 1974, 1976, and Statistički godišnjak, 1980, Federal Institute of Statistics, Belgrade; annual averages from B. Radivojević, "Smrtnost stanovništva Jugoslavije prema starosti i polu u razdoblju 1952-1976," Stanovništvo, Belgrade, 1978, no. 1–4.

more developed regions, whereas the female rates are more even. In some of the less-developed regions, mortality of the elderly groups is very low, which some authors ascribe to greater natural selection and others to defective data on both the age structure of the population according to the censuses or estimates and on the age structure of deaths.

Infant mortality has dropped significantly since World War II, even though its present level — particularly in Macedonia and Kosovo — is still high in comparison with certain countries with low infant mortality (Table 8).[9]

The level of infant mortality is rather closely related to the

Table 6

Number of Male Deaths per 1,000 Female Deaths by Age

Age group	1952-54	1974-76
Total	1,062	1,125
0	1,114	1,115
1-4	949	1,065
5-9	1,058	1,250
10-14	1,200	1,666
15-19	941	2,000
20-24	1,000	2,600
25-29	1,037	2,142
30-34	1,000	2,000
35-39	1,629	2,000
40-44	1,166	1,950
45-49	1,396	1,906
50-54	1,409	1,860
55-59	1,439	1,762
60-64	1,333	1,714
65-69	1,264	1,553
70-74	1,202	1,420
75-79	1,177	1,257
80-84	1,175	1,181
85 and over	1,106	1,070

Source: as Table 5.

level of socioeconomic development, that is, the development of curative and preventive health services. High infant mortality is still one of the country's major demographic, social, and health problems.

The level of mortality — with reference to all age groups and excluding the influence of the age structure — is measured by means of the index of mean life expectancy at birth as a synthetic index (Table 9).

Mean life expectancy at birth has increased most where it was low before (Kosovo). Still, in all regions the upward trend — in line with the described trends in age-specific mortality — has been pronounced, although differences between the sexes are growing. Differences in mean life expectancy still obtain between Yugoslavia and countries with the lowest level of mortality by age.

According to data on causes of death, overall national pathology is changing concurrently with the decline in mortality and the changes in the population age structure. The proportion of deaths

Table 7

Age and Sex-specific Mortality Rates by Region
Annual Average 1974-76

Age group	Deaths per 1,000 population by age and sex								
	Bosnia-Herzegovina	Montenegro	Croatia	Macedonia	Slovenia	Serbia			
						Total	Proper	Kosovo	Vojvodina
	Males								
Total	6.6	6.2	10.7	7.5	10.9	9.3	9.1	7.4	11.3
0	48.1	27.2	27.8	67.0	21.9	46.4	33.3	80.3	27.0
1-4	1.6	1.1	0.8	2.0	0.8	1.9	1.0	4.2	0.8
5-9	0.6	0.4	0.5	0.6	0.4	0.6	0.5	0.8	0.4
10-14	0.4	0.3	0.4	0.4	0.4	0.5	0.4	0.5	0.5
15-19	0.8	0.5	1.0	0.7	1.1	0.8	0.8	0.8	0.8
20-24	1.3	1.0	1.5	1.0	2.1	1.1	1.1	1.0	1.2
25-29	1.6	1.1	1.7	1.0	2.0	1.4	1.3	1.3	1.5
30-34	1.9	1.4	2.1	0.9	2.3	1.7	1.6	1.5	2.0
35-39	2.7	1.9	3.1	1.9	3.5	2.2	2.0	2.4	2.9
40-44	3.9	2.7	4.8	3.0	5.4	3.4	3.1	3.2	4.2
45-49	6.1	4.9	7.2	4.6	8.0	5.4	5.1	4.8	6.7
50-54	10.0	7.2	10.7	7.2	11.4	8.5	7.9	8.0	10.4
55-59	14.6	10.3	16.1	12.1	16.9	12.9	11.7	13.1	15.7
60-64	23.3	16.8	25.1	10.5	26.1	21.5	28.1	19.0	25.3
65-69	37.6	26.0	40.7	31.3	41.6	34.4	32.8	29.3	40.4
70-74	58.4	35.1	64.3	48.2	66.1	55.7	54.1	42.7	64.8
75-79	99.1	62.6	104.3	79.6	108.8	94.8	93.7	63.9	107.8
80-84	150.7	89.1	171.0	110.0	175.0	152.1	152.7	95.2	173.9
85 and over	180.7	187.9	236.1	211.3	273.9	216.6	210.3	158.5	252.2
	Females								
Total	5.8	5.6	9.3	6.5	9.7	8.5	8.4	6.9	9.9
0	38.3	26.9	19.9	66.4	15.6	43.5	26.5	86.9	20.6
1-4	1.5	1.1	0.7	2.0	0.6	2.0	0.9	4.8	0.7
5-9	0.5	0.5	0.3	0.4	0.2	0.4	0.4	0.6	0.4
10-14	0.3	0.2	0.3	0.2	0.2	0.3	0.3	0.3	0.2
15-19	0.4	0.4	0.5	0.3	0.5	0.4	0.5	0.3	0.4
20-24	0.6	0.5	0.5	0.5	0.5	0.5	0.5	0.7	0.4
25-29	0.8	0.5	0.7	0.6	0.6	0.7	0.7	0.9	0.7
30-34	0.9	0.7	0.8	0.9	1.0	0.9	0.9	1.4	0.9
35-39	1.4	1.0	1.3	1.2	1.2	1.4	1.3	1.7	1.3
40-44	2.2	1.9	2.0	1.8	2.2	2.0	1.9	2.4	2.1
45-49	3.5	3.0	3.3	2.8	3.5	3.2	3.0	3.2	3.6
50-54	5.4	3.7	5.7	4.8	5.0	5.0	4.8	4.4	5.7
55-59	9.1	6.9	7.7	7.4	8.1	8.0	7.9	7.5	8.6
60-64	15.8	10.0	12.8	13.0	12.0	13.5	13.3	12.4	14.3

Table 7 - continued

65-69	27.9	15.8	22.1	24.0	21.3	24.0	24.7	18.9	24.4
70-74	46.1	16.0	39.4	37.4	39.0	42.3	42.6	31.4	44.6
75-79	83.9	48.7	78.0	70.6	72.5	78.8	80.8	57.9	79.5
80-84	119.1	76.7	138.7	107.8	134.0	130.6	133.7	80.5	138.8
85 and over	162.1	158.6	217.0	205.4	247.3	200.2	203.7	119.6	231.1

Source: Demografska statistika, 1974, 1975, 1976, Federal Institute of Statistics, Belgrade.

Table 8

Postwar Infant Mortality in Yugoslavia, 1950-78

Year	Infant deaths per 1,000 live births									
	Yugoslavia	Bosnia-Herzegovina	Montenegro	Croatia	Macedonia	Slovenia	Serbia total	Serbia proper	Kosovo	Vojvodina
1950	118.6	125.6	101.9	118.1	136.7	80.6	119.1	101.7	141.3	145.1
1960	87.7	107.0	66.4	70.4	114.6	35.1	86.2	66.7	132.5	73.4
1970	55.5	69.1	29.0	34.2	88.0	24.5	56.3	39.0	96.3	36.7
1978	33.6	32.4	21.6	21.6	57.5	16.2	37.8	26.3	69.8	16.4
Index: 1978/1950	28.3	25.8	21.2	18.3	42.1	20.1	32.0	25.9	49.4	11.3

Sources: Demografska statistika, 1950, 1960, 1978; Savezni statistički godišnjak, 1980, Federal Institute of Statistics, Belgrade.

due to infectious diseases, tuberculosis, and diseases of the respiratory and digestive organs has dropped significantly, while cardiovascular diseases, cancer, and cerebrovascular diseases (Table 10) are growing in frequency. Deaths due to accident have increased in recent years.

2. Migration

In the postwar period long-distance internal migration in Yugoslavia proceeded along the traditional routes traced out earlier. Emigratory regions were characterized by a high natural increase, poor economic development, few employment opportunities, etc.

Table 9

Mean Life Expectancy at Birth in Yugoslavia and Regions, 1952-54 and 1974-75

	1952-54		1974-75	
	m	f	m	f
Yugoslavia	56.9	59.3	66.9	71.7
Bosnia-Herzegovina	52.6	54.8	66.5	70.9
Montenegro	58.4	59.9	69.2	73.9
Croatia	59.1	63.2	66.7	73.5
Macedonia	55.0	55.1	66.6	70.2
Slovenia	63.0	68.1	66.7	74.2
Serbia, Total	57.1	58.8	67.3	71.1
Proper	59.1	61.1	68.5	72.1
Kosovo	48.6	45.3	65.5	67.4
Vojvodina	53.3	62.1	67.1	72.7

Source: Demografska statistika 1977, Federal Institute of Statistics, Belgrade.

Table 10

Most Common Causes of Death, Yugoslavia, 1962, 1971, and 1978

	Males			Females		
	1962	1971	1978	1962	1971	1978
Number of deaths	93,889	93,944	101,135	92,954	85,097	89,952
Percentage structure:	100.0	100.0	100.0	100.0	100.0	100.0
Infectious diseases	2.2	0.9	0.5	2.2	0.8	0.5
Tuberculosis	5.4	2.6	1.4	3.7	1.4	0.7
Cancer (malignant tumor)	8.7	12.2	15.0	8.3	11.0	13.0
Pneumonia and bronchitis	8.8	4.5	4.7	8.4	4.4	4.1
Cardiovascular diseases	18.0	22.1	32.1	21.7	26.3	38.3
Cerebrovascular diseases	5.6	7.5	8.8	7.1	10.3	12.2
Diseases of digestive organs	5.1	4.7	5.0	2.8	3.2	3.4
Insufficiently defined diseases	23.2	24.6	12.8	28.3	30.0	14.8
Other diseases	15.8	9.8	9.8	14.9	8.6	8.9
Unnatural deaths	7.2	11.1	9.9	2.6	4.0	4.2

Source: Statistički godišnjak Jugoslavije, 1973 and 1980, Federal Institute of Statistics, Belgrade.

Following World War II, spatial mobility very frequently ran parallel to occupational and social mobility and was a by-product of industrialization and the development of other nonagricultural activities. Population transfer out of agriculture into nonagricultural sectors was very rapid, as is seen from the dynamics of the proportion of the agricultural population in the total. Just twenty-five to thirty years ago it amounted to about 70% of the total population, yet today (1980) — according to estimates — it has dropped to less than 30%. Urbanization, that is, the growth of the urban population, similarly has been accelerated, although slower than the shift in the relative size of the agricultural population. Namely, according to the 1971 census, the share of the urban in the total population of Yugoslavia was about 38%, while the share of the nonagricultural population was 62%.

The greatest organized internal movements of the population just after World War II went from underdeveloped to developed areas. In the main they had a south or southwest to north direction. About 41,600 households with 246,000 members moved from various localities, predominantly economically depressed, to the flatlands of Vojvodina, the fertile plains of the Banat, Bačka, and Srem which had been vacated by German nationals in fear of retribution connected with their collaboration with the Nazi wartime occupiers.

Subsequent interrepublic (and interprovincial) migrations also encompassed substantial numbers. Today two republics (Bosnia-Herzegovina and Montenegro) and one province (Kosovo) have a negative internal migration balance, Macedonia breaks even, while the other regions have a positive balance. According to the findings of the census, on March 31, 1971, there were 1.68 million persons in the country living in a republic or province different than the one in which they had previously been permanently resident.

The extent of the impact of the migration balance between the republics and provinces on the dynamics of the total population can be seen from Table 11.

However, interrepublic or interprovincial migration constitutes only less than a fifth of total internal migration. The remainder takes place within a narrower framework, between localities within the republics and provinces. Reasons of an economic nature (level of development of the region and the rate of natural increase) were preeminent in these migrations. The shares of native-born and various categories of migrants in the total

Table 11

Annual Migration Balances of the Republics and Provinces (1948-71)

	Annual average migration balance		
	1948-53	1953-61	1961-71
Bosnia-Herzegovina	−3,800	−13,200	−18,300
Montenegro	− 400	− 1,630	− 1,550
Croatia	+ 500	+ 2,100	+ 6,400
Macedonia	−1,200	+ 2,200	− 200
Slovenia	+ 200	+ 1,800	+ 3,300
Serbia, Total	+ 4,700	+ 8,800	+ 10,200
Proper	. . .	+ 400	+ 7,300
Kosovo	. . .	− 3,300	− 3,900
Vojvodina	. . .	+ 11,700	+ 6,800

Note: The balance is estimated from data on the distribution of the total population by place of permanent residence and place of birth based on the censuses of 1948, 1953, 1961, and 1971.

population are presented in Table 12.

The percentage of native-born is correlated with the level of economic development. For example, Slovenia, the most developed region, has a low percentage of native-born inhabitants. In Vojvodina this percentage is even lower, but this is related to the heavy immigration from depressed regions following the war. The less-developed regions (Montenegro, Macedonia, Bosnia-Herzegovina, and Kosovo) have higher shares of native-born inhabitants. Local migration — the incidence of which is dependent to a considerable degree on the average size of settlements in each region — includes migrations stemming from marriage and migrations toward local centers. This also holds for movement to other communes within the same first-order region. In the remaining migration categories, economic motives predominate. Immigration from abroad is negligible.

When migrations are classified according to type of settlement (urban, mixed, and rural), it can be concluded that the most significant has been rural-urban migration, followed by interurban and then interrural. Although urbanization has proceeded directly (rural-urban migration) for the most part, the remaining types of migration (e.g., rural-mixed settlement and mixed settlement-urban) have also contributed to urbanization. These processes in the country as a whole can be seen from the data in Table 13.

Table 12

Native-born and Migrant Categories in the Total Population

	Total pop. (000)	Percentage						
		Native born	Immigrated from					
			same commune	same first-order region	another first-order region	another republic or province	abroad	unknown
Yugoslavia	20,523	59.9	14.3	6.0	10.8	8.2	0.5	0.3
Bosnia-Herzegovina	3,476	69.7	13.5	4.3	9.0	3.3	0.0	0.2
Montenegro	530	60.7	18.8	9.2	4.7	6.2	0.3	0.1
Croatia	4,426	56.6	13.6	5.0	15.9	8.0	0.5	0.4
Macedonia	1,647	62.3	17.4	4.0	10.2	4.7	1.3	0.1
Slovenia	1,727	53.8	19.8	7.4	12.2	5.4	1.2	0.2
Serbia, Total	8,447	57.9	13.2	7.2	13.1	8.0	0.3	0.3
Proper	5,250	56.9	14.6	6.4	12.4	9.2	0.2	0.3
Kosovo	1,244	69.3	15.0	7.0	3.7	4.3	0.2	0.2
Vojvodina	1,855	53.4	8.3	9.3	4.4	23.8	0.6	0.2

Source: "Vitalna, etnička i migraciona obeležja," Popis stanovništva, 1971, vol. 1, Federal Institute of Statistics, Belgrade, 1974.

Note: "Native born" includes all persons living in their place of birth. "Immigrants" are classified into five groups: the group immigrating from "another place in the same commune" are local migrants; the other groups include migrants from within the same first-order region (there are 79 such regions in Yugoslavia) or from another first-order region (but within the same republic or province), or from another republic/province.

Table 13

Migration by Type of Settlement, Yugoslavia, 1961-70

	1961	1962	1963	1964	1965	1966	1967	1968	1969	1970
Rural-urban	114,695	107,114	121,645	123,606	115,382	88,678	85,910	93,462	99,442	134,756
Urban-urban	58,401	52,008	62,213	69,160	69,661	55,777	60,201	70,762	77,403	100,290
Rural-rural	56,940	58,549	66,947	66,070	74,236	62,319	64,195	66,884	67,846	95,830
Rural-mixed	29,568	29,197	33,961	34,795	36,904	29,945	28,859	30,445	32,214	48,645
Mixed-urban	20,476	19,279	21,739	22,473	21,359	17,523	17,619	19,911	20,746	27,308
Mixed-mixed	5,216	4,845	5,684	5,858	6,278	5,867	6,060	6,482	7,217	10,239
Urban-rural	4,782	5,261	6,304	6,969	8,420	7,860	8,987	10,508	12,373	19,284
Mixed-rural	3,286	3,372	3,755	4,189	4,448	4,031	4,561	4,930	5,513	7,902
Urban-mixed	6,520	6,877	8,129	9,146	10,125	8,843	10,164	12,159	14,442	21,419

Source: as for Table 12.

Note: Data derive from census question as to type of settlement the person came from (if a migrant) and when he moved (1971 census). The question referred to the last place lived in, which means that only one migration was taken into consideration if the person had moved more than once. Hence the data are more accurate for years immediately preceding the census. The influence of mortality, which is higher for persons who have migrated, must also be noted. Nevertheless the data in the above table give an accurate picture of the structure of migration according to type of settlement and to a certain extent the dynamics of migration, similarly by type of settlement.

The economic reform (1964-65) in particular had an impact on rural-urban migration flows, which was primarily evident in 1966 and 1967. It also had a significant impact on the other types of migration constituting the urbanization process (rural-mixed and mixed-urban).

Population migrations in Yugoslavia have produced great changes in the regional distribution of the population. The number of inhabitants in predominantly agricultural settlements, particularly those in highland and depressed regions (except those with a high natural increase), is falling owing to emigration of the young and young middle-aged and a declining birth rate. In these regions the age composition of the population is also changing rapidly. The sequelae are not just demographic but economic as well because of the aging of the agricultural population.

The shifts that have taken place in the settlement pattern can be seen from the data on population by size of settlement (Table 14).

The proportion of the population living in settlements with more than 5,000 inhabitants rose from 23.2 to 37.3% in the period observed, while it declined in settlements in the other size groups. The index of population growth rose very rapidly, especially in settlements with 15,000-49,999 and over 50,000 inhabitants, attesting to the trend toward substantial concentration in major urban centers.

Table 14

Population Pattern by Size of Settlement, Yugoslavia, 1948 and 1971

Size of settlement by number of inhabitants	1948		1971		Index
	in 000	%	in 000	%	
Total	15,842	100.0	20,523	100.0	129.5
299	2,070	13.0	1,966	9.6	95.0
300-599	2,598	16.4	2,590	12.6	100.3
600-1,199	3,554	22.5	3,613	17.6	101.7
1,200-4,999	3,939	24.9	4,701	22.9	119.3
5,000-14,999	1,156	7.3	1,925	9.4	166.5
15,000-49,999	1,071	6.7	2,278	11.1	212.7
50,000 and over	1,453	9.2	3,449	16.8	237.4

Source: Materijalni i društveni razvoj Jugoslavije 1947-1972, Federal Institute of Statistics, Belgrade, 1973.

With respect to external migration, Yugoslavia has been an emigratory region in the postwar years. Statistical data are not complete, except on immigrant data from the censuses and on emigrants requesting emigrant passports on departure from the country. Estimates have been complied on external migration on the basis of these and data on the total population according to successive censuses, coupled with data on natural increase. According to them, the annual migration balance in the period 1948-53 was about –25,000, in 1953-61 about –34,000 (generally emigration to Turkey), and in 1961-71 about –23,000. On the hypothesis employed in population projections by the Demographic Research Center, the balance in external migration has amounted to about –18,000 a year in the post-1971 period.

From 1964 onward there was a steady increase in departures by Yugoslavs to work temporarily abroad. This came about, on the one hand, because of the abundance of manpower and insufficient employment opportunities in the country, and on the other hand, because of the increased demand for manpower in Western Europe, as well as the higher earnings available abroad. Besides this, it must be noted that in Yugoslavia there were no restrictions on leaving the country to seek work temporarily abroad. The findings of the 1971 census show that there were about 672,000 Yugoslav citizens working abroad temporarily, which is probably an underestimate. The number of persons working abroad rose right up to 1973 and then gradually began to drop. The Center for Migration Research (Centar za ispitivanje migracije) in Zagreb estimates, using the statistics of the recipient countries, that in 1973 there were 860,000 workers from Yugoslavia in the developed countries of Western Europe but that by the end of 1977 this figure had declined to about 705,000. In recent years there has been an uptrend in the number of supported family members of these workers. Whereas in 1973 there were 250,000, in 1977 it is estimated that there were 385,000. In research concerning the total population in Yugoslavia, the principle of "permanent" population is employed, which means that workers temporarily employed abroad, and their family members, are included in the total population, and only permanent emigrants are excluded. In the aforementioned estimate of permanent migration (negative annual balance in the post-1971 period of –18,000), the possibility of shifts from temporary to permanent emigrant status is taken into account, but the extent to which the estimate is acceptable is open to discussion.

3. Growth of the Population of Yugoslavia since 1880

Although strictly speaking only demographic processes in the period since World War II are under examination here, a longer period will be reviewed in this section, namely, the growth of the population on the present territory of Yugoslavia over the past 100 years. During this time total population dynamics was strongly influenced by war losses (the Balkan and then World Wars I and II), external migration (overseas, continental), internal migration, and further major shifts in the components of natural population movement. Very great changes took place in the development of the population during this long period which coincide with demographic transition. This process of demographic transition — declines in fertility and mortality, changes in the composition of the population — began at various times in the different parts of the country, at the end of the nineteenth century in some, between the world wars in others, and after World War II in yet others. In the period 1880-1980, the population of Yugoslavia (on its present-day territory) more than doubled (Table 15).

With the exception of Macedonia and Kosovo, the annual rate of population growth in all parts of the country is declining — as far as the periods 1948-61 and 1961-80 are concerned. Whereas over 1948-61 it amounted to 1.22% for the country as a whole, over 1961-80 it was 0.92%.

The index of population growth in the country as a whole in the period 1948-80 was 140. In the individual regions it was considerably lower than the country average in Croatia, Slovenia, Vojvodina, and Serbia Proper (from about 122 to 135), while in the other regions it was above average, the indices ranging from about 151 to about 163 (Montenegro, Bosnia-Herzegovina, Macedonia), or considerably above average (Kosovo: 207). These regional differences are even more pronounced when examined over a period of 100 years (Table 15). They can be attributed in the first place to trends in and the level of natural increase and in some intervals to migrations.

4. Changes in Population Structures

Under the impact of the considerable shifts in birth and death rates, migration, and occupational and social mobility, the expan-

Table 15

Population of Yugoslavia, 1880-1980
(in thousands)

Year	Yugoslavia	Bosnia-Herzegovina	Montenegro	Croatia	Macedonia	Slovenia	Serbia			
							Total	Proper	Kosovo	Vojvodina
				Absolute numbers						
1880	8,877	1,158	(207)	2,479	(528)	1,182	3,323	1,896	(240)	1,187
1910	12,962	1,898	344	3,375	876	1,321	5,148	3,147	475	1,526
1921	12,545	1,890	311	3,427	809	1,288	4,819	2,843	439	1,537
1931	14,534	2,324	360	3,789	950	1,386	5,726	3,550	552	1,624
1948	15,842	2,564	377	3,780	1,153	1,440	6,528	4,154	733	1,641
1953	16,991	2,843	420	3,936	1,305	1,504	6,979	4,464	816	1,699
1961	18,549	3,278	472	4,160	1,406	1,592	7,642	4,823	964	1,855
1971	20,523	3,746	530	4,426	1,647	1,727	8,447	5,250	1,244	1,953
1980	22,080	4,034	569	4,595	1,882	1,846	9,155	5,593	1,517	2,045
				Indices						
1980/1880	248.7	348.4	274.9	185.4	356.4	156.2	275.5	295.0	632.1	172.3
1980/1921	141.3	163.2	150.2	138.2	153.2	109.0	145.0	149.9	182.9	129.5
1980/1948	139.4	157.3	150.9	121.6	163.2	128.2	140.2	134.6	207.0	124.6
				Average annual growth rates (%)						
1880-1910	12.7	16.6	17.1	10.3	17.0	3.7	14.7	17.0	23.0	8.4
1921-31	14.8	20.9	14.7	10.1	16.2	7.4	17.4	22.5	23.2	5.5
1948-61	12.2	19.1	17.4	7.4	15.4	7.8	12.2	11.6	21.3	9.5
1961-80	9.2	11.0	9.9	5.3	15.5	7.8	9.6	7.8	24.2	5.2

Sources: Estimates only for Macedonia, Montenegro, and Kosovo for 1880 and 1910. All other data drawn from census findings. Estimates for 1980 by the Demographic Research Center.

Note: In 1971 the "permanent" population included about 672,000 persons temporarily working abroad.

sion of schooling of children and young people, rising urbanization, etc., population structures have altered very rapidly in Yugoslavia in the postwar period. In this section only the shifts in major structures will be reviewed.

Age structure varies widely in the different republics and provinces as a function of when the downtrend in birth rate commenced. An aging process is already in evidence in some regions, while others are still characterized by a young age structure. There is a readily apparent interrelationship between trends in the birth rate and the age structure of the population when shifts in the age structure in the country as a whole (Table 16) are examined, and when they are compared to trends in the birth rate (Table 1).

Aging has reached a relatively advanced stage in Croatia, Slovenia, Serbia Proper, and Vojvodina, which means that account must be taken of the repercussions (demographic, social, economic, and others) of this process. With regard to Bosnia-Herzegovina, Montenegro, and Macedonia, a process of demographic aging must also be expected in view of current trends in the birth rate. In Kosovo, on the other hand, the present youthfulness of the population will continue for some time.

The structure of the population by economic activity[10] is deter-

Table 16

Age Structure of the Population of Yugoslavia (1921-80) and the Regions (1980) (in %)

	Total	0-14	15-64	65 and over	Aging index
a) Yugoslavia (1921-80)					
1921	100.0	34.6	60.1	5.3	0.15
1931	100.0	34.5	60.2	5.3	0.15
1953	100.0	30.5	63.6	5.9	0.19
1971	100.0	26.8	64.9	7.8	0.29
1980	100.0	24.7	66.3	9.0	0.36
b) Regions (1980)					
Bosnia-Herzegovina	100.0	28.2	66.1	5.7	0.20
Montenegro	100.0	27.4	64.3	8.3	0.30
Croatia	100.0	20.9	67.8	11.3	0.54
Macedonia	100.0	29.7	63.5	6.8	0.23
Slovenia	100.0	23.6	65.6	10.8	0.46
Serbia, Total	100.0	24.1	66.4	9.5	0.39
Proper	100.0	21.3	68.6	10.1	0.47
Kosovo	100.0	41.0	54.6	4.9	0.12
Vojvodina	100.0	19.8	68.8	11.4	0.58

Sources: For 1921, 1931, 1953, and 1971, from the censuses; for 1980, according to estimates by the Demographic Research Center.

mined by the age and sex structure, extent of schooling of the young age groups, the pension system, level of economic development, proportion of agricultural population, the level of female economic activity, and many other factors of a demographic (e.g., fertility level), social, health (e.g., invalidity rate, incapacity for work, etc.), sociological, and other character. As a consequence of the differentiated action of these factors, there are very wide regional differences in the economic activity structure in Yugoslavia (Table 17).

In the period under observation the activity rate has declined

Table 17

Population of Yugoslavia by Economic Activity, 1953 and 1971

	1953			1971		
	total	male	female	total	male	female
a) Active population (in 000)						
Yugoslavia	7,849	5,169	2,680	8,890	5,686	3,204
Bosnia-Herzegovina	1,210	816	394	1,374	940	434
Montenegro	153	109	44	173	119	54
Croatia	1,870	1,212	658	2,016	1,239	777
Macedonia	532	384	148	630	440	190
Slovenia	704	429	275	837	473	364
Serbia, Total	3,381	2,218	1,163	3,859	2,474	1,385
Serbia Proper	2,234	1,452	882	2,703	1,635	1,068
Kosovo	268	225	43	323	272	51
Vojvodina	778	541	237	833	567	266
b) Percentage of active persons						
Yugoslavia	46.3	63.0	30.7	43.3	56.4	30.7
Bosnia-Herzegovina	42.5	58.9	26.9	36.7	51.3	22.7
Montenegro	35.4	53.8	20.3	32.7	46.1	19.9
Croatia	47.7	65.4	31.8	45.5	57.9	34.0
Macedonia	40.8	58.3	22.9	33.3	52.7	23.4
Slovenia	48.0	61.9	35.5	48.4	56.6	40.8
Serbia, Total	48.4	65.0	32.6	45.7	59.3	32.4
Serbia Proper	52.4	66.7	38.6	51.5	63.2	40.1
Kosovo	33.2	54.6	10.9	26.0	42.7	8.4
Vojvodina	45.4	65.7	26.7	42.7	59.7	26.5

Source: 1953 and 1971 census data taken from Ekonomska obeležja stanovništva, Federal Institute of Statistics, Belgrade.

in Yugoslavia as a whole, as it has in the individual republics (with the exception of Slovenia) and provinces. The downtrend has been pronounced for the male population in all regions. The female activity rate, by contrast, has been rising in the three developed regions (Croatia, Slovenia, and Serbia Proper) as well as in Macedonia. The female activity rate for Yugoslavia as a whole has remained constant.

A number of factors have been operative in the decline in the activity rate. In the first place, a growing proportion of the young are continuing schooling. Then there has been a rapid drop in the proportion of the agricultural population, whose activity rates are high, which is related to the pension system (nonagricultural persons are entitled to a pension at 60 for males and 55 for females, and they are entitled to invalid pensions, while discussion has only recently begun on the question of instituting a pension scheme for the agricultural population), and to the higher activity rate of the female agricultural population. Furthermore there has been an uptrend in the activity rates of women 20 and more years of age.

The data on activity rates by age and sex in the agricultural and nonagricultural population confirm the above assertion (Table 18).

The proportion of active persons in the primary sector (agriculture and forestry) has declined, while it has risen in the secondary (industry, mining, construction, and production crafts and

Table 18

Age-specific Male and Female Activity Rates

	Total population				Agricultural and nonagricultural population in 1971			
	1953		1971		agricultural		nonagricultural	
	m	f	m	f	m	f	m	f
Total	63.0	30.7	56.4	30.7	62.5	42.9	51.1	22.6
10-14	20.0	20.3	2.9	4.9	7.4	12.4	0.3	0.3
15-24	87.6	63.0	60.4	46.3	70.5	64.4	54.8	35.5
25-34	96.8	45.0	96.5	53.6	97.6	63.2	96.1	48.7
35-49	97.7	34.9	94.1	46.2	99.2	60.0	96.6	36.6
50-64	87.5	23.0	72.9	28.5	98.4	46.9	49.6	10.8
65 and over	60.3	50.9	11.8	15.5	88.2	32.8	6.8	1.2

Source: Computed from the 1953 and 1971 census data.

trades) and tertiary (all others) economic sectors (Table 19).

The proportion of active persons in agriculture is only 1-2% less than the proportion in the primary sector (the difference is accounted for by forestry). On the other hand, however, the percentage share of agriculture in the total population is considerably lower than its share of the total active population (Table 20).

The agricultural population is decreasing not only in terms of relative share but in absolute terms as well. In just the period from 1953 to 1971 it dropped from 10,646,000 to 7,840,000 in the country as a whole. The transfer to nonagricultural activities involved, according to estimates, about 229,000 persons per year over 1953-61 and then about 217,000 per year during 1961-71. The deagrarianization process is unfolding much faster than urbanization, since, as already pointed out, the percentage of nonagricultural population in 1971 was 61.8% and of the urban 38.6%. This indicates that a considerable number of people working outside agriculture reside in rural or mixed settlements. For example, the data from the 1969 agricultural census show that there were

Table 19

Active Population by Economic Sector, 1953 and 1971
(in %)

	1953			1971		
	primary	secondary	tertiary	primary	secondary	tertiary
Yugoslavia	70.9	16.1	13.0	48.7	28.7	21.6
Bosnia-Herzegovina	73.0	15.9	11.1	52.6	28.2	19.2
Montenegro	70.6	14.4	15.0	46.5	26.2	27.4
Croatia	67.2	18.2	14.6	42.4	31.7	25.9
Macedonia	72.4	14.9	12.7	49.9	29.0	21.1
Slovenia	53.6	28.7	17.7	27.2	46.0	26.7
Serbia, Total	75.6	12.8	11.6	55.1	25.6	19.3
Proper	76.6	12.2	11.1	56.9	24.5	18.6
Kosovo	78.6	11.7	9.7	58.8	23.9	17.3
Vojvodina	71.4	14.9	13.7	48.0	30.1	21.9

Source: Computed from 1953 and 1971 census data.

Notes: The following categories are included in the active population: unemployed and unknown and, in 1971 alone, workers temporarily employed abroad.

1980 is expected to show a further significant drop in the primary sector's share (the Demographic Research Center estimates the share of the primary in the total active population to be 38%).

Table 20

Share of Agricultural and Urban Population
(in %)

	Agricultural population			Urban population
	1953	1971	1980	1971
Yugoslavia	60.9	38.2	28.8	38.6
Bosnia-Herzegovina	62.2	40.0	29.6	27.9
Montenegro	61.5	35.0	25.4	34.2
Croatia	56.4	32.3	22.1	41.1
Macedonia	62.7	39.9	30.2	48.1
Slovenia	41.4	20.4	10.3	37.7
Serbia, Total	66.7	44.0	35.5	40.6
Proper	67.2	44.1	34.7	40.8
Kosovo	72.4	51.5	43.2	26.9
Vojvodina	62.9	39.0	32.0	48.8

Sources: 1953 and 1971 from census data; 1980 estimated by the Demographic Research Center.

1,420,000 active persons living on farms but not working in agriculture that year. In the main they were engaged in nonagricultural activities. These persons have "worker-farmer" status, which has its good sides (they have assured housing and supplementary means of living, which is important if their income is low) and its bad sides (productivity and labor efficiency are generally low).

The postwar socioeconomic transformation has been very rapid, which has meant that the economy and social services have not been able to completely absorb both the influx of farmers and the new generations of educated people trained for nonagricultural professions. In addition to this, after 1966 demographic pressures began to grow because the contingents entering the labor force were bigger than before as a consequence of the high birth rate in the period just after the war. This all led to increases in unemployment in the country and considerable incidence of temporary employment of Yugoslav citizens abroad, especially in the developed Western European countries. The increases in unemployment and employment abroad coincide with the beginning of the Economic Reform (1965), when efforts were stepped up to switch from an extensive to an intensive employment policy in the social sector, and when the employment rate in this sector was very low;

it only began to rise more substantially after 1970.

The entire postwar period has been characterized by surging growth of the educational system. Obligatory eight-year elementary schooling was introduced, and a rising proportion of young people, as well as adults, complete secondary, college, and higher education. The total number of persons with completed elementary school (eight years) in the country in 1953 was 556,000, and in 1971, 2,548,000. The number with completed secondary school (eleven to twelve years of schooling) rose from 877,000 to 2,575,000; and those with college or higher education from 81,000 to 473,000 in the same period, according to the census data for 1953 and 1971. Since 1971 this process has become even more pronounced.

There has been a rapid rise in the number of employed persons in the postwar period. In 1953, 31.6% of the total active population was employed, and in 1971, 49.5%. The bulk of the employed were engaged in the social sector — about 98% (of which more than 95% in the nonagricultural sector). In 1971, 51.5% of the total active population was in other occupational categories, of which 22.3% were own-account workers (predominantly private farmers, tradesmen and craftsmen, free-lance professions, etc.), 0.4% employers, 21.1% unpaid family workers (predominantly on private farms), and 6.6% persons temporarily employed abroad.

In 1939, when the total population was 15.6 million, there were only 920,000 employed. In 1979, in a population of 21.9 million there were 5,615,000 employed, of which 5,506,000 were in the social sector and 109,000 in the private. The significance of the social sector for the economy is best seen from its share in national income, which was 67.7% in 1952 and 85.2% in 1979. Over the same period the national income of the social sector rose from 37,015 to 283,882 million dinars, while the private sector's grew from 17,689 to 49,484 million dinars (all in 1972 prices). The income of the social sector is generated by persons employed in that sector, while the private sector's income derives from all the other occupational categories (own-account workers, unpaid family workers, employers) and those employed in the private sector.

The dynamics of employment in the postwar period in both the social and private sectors is reviewed in Table 21.

Growth in the total number of employed was fastest directly following the war. After a mild slowdown the annual rate dropped to its lowest level in the wake of the Economic Reform (1965). There was an upturn after 1972, but the rate remained below the prereform level. Annual female employment growth was lower in

Table 21

Employed Persons in Yugoslavia, 1947-79

	Total (in 000)	Growth rate (%)	Females (in 000)	Growth rate (%)	Social sector												Private sector (in 000)
					number employed (in 000)						Growth rate (%)						
					total	(1)	(2)	(3)	(4)	(5)	total	(1)	(2)	(3)	(4)	(5)	
1947	1,167	-	337	-	1,132	382	51	142	355	202	-	-	-	-	-	-	35
1953	1,836	7.8	438	4.5	1,784	567	152	307	445	313	7.9	6.8	20.0	13.7	3.8	7.6	52
1965	3,662	5.9	1,105	8.0	3,583	1,375	305	381	948	574	6.0	7.7	6.0	1.8	6.5	5.2	79
1972	4,210	2.0	1,371	3.1	4,115	1,591	238	430	1,163	693	2.0	2.1	–3.5	1.7	3.0	2.7	93
1979	5,615	4.2	1,976	5.4	5,506	2,102	267	602	1,589	946	4.2	4.1	1.7	4.9	4.6	4.5	109

Source: Savezni statistički godišnjak Jugoslavije 1980, Federal Institute of Statistics, Belgrade.

(1) Industry and mining; (2) agriculture, fishing, forestry and water resources; (3) construction; (4) other economic activities (transport and communications, trading, catering, tourism, trades and crafts, housing and communal services, financial and other services); (5) noneconomic activities (education and culture, health and social welfare, sociopolitical communities and organizations).

the period from 1947 to 1953 but then followed a pattern similar to total employment, although at a slightly higher level. Employment grew somewhat faster in industry than in the other economic and noneconomic sectors up to 1965, after which it was a little slower. The employed in the social sector of agriculture (socialist agricultural properties) constitute only a small part of the total number active in agriculture (the private sector accounts for about 85% of arable land; only 15% is in the social sector), but they produce very large market surpluses of certain crops (wheat, sugar beets, sunflower) compared with the private sector.

Since 1965 the problem of unemployment has become an increasingly important one, particularly in the less developed regions. In 1965 there were 237,000 persons seeking employment and in 1979 about 762,000 (Table 22).

The greatest surge in unemployment occurred after 1972 despite the resumed uptrend in employment at that time. The factors underlying the growth in unemployment continue to be the rapid transfer out of agricultural activities, the pronounced vocational orientation of the young toward nonagricultural activities, growing pressure by the female population on employment (an increasing number of young females are training for nonagricultural professions), and the relatively low simple reproduction of the employed as a result of their relatively young age structure. Only after 1985 are more substantial age retirements of the employed expected, thereby raising currently low simple reproduction (replacement of the employed through retirement, death, etc.) to a higher level.

In any examination of population structures it is essential to bear in mind that the Socialist Federal Republic of Yugoslavia is a multiethnic community. According to the 1971 census many

Table 22

Number Seeking Employment from 1953 to 1979 in Yugoslavia

	Number seeking employment, in 000					Unemployed as a percentage of total number employed
	total	females	%	unskilled	%	
1953	92	45	54.9	51	62.2	4.5
1965	237	126	53.2	199	84.0	6.5
1972	315	156	49.5	220	69.8	7.5
1979	762	409	53.7	449	58.9	13.6

different nations and national minorities were living in Yugoslavia at that time:

	in thousands	%
Total	20,523.0	100.0
Nations of Yugoslavia		
Montenegrins	508.6	2.5
Croatians	4,526.8	22.1
Macedonians	1,194.8	5.8
Moslems (ethnic)	1,729.9	8.4
Slovenes	1,678.0	8.2
Serbs	8,143.2	39.7
National minorities		
Albanians	1,309.5	6.4
Bulgarians	58.6	0.3
Czechs	24.6	0.1
Italians	21.8	0.1
Hungarians	477.3	2.3
Romanians	24.6	0.1
Slovaks	87.7	0.4
Turks	127.9	0.6
Others*	551.1	2.7

*273,100 respondents did not declare any specific nationality, describing themselves as "Yugoslav."

The demographic development of the various nations and national minorities is constantly under study, particularly from the standpoint of changes occurring in their natural components, demographic structures, especially their economic, occupational, and educational structures, and others.

The population of Yugoslavia in the coming period

Projections indicate that in the coming period natural increase will further moderate. The total population will most probably rise to 24.5 million by 2000, with a somewhat lower natural increase than today's and a slightly lower migration balance.

The proportion of the agricultural population will go on declining, most probably to about 11% in 2000. Similarly, further increases in the urban population are to be anticipated (to over 70%, likewise in 2000). Illiteracy will disappear, and the educational structure of the population and the skills structure of the labor force will rise substantially as a direct consequence of the present very rapid expansion of education.

In the long-term projections, full employment will most likely be achieved by the end of the millenium, with quite a different socioeconomic structure of the population. The problem of unemployment, it is expected, will be considerably mitigated in the period after 1985 as a consequence of lower transfer out of agriculture and a rise in the simple reproduction of the employed part of the labor force. In addition to the problems discussed earlier (low fertility in many areas; a pronounced process of demographic aging; continuing high infant mortality in some regions; very high fertility in certain smaller regions; considerable labor force emigration; relatively high unemployment, which is gradually becoming structural, etc.), from the standpoint of demographic development, a number of other issues should especially be borne in mind — those related to the aging of the agricultural labor force, the growing number of farms with only elderly manpower, and the need for greater synchronization of the process of training young people for various professions (vocational orientation) with expected needs in the economic and noneconomic sectors in the coming periods.

Population policy in Yugoslavia

The bases of Yugoslav population policy are laid down in a separate section of the Federal Assembly Resolution on "Foundations of Common Longterm Development Policy in Yugoslavia to 1985," which was adopted at a session of the Chamber of Republics and Provinces on October 14, 1975 (Službeni list SFRJ, No. 51, October 24, 1975). It follows from this resolution that "within the framework of common policy, changes in the population should be sought which will: (1) promote economic and social development; (2) affirm general human values and consolidate the position of women in society; (3) further humanize biological reproduction of the population; and (4) be conducive to a population model appropriate to a developed socialist society." The resolution goes on to elaborate the various areas of demographic development in more detail (fertility, mortality, migration, responsible parenthood, etc.). Generally speaking, the problems that arise in the development of the population are to be resolved in the context of general economic and social development.

Notes

[1]For a more detailed account, see the Demographic Research Center's study Fertilitet stanovništva Jugoslavije, Belgrade, 1972.

[2]The work cited in Note 1 gives an extensive bibliography of works dealing with the process of fertility decline in various regions of the country.

[3]Total fertility rates in Europe and North America were:

Country	Year	F_0	Country	Year	F_0	Country	Year	F_0
Canada	1976	1.82	FRG	1978	1.39	Switzerland	1978	1.50
USA	1978	1.80	Greece	1977	2.28	UK	1977	1.70
Austria	1978	1.63	Hungary	1978	2.08	USSR	1977	2.32
Belgium	1977	1.73	Italy	1977	1.93	Yugoslavia	1978	2.15
Bulgaria	1977	2.21	Netherlands	1978	1.59	Australia	1977	2.04
Czechoslovakia	1977	2.38	Poland	1977	2.23	Japan	1978	1.80
Denmark	1978	1.67	Portugal	1978	2.11	Yugoslavia	1977	2.15
France	1978	1.84	Romania	1977	2.54			
GDR	1976	1.64	Spain	1975	2.77			
			Sweden	1978	1.59			

[4]The social, legal, demographic, medical, and other aspects of family planning are set out in detail in Fertilitet i planiranje porodice u Jugoslavije, published in Belgrade in 1980 by the Demographic Research Center. This study has also been published in English under the title Fertility and Family Planning in Yugoslavia. It presents demographic survey findings on fertility and family planning (1970, 1976), namely: fertility levels, public awareness, and knowledge about contraception, incidence of abortion, use of contraceptives (classical and modern methods), attitudes toward family size, abortion, contraception, etc.

[5]Article 191 of the Yugoslav Constitution states: "It is a human right to freely decide on childbirth. This right may only be restricted for the purposes of health protection."

[6]The constituent republics and provinces are competent for regulations in the sphere of family planning and family law in general (marriage, the family, parent-child relations), which assures greater consideration for regional disparities. With respect to family planning, the fundamental principles have been laid down in the Resolution of the Federal Assembly on Family Planning, adopted at sessions of the Federal Chamber and the Social-Health Chamber of the Assembly on April 25, 1969 (published in Službeni list SFRJ, No. 20, May 8, 1969).

[7]With the exception of infant and small-child mortality, in most age groups in Yugoslavia mortality is gradually approaching the level attained in countries with very low mortality (Sweden, Norway, United States).

	Deaths per 1,000 population by age, 1976											
	0 years		1-4		10-14		30-34		50-54		70-74	
	m	f	m	f	m	f	m	f	m	f	m	f
Yugoslavia	39.5	35.0	1.5	1.4	0.5	0.3	1.8	0.9	9.5	5.0	58.7	42.0
Sweden	8.9	7.3	0.4	0.4	0.3	0.3	1.3	0.7	7.0	3.7	50.0	27.2
Norway	11.0	9.6	0.8	0.5	0.3	0.2	1.2	0.6	7.5	3.8	50.0	26.0
USA (1974)	19.7	15.3	0.8	0.7	0.5	0.3	2.1	1.0	10.7	5.6	57.2	30.7

Source: Demographic Yearbook, 1975, 1976, and 1977, United Nations, New York.

[8]In 1977, for example, the proportion of deaths due to unnatural causes (accidents, suicides, murders) in the total number of deaths by age and sex was as follows:

Age group	Male			Female		
	total number of deaths	number of unnatural deaths	%	total number of deaths	number of unnatural deaths	%
Total	96,504	9,832	10.2	86,299	3,587	4.2
0-4	8,458	275	3.3	7,202	208	2.9
5-14	990	434	43.8	645	218	33.8
15-24	2,198	1,432	65.2	926	362	39.1
25-34	2,507	1,404	56.0	1,124	259	23.0
35-44	5,104	1,666	32.6	2,585	396	15.3
45-54	9,849	1,712	17.4	5,658	474	8.4
55-64	11,920	1,036	8.7	8,606	400	4.6
65 and over	55,448	1,865	3.4	59,539	1,269	2.1
Unknown	30	8	26.7	14	1	7.1

Source: Demografska statistika za 1977, Federal Institute of Statistics, Belgrade.

Breakdown of Unnatural Deaths

	Males	%	Females	%
Total	9,832	100.0	3,587	100.0
Accident	7,270	73.9	2,449	68.3
Suicide	2,189	22.3	988	27.5
Murder	373	3.8	150	4.2

[9]The number of infant deaths per 1,000 live births in various countries in 1977 was:

Austria	16.9	Netherlands	9.5
Belgium	14.0	Italy	14.0
Bulgaria	24.0	Poland	24.5
France	12.4	USA	14.0
Denmark	8.9	Hungary	31.2

[10] The classification of "economic activity" is trichotomous, with the following divisions:

a) economically active persons — includes all persons engaged in an occupation as well as persons temporarily not engaged in their occupation (unemployed persons, persons on sick leave, persons currently doing military service if active before entering, etc.);

b) persons with personal incomes (age, invalid, and family pensioners, persons receiving social welfare aid, etc.);

c) dependents — persons supported by economically active persons and persons with private incomes.

12
FINANCING PERSONAL AND PUBLIC CONSUMPTION

Berislav Šefer

Consumption is an essential factor in economic development and the operation of all socioeconomic systems. As the final phase of the process of reproduction, consumption defines the scope of production and its structure, and is thus an essential factor not only of the scope and structure of production but of its costs and business savings. It is evident that more developed consumption expands the market, i.e., demand, and on this basis greater chances are created for expanding the economy and its more effective operation. When speaking of personal and public consumption, it is evident that one is speaking of satisfying the needs of the population on which the standard of living and quality of life very largely depend. Very often economic science tried to prove that needs are the single goal of all production, basing its arguments on the fact that the growth of production means a growth of consumption, that the level of satisfying human needs is increased. There is, of course, no question about the fact that higher levels of production guarantee higher levels of consumption and satisfaction of needs. However, one cannot infer from this any conclusion on the universality of the motivation of production to satisfy human needs. The motives of production can only be derived in each socioeconomic system from the character of socioeconomic relations. Under conditions of social ownership of the means of production, the position of consumption undergoes a change, and satisfying human needs genuinely becomes the motive of economic activities, so that consequently, consumption is an exceptionally important area of the overall process of reproduction in terms of the general functioning of the economic system.

1. The Significance of Personal and Public Consumption in the Self-management Socialist Economic System

1.1 In the self-management socialist economic system, the means of production are socially owned and managed directly by the workers.[1]

The workers directly manage the means of production according to their own interests. Since the means of production are highly developed, workers cannot use them individually. They must be associated in the production process with a certain number of other workers.[2] The workers therefore associate into corresponding work collectives with the aim of social production.[3] They cannot sell the means of production. They enjoy the right to manage the means of production and appropriate the results of labor only when, and as long as, they are working with these means of production. Work with socially owned means of production, in such economic conditions, is the precondition of the workers' existence, their standard of living, i.e., the satisfaction of their needs.

Naturally, under conditions of developed productive forces and a correspondingly developed division of labor, workers cannot satisfy their needs through the direct production of the material goods they need, i.e., through the direct appropriation of the use values they produce. The impossibility of all people satisfying their needs equally (given the disproportionately high quotient of needs in relation to possibilities) under conditions of a developed division of labor makes commodity production in the self-management socialist system unavoidable. Workers therefore produce corresponding material goods as commodities which, through exchange and recognition of their value on the market, give them an income in monetary form, which in turn provides the means of satisfying their needs. They are in a position to secure the material means for meeting their needs both as producers and as consumers only if and as long as they are economically sufficiently competitive in their field of production to be able, through exchange on the market, to secure such a monetary countervalue as will enable them to cover material expenditures for production, the expended means of production, and their own labor. In order to be competitive on the market, however, they must secure more than this through commodity exchange: they must secure the means to promote and expand production as a precondition for their more complete satisfaction of needs in the future.

1.2. Under such socioeconomic conditions, satisfaction of needs through extensively developed consumption becomes the ultimate goal of production. However, this goal has to be attained, under conditions of commodity production, through the exchange of commodities, i.e., under conditions of production not only of use values but also of values. For the goods produced, as has been stated, workers must receive corresponding monetary countervalues on the market. This countervalue is, in fact, the sum of the selling prices of their goods. This sum of money effected through exchange, this total revenue is at the disposal of the workers of each production entity (basic organization of associated labor). Out of this revenue they must cover all material expenditures and make up for expended means of production (depreciation). The remainder is the monetary income of that particular work collective. It is out of this income that the workers receive their personal incomes (in monetary form), i.e., the purchasing power to buy the goods and services they need. Out of this same income, however, workers set aside means for the expansion and promotion of production, for under conditions of a commodity economy, this is an obvious condition for increasing incomes, including personal incomes, i.e., personal consumption.

Therefore, in a self-management economic system the satisfaction of human needs is the ultimate goal of production. Consumption is a form of satisfying needs, and its importance obviously increases in such a system. The acquisition of monetary income is the motive of economic activities, as under conditions of commodity production, it allows for the optimal satisfaction of needs.

1.3. Under conditions of a self-management socialist system, the increase in consumption (personal and public) with a view to meeting human needs becomes the direct objective of production and economic activities. Under such social conditions workers are not separated from the means of production; they use them as a common social asset and for creating better material foundations for consumption — i.e., for the satisfaction of needs. Under such conditions consumption acts as an objective material force boosting economic development. The possibility of increasing consumption (i.e., of satisfying needs to a greater degree) makes every worker, as a member of the collective in which he works, interested in the results of economic activities. An increase in consumption in keeping with the increase in production is no mobilizing slogan but a law immanent to socialist social relations. This is evident in the self-management socialist system. The greater satisfaction of the workers' needs is the genuine motive of better operations and the generation and acquisition of a higher income in organizations of associated labor.

It should be pointed out that the countries which have so far embarked on the road of socialist construction have not, in their development policies, shown due respect for the laws governing relations between production and consumption in the socialist socioeconomic system. This has been the result of a number of factors, including the backwardness of the material base in the majority of these countries at the time they began the process of socialist development. However, the basic reasons for this phenomenon should be sought in the essential problems resulting in these countries from the administrative regulation of economic processes based on state ownership of the means of production and state management of economic processes. Lack of respect for the economic laws governing relations between consumption and production in these countries leads to major contradictions and considerable inequalities and disproportions in the development of individual economic branches. The obvious material difficulties and problems in the sphere of consumption in these countries are in fact a reflection of the contradictions stemming from the state's regulation of the course of reproduction.

1.4 Naturally it is due to this role of consumption (personal and public) in the self-management economic system that specific mechanisms are encountered for financing all monetary incomes which determine the purchasing power for personal and public consumption. The sources of consumption financing (both personal and public) as well as the decision-makers on financing are different than in other systems. All these are specific features in relation to other socioeconomic systems, particularly the capitalist, but also the state socialist system.

2. Consumption and Distribution in Self-management Socialism

2.1 There are two basic principles of distribution under socialism, which also determine the distribution of consumption, i.e., the degree of satisfaction of people's needs. They are: distribution according to the results of work, and distribution on the basis of reciprocity and solidarity. How are these two principles implemented under conditions of the self-management socialist system?

2.2. Work and the results of work are the basis of the social position of the individual and people in general in the self-management socioeconomic and political system. The results of work are valorized in the socialist economy and society as values, and they become the basic criterion of distribution, for there is no class relationship such as would prevail if the basis for distribution were property. Under conditions of the self-management economic system, distribution according to work performed is therefore implemented through the mediation of commodity exchange, through the distribution of the total value produced. Associated workers, as a work collective, through the sales of their products on the market, acquire a total monetary revenue and receive general social recognition of the value of their products. Depending on the concrete relationships on the market, they may obtain the monetary equivalent of their expended labor (past and value-added) — which is the exception, not the rule — or they may obtain more or less than this. In fact, as a collective of associated workers, the workers appropriate income on the basis of jointly expended labor, but its volume depends on the labor recognized through exchange. The appropriation of income by the work collective on the basis of the principle of socially recognized value decisively influences the interest of associated labor as a collective in promoting production and competitive ability. Therefore, as a collective of associated labor, the workers appropriate the results of their labor in the form of monetary income through exchange on the market.

Personal distribution according to work performed is carried out within the framework of each work collective of associated labor. After covering material expenditures and depreciation, each collective decides how much will be appropriated as the personal incomes of workers, and how much the share of each individual worker will be. This will be considered in greater detail later.

The principle of distribution according to work performed is necessarily linked to relations in associated labor which exclude any other basis for distribution and assert work as the only possible basis for appropriation. This is also conditioned by the fact that there are not sufficient material means to satisfy all needs and to permit distribution based on needs, and by the limited and uneven spread of the means of production, know-how, information, etc. This is the reason for the existence of the commodity economy in the self-management socialist system.

The mechanism of a commodity economy allows for the appropriation of the results of work in the form of monetary income by the work collective, without the mediation of the state. Although this still implies the appropriation of the results of work in a monetary form, it nevertheless opens the way to overcoming the workers' alienation from the results of their labor. For, with the development of the integral self-management structure as the basic form of economic, social, and political organization of society, the direct producers and working people in general, associating and pooling their labor and resources directly or indirectly, also determine and satisfy their needs outside their work collectives. Finally, the mechanism of the commodity economy alone enables personal consumption to be formed on the basis of peoples' preferences, and for its optimalization depending on the needs and possibilities of individuals, families, and corresponding groups of people. This is of essential significance in terms of satisfying human needs; it is an essential element of human freedom. However, it is also an essential element affecting production and the subordination of production to the demands of consumption, i.e., demands which stem from human needs.

However, in connection with distribution according to work performed, certain significant difficulties and limitations are in evidence. Distribution according to the results of work is not a definitive ideal but an objective economic and social need under conditions which do not permit all needs to be equally satisfied due to the limitation of available means. Distribution according to work is not an ideal form of distribution, but given limited resources, it is the only just and possible one.

As has already been stated, distribution according to work is effected as distribution according to socially recognized, and not invested, labor. This, in fact, boosts economic and technological progress. The fact that distribution is carried out on the basis of socially recognized labor, and not invested labor, causes dilemmas, conflicts, and difficulties in practice.

Namely, due to such a nature of distribution, income profiles of individual work collectives, commodity producers, branches, and groupings differ. Resources set aside for living standards (personal incomes and joint consumption funds), however, depend on the income realized by individual organizations of associated labor. Therein lies the incentive immanent to these organizations: the higher the income, the more there will be for the standard of living. Since a higher income is decisively tied in with accumulation and the expansion and promotion of production (which includes modernization and innovations), personal incomes are also tied in with higher accumulation. Consequently, in keeping with the economic laws of a commodity economy, this naturally leads to differences in the personal incomes of the same category and type of labor, since the actual results of work of the same category of labor differ. However, due to traditional views of wages and salaries as a form of pricing labor, there are problems and difficulties, and even lack of understanding, in practice. Demands are frequently heard for equal personal incomes for equal qualifications, which, in fact, boils down to salaries regardless of the results of work. This naturally has certain social, economic, and political repercussions.

Distribution according to the results of work means reproducing inequalities between people. These inequalities are caused by differences in work contribution. Under conditions of limited production resources, knowledge, information, and the like, the reproduction of these differences can also be the result of various forms of monopolies. Differences between socially recognized and invested labor may be an expression of monopoly situations and may in turn cause a distortion of the principle of distribution according to work performed with unfavorable economic and social consequences. Differences would then be reproduced not only through the system of distribution according to work but also outside that system; they would most probably expand significantly, particularly when the means of production as well as other production factors are still unevenly distributed. Under such conditions various forms of group ownership may emerge, and income acquisition and appropriation may not be founded on work. Consequently, distribution according to work is not a spontaneous process but must be socially channeled. Hence the great significance of all solutions in the Yugoslav economic system which directly connect the distribution of the results of work to the association and pooling of the labor and resources of various organizations of associated labor in production, trade, social, and other services and prevent exceptionally favorable natural and other conditions of work from affecting the social position of workers.

Distribution according to the results of work under conditions of insufficient means of consumption is an economic law of the socialist society. However, it also has its social aspect, its social dimension. Namely, the option for income to be acquired and distributed only on the basis of work and its contribution to revenue is an essential social characteristic of an epoch in which society is being transformed on the basis of the association of labor. Consequently, the process of distribution according to the results of work is not, and cannot be, a spontaneous process but is the result of society's conscious orientation and activity. Just as securing distribution according to the results of work is an essential prerequisite for the functioning of an integrated socialist system, by the same token the realization of this principle (which, in fact, means a measure of satisfying personal needs) represents a significant social issue. Proceeding from social ownership, the association of labor and income, it is evident that the realization of the principle of distribution according to work must be the subject of social action and conscious channeling. In the Yugoslav economic system, society's influence in that sense is effected through social compacts and self-management agreements. These are essential instruments of the conscious regulation of economic relations, but also of social policy. It is precisely through social compacts and self-management agreements that conditions are secured for overcoming the spontaneous effect of commodity laws and for introducing into distribution elements which are not exclusively linked to work but to other factors as well.

Another principle on which satisfaction of needs and consumption is based is solidarity and distribution based on the principle of solidarity. Solidarity has its humane and ethical aspects and represents, in itself, a significant value-principle in a socialist society. It has its economic and social components. That is, if the socialist society were to regulate relationships in distribution (and they stem from relationships in production) exclusively on the basis of the principle of distribution according to the results of work, that very principle would be infringed on, since reproduction would increasingly favor those strata of the working class and population which happen to find themselves in conditions which offer, or rather guarantee, them a more advantageous economic position in the process of reproduction. In that case distribution according to work would be distorted, as the terms of exchange would increasingly be formed on the basis of various types of monopoly (know-how, control over certain means of production, and the like). This would mean a continuous violation of the principle of distribution according to work performed. It would also undermine the social nature of property and income, lead to the development of elements of group ownership of the means of production, and the management of production resources (without formal ownership) would become a source of income and of the exceptionally favorable economic and social position of certain sections of associated labor and of individuals. Consequently there is also an economic and social need for part of the income to be distributed on the basis of the principle of solidarity. That is, aside from its humane-ethical component, solidarity also contains an economic and social component. The implementation of the principle of solidarity is an essential precondition for the realization of distribution according to the results of work as the predominant form of distribution and criterion for satisfying needs in a socialist system.

However, setting aside and using part of revenues in keeping with the principle of solidarity must not primarily be aimed at reducing differences in current distribution of income which are the result of the principle of distribution according to work. If the main purpose of distribution based on solidarity were the quantitative and direct reduction of current differences resulting from distribution according to work, this would be very dangerous for economic and technological progress, since it would reduce, or even eliminate, incentives for such progress inherent in distribution according to work performed. The object of forming, distributing, and using certain funds on a solidarity basis must be to even out the starting positions of working people in the work and distribution processes and their social security. Globally speaking, this implies the following areas: first, the equalization of working conditions (the expansion of the economic bases of work, accessibility of education, etc.); second, joint risks in the field of health insurance, in restructuring and readaptations (as a result of economic development and the effects of the scientific-technological revolution) and the like; third, securing of minimum living conditions (both for persons who are employed and for those who for various reasons of an objective or subjective nature are not in a position to earn their own living); fourth, securing living conditions in old age on a solidarity basis.

All these matters are taken into consideration by the Law on Associated Labor, which adopts the position that means pooled on the basis of solidarity and reciprocity represent not only the material preconditions for social welfare and social security but also one of the essential conditions for work and development. The funds which are set aside from the income of the basic organization of associated labor, on the basis of a self-management agreement or the law, for the needs of implementing social policy enjoy equal treatment with those parts of income earmarked for other purposes.[4]

Furthermore special stress is laid on the importance of the principle of solidarity. "Apart from the principle of distribution according to work, the workers in the basic organization shall apply the principle of solidarity, primarily through the use of social consumption funds with a view to contributing to the satisfaction of certain social and other needs of workers with low personal incomes and of the members of their families."

Solidarity must therefore be steered toward creating objective conditions leading to the greater homogenization of society and its social structures and, in conditions of distribution according to work, causing an intensification of the process of reducing differences in the economic and social position of individuals. The role of solidarity thus conceived leads to a reduction in differences without eliminating economic and social incentives inherent in distribution according to work, this being of exceptional importance for a socialist society. This kind of solidarity guarantees (and increases) social security. However, both the reduction in differences and guarantees of social security are done in such a way as to ensure dynamism of development and change and not to lead to the stagnation of existing or reproduction of old relationships.

3. Personal Incomes of the Population as a Source of Financing Personal Consumption

3.1 Under conditions of a socialist self-management economic system, personal consumption is financed through personal incomes, as the purchasing power through which, by means of the purchase of goods and services, conditions are created for personal consumption or a process of consuming material goods and services to satisfy needs.

The predominant source of personal incomes of the population are incomes derived from the work of those employed in the social sector (economic and noneconomic). This is natural in a self-management socialist society, for, as has already been said, work represents the principal determinant of the economic and social position of the individual.

The personal incomes of workers in the economy depend on the overall income at the disposal of their organization of associated labor and the division of that income into a part to meet general social obligations and net income. It is perfectly clear that the total revenue of the work organization has a decisive influence on the level of personal incomes. The revenue is acquired through the production of goods and their sale or exchange on the market. The total revenue which the workers of an organization of associated labor acquire through exchange on the market is the form in which distribution according to the results of work is carried out under conditions of socialist commodity production. This was discussed earlier. This form of distribution has certain limitations, for, as was pointed out earlier, distribution is effected on the basis of socially recognized, and not invested, labor, which means that many factors may influence the difference between invested and socially recognized work results, aside from greater effort or higher quality of work, such as monopoly situations (in various forms), natural advantages, and the like. Hence the need for social and self-management agreements on the conditions of income generation as well as on its distribution and division.

Given the fact that workers in associated labor generate total revenues through the exchange of the fruits of their labor, personal incomes in the self-management socialist system lose the attributes of wages (i.e., salaries) as a form of the price of labor. The socioeconomic content of personal incomes can consequently be defined as the monetary expression of participation in the distribution of the total newly created value. In this respect the socioeconomic content of the personal income of workers employed in noneconomic activities is the same, with the stipulation that this income is tied in with the free exchange of labor, or budgetary forms of income generation, and not with the sale of goods produced on the market. Personal incomes in noneconomic activities are far more reminiscent of wages than in the economy. To a very great extent, in the noneconomic areas the budgetary method of income generation still prevails rather than the free exchange of labor (in its full socioeconomic meaning).[5]

The funds for personal incomes set aside by organizations of associated labor from their net income are distributed among the workers as individuals on the basis of the principle of distribution according to work contribution. Therefore the criteria of distribution must proceed from the implementation of the principle of distribution according to the work results of each individual, which should encourage interest in the organization's performance on the part of both the individual and the organization of associated labor as a whole. The criterion of work contribution should take into consideration both the worker's contribution through his current labor and through his past labor.

The fact that personal incomes depend directly on work leads to their inequality, both among workers in various fields of associated labor (among various branches and groupings) and among workers in the same grouping of associated labor (the same type of production, i.e., the same branch of the economy), but in different organizations of associated labor. These differences also appear among workers in the same organization of associated labor. However, on the basis of his work, every worker in associated labor is guaranteed a personal income sufficient to ensure his material and social security. The amount of this lowest, guaranteed personal income is defined by workers in organizations of associated labor in an appropriate self-management act.

3.2. The personal incomes of retired workers — pensions — are of considerable significance. In terms of their socioeconomic content, pensions are a monetary expression of the pensioners' participation in the distribution of current income on the basis of their past labor. Throughout their working life workers set aside a part of their income as the basis of their livelihood when their active working days are over. These means form special funds and are proportionate to the personal incomes they earn during their years of service. However, in the course of their working lives, workers invest another part of their income in the material expansion of production. The accumulated social means of production are the result of the labor of the workers of several generations. Pensioners consequently are entitled to an increase in their personal income in the form of pensions after retirement, in keeping with the increases in total revenue resulting from the expansion and improvement of the material basis of labor, in which they had also invested during their years of active service. Thus during retirement pensions are adjusted to the general fluctuations in the personal incomes of workers.

Finally there are a few other forms of monetary earnings of the population. These are earnings from the sale of goods and services based on work with means in private ownership (individual agricultural producers, craftsmen, the liberal professions, etc.), from the sale of personal property, various forms of social welfare, etc. But the dominant feature of all forms of the population's income is that in the vast majority of cases, it is derived from work, in the social or in the private sector. However, due to the existence of a commodity economy and the private sector, income is not exclusively the result of work; there are forms of income which are generated by syphoning off and using the labor of others. Under the conditions of a commodity economy, this is, up to a certain point, inevitable and even economically stimulating. But through the influence of social policy, such syphoning off of income must be reduced within social and economic bounds which will not encroach on the integrated character of distribution.

3.3. The practice of implementing a system of personal incomes thus conceived naturally involves numerous problems related to personal income acquisition and distribution. It may be useful to distinguish some of the essential features involved as an indication of the degree to which personal incomes are acquired on the basis of the mentioned principles, and with a view to stressing the basic practical issues inherent in the functioning of distribution on the basis of the results of work.

Personal incomes based on work have been, and still are, the most dynamic factor determining the purchasing power of the population. The reasons for this dynamism are to be found in the very rapid development of the social sector of the economy and social activities, which led to an exceptionally rapid increase of the number employed in the social sector (both in the economy and in noneconomic activities). In the course of thirty years (1947-77) the number employed went up from 1.167 million to 5.161 million (that is, 4.42 times or by 4.6% annually). It is easy to imagine how much this contributed to the growth of personal incomes. Another factor which affected the growth of purchasing power through personal incomes based on work is their average (real) increase. Real personal incomes per employed increased in the past twenty years (1957-77) by 4.7% a year (or over 150% for the entire period).[6] Finally, the growth of the mass of personal incomes derived from labor was also affected by prices. It is well-known that the past two decades have been characterized by a rapid growth of prices, which has also been a factor in the nominal growth of the mass of personal incomes. The cost of living has been going up at a faster rate than manufacturers' prices, which is another reason for the more rapid growth of nominal personal incomes than total revenues.

However, in the past few years the growth of the real personal incomes of the employed have run ahead of the growth of labor productivity. Analyses and research indicate, however, that this phenomenon is connected with and conditioned by the overall socio-economic setting of this period rather than economically inappropriate behavior in income distribution within the work organizations themselves. That is, although the law provides for the free acquisition of income by the workers of work organizations and their decisive influence on overall distribution, in reality this has not been fully achieved. First of all, prices have remained under the considerable influence of the administration at all levels, and they essentially affect the total revenues of work organizations. The distribution of income itself is still strongly influenced by administrative measures, with a marked tendency to burden the work organization more and more with various taxes and contributions, which has led to the reduction of their share of income in real terms over the past years, generally at the expense of accumulation in the basic organizations of associated labor. To this one should add that in the very tight distribution of the total national income, which gave priority to investments which were decided on outside the organizations of associated labor, work organizations were left with less and less income, virtually with only the means for their own personal incomes. Such a situation influenced the high growth of the cost of living, which grew faster than the administratively regulated selling prices of manufacturers. All this weakened the economic position of the work organizations themselves and led to problems in the overall distribution of the national income, which was generally disrupted.

The personal incomes of workers differ considerably among industries. For the same qualification level, in the economic branch where they are highest, they are 50% higher than in the economic branch where they are lowest. If one takes into account five branches with the highest and five branches with the lowest personal incomes per worker, the difference is still high, amounting to approximately 40%. Furthermore, from year to year practically the same branches of the social sector have the highest and the same the lowest personal incomes, so that we are evidently dealing with stable differences and not accidental deviations. It should, however, be said that in the past several years these differences have been somewhat reduced. Yet they still remain such that they cannot be explained only by differences in work contribution but are obviously the product of the conditions of business (prices, differences in social overheads, etc.). This is, understandably, a major social and economic problem. It has not been resolved so far through social compacts and self-management agreements on the policy of incomes and personal incomes. The reasons lie partly in lack of respect for compacts and agreements. But the methods used so far in reaching agreements on income policy and the policy of personal incomes have not proved capable of resolving these problems of interbranch relations of personal incomes. For the agreements deal only with the division and distribution of income and personal incomes, and not their acquisition. Furthermore, agreements are between organizations of associated labor in more or less homogeneous economic groupings, and not between groupings which are income interdependent, so that they determine each other's income conditions and thus also (justifiably or not) personal incomes. For it is evident that income policy and the policy of personal incomes should not be the subject of mutual agreement among the organizations of associated labor, for instance, of the clothing industry but rather between, first and foremost, the producers of raw materials (in this case cotton, wool, and fibers), then manufacturers of semi-finished products (textiles), clothing manufacturers (producers of the finished product), and sales organizations selling these products. If the process of compacts and agreements on income and the policy of personal incomes were to follow this logical process, the leveling of differences in personal incomes between individual spheres of labor would also be more effective.

In terms of qualification levels, the ratio of highest to lowest rates of personal incomes is 1: 2.5 (unskilled worker as compared to a worker with a university degree), with a tendency toward reduction. Whatever the basis for comparison, these differences are modest and are not a satisfactory reflection of the differences in contribution. Interqualification earnings have a tendency toward general leveling, as do personal incomes within a given work organization. That is, the average range of personal incomes in individual work organizations for the whole Yugoslav economy is 1: 3.9, with the stipulation that in almost three fourths of work organizations this ratio is 1: 2.9. This is obviously not a stimulating ratio, as evidenced by comparison with ranges in other countries, of either the capitalist or the socialist system. There is another indication of the tendency toward "*uravnilovka*," or forced leveling: differences in personal incomes in the same qualification group (i.e., the difference between the highest and lowest personal incomes of those with identical qualifications) are only 13-30%, which is also very little given the fact that the contributions of workers with the same qualifications are also, obviously, quite different.

Consequently in practice there are notable deviations in relation to the system and vehicles of decision-making and to the criteria according to which workers should acquire their personal incomes. There are violations of the principle of distribution according to the results of work, leading both to unjustifiably high differences in personal incomes derived from labor and to unjustifiable equalization of incomes. In such a situation personal incomes perform mainly their consumer function, i.e., they lead to the creation and financing of personal consumption, while their incentive role in development, in maintaining and constantly increasing interest in higher productivity, in productive and creative work, is not satisfactory. Consequently this is the root cause of significant difficulties in relations between consumption and income, as there is a growing tendency toward greater spending which is not matched by a corresponding increase in productivity and effectiveness of operations. It is evident that a great deal has yet to be done to ensure a consistent application of the principle of distribution according to the results of work.

4. Financing Public Consumption

4.1 While in the field of personal consumption the satisfaction of needs is individualized and is achieved through financing from personal incomes, social consumption is not subject to this method of financing. The sector of social consumption is organized on a broader social level. This is not inherent only in socialism. The jointly organized satisfaction of needs, which means that there are no prices for individuals in the case of consumption financed socially, also exists in capitalist society. However, in capitalist society the main organizer of social consumption is the state, and the financing is of a budgetary character, so that consumption thus socialized cannot be treated as "joint." In the capitalist system this is what is known as "public" spending.

4.2. In the socialist self-management system, public consumption is effected through the implementation of the principles of solidarity and reciprocity, which have already been discussed. As has been said, solidarity and reciprocity are, above all, humane and ethical principles, principles whose inference is mutual assistance, a feeling for the needs and interests of others, and not just one's own. Solidarity in the modern system is not identifiable with the principle of charity but is a complex value-principle, a social law of socialism. It is complementary to distribution according to work performed and is one of the preconditions for its consistent implementation.

4.3. In the Yugoslav self-management society, public consumption covers the following areas of consumption (implying also the social services for effecting consumption and satisfying needs): education, health protection, child welfare, social welfare, recreation and physical education, certain communal needs. All these needs are generally met without payment for services by the individual. But in each of the listed sectors of consumption, there is partial payment by the individual user through his personal income for the use of these service or others which are not covered on a solidarity basis, or when it involves citizens who are still not fully included in the system of satisfaction of needs on a solidarity basis or are only partially included (for instance, in the care of certain needs of private farmers, craftsmen, or the liberal professions). The area of housing is also partly included in the field of social consumption.

It is quite evident that through public consumption, exceptionally important needs of workers and citizens are satisfied. It is probably not at all necessary to elaborate on the role and significance of the individual sectors of consumption and the needs which are jointly satisfied, both in terms of the living standard of the people and in terms of economically efficient development. Each of these needs is covered by a corresponding social service. For instance, educational services are rendered by workers employed in schools and other educational institutions, which are also constituted in the Yugoslav system as basic organizations of associated labor. Characteristic of all these activities which offer services within the frameworks of social consumption is that they are very labor intensive, and that most of the manpower employed has high qualifications.

4.4. The development of the material basis of society and of society itself leads to a rise in the population's need for education, health protection, and other areas of activity which ensure satisfaction of these common needs. This is the rule today in the capitalist countries, and even more so in the socialist countries. Consequently these activities are playing an increasingly important part in the overall distribution of the national income, and as a rule social consumption grows more rapidly than personal consumption. This is why their share in the national income is constantly increasing. Under conditions of a self-management socio-economic system, financing social services consequently constitutes an exceptionally important and complex issue. That is, if growing social consumption were to be financed through the state, i.e., through budgets, this would mean the alienation of a growing portion of income from the workers. On the other hand, a great many workers employed in the social services would not acquire personal incomes on the basis of their free activities and the valorization of the results of their labor, but on the basis of a sort of wage-earning relationship with the state. This would call for deep-rooted changes in the field of financing social activities, which also means in social consumption. For if solidarity and reciprocity in social consumption are effected through the mediation of the state budget, then they have the character of an etatized activity and are obviously in conflict with the overall self-management character of economic and social development.

4.5. In advanced self-management relations, such a dichotomy in the methods of income acquisition in the economy and in the social services is unacceptable, and it has no real economic or political justification.[7] For, through their operations these services directly satisfy the needs of workers in terms of safeguarding health, promoting knowledge, and the like, contributing thereby to production and income generation as well. Income is generated in the material sphere, but it is obvious that its generation is decisively affected by such activities as education, health protection, etc. Consequently there are no economic or political reasons to justify differences in the economic and political position of workers in education, health, and other related activities from that of workers engaged in material production. Viewed superficially, one might think that redistribution of income by the state through budgets would put associated labor in the social services in a privileged position. It would not have to struggle for income generation as it would acquire the means of labor from fiscal sources. In fact this is a mistaken concept. Associated labor, i.e., those employed in the social services, would, in such a situation, in fact be in an unequal position in relation to the economy. Their income would depend on the decisions of state organs, and the possibilities of associated labor in the social services to acquire an income on the basis of the results of work and its contribution to general progress would thus be completely thwarted. Under such conditions the social services would not earn income which they could freely manage but would be paid by the state. In other words, workers employed in the social services would remain in a wage-labor relationship with the state. It is clear that it is impossible to maintain two essentially different types of socioeconomic relations: one type in material production and another in the social services. As the share of social services in the distribution of the national income has a constant upward tendency, this means that an increasingly large portion of the income created in material production would be redistributed through the state. Hence through distribution the state would have independent control over a large portion of income, which would strengthen its role in development and lead to bureaucratization, which in turn would have a feedback effect on social relationships in material production as well. The state apparatus would decide on the development of social services, while the workers in material production, who generate income, would not be able to influence the development of those services according to needs and possibilities.

4.6. All these are the reasons why in the self-management socialist system, the principle of income is equally valid in relation to the social services. Namely, in the same way that workers in material production acquire an income through the exchange of goods on the market and distribute it themselves, there is no reason for relations between material production and the social services not to be effected equally on the principle of exchange of labor, given the fact that this labor is useful to workers in material production, that it contributes to economic development and the greater degree of satisfaction of workers' needs. As opposed to income acquisition in material production, where the market and exchange via the market are the basic mechanism, the exchange of labor between the social services and material production and other users is free; it is effected through agreements and compacts between these services and their users, primarily the work organizations in the economy.

The principle of free exchange of labor within the framework of a comprehensive system of expanded reproduction of the self-management socialist society and economy means a transition to a system of unified income distribution for clearly defined purposes in all areas of consumption, and thereby the initiation of the process of transforming surplus labor into necessary labor. This is a major economic and social process which implies an in-depth revision of the overall character of social reproduction. Under these conditions the economic and social position of all the working people is determined through the exchange of labor as the basic criterion, while they themselves decide on their share in the distribution of income. Relations in the process of reproduction between workers employed in material production and workers in the social services, being based on the principle of the free exchange of labor, are freed of all form of mediation, particularly the mediation of the state. The exchange of labor is carried out either on the basis of common interests and the direct mutual linkage of individual sectors of associated labor, or through interest-motivated self-management association with a view to realizing common interests. As these services operate on the basis of the principle of solidarity and reciprocity, this also implies de-etatization in the realization of this important principle of socialist society.

The realization of the principle of the free exchange of labor and interest-motivated association of workers in material production and social services is of the utmost importance. Such a process has not been realized to date in any socioeconomic system. Relations between the material and nonmaterial spheres of labor in modern social systems are, as has been stated, effected through coercion, decision-making, and the redistribution of income by the state, so that in terms of their socioeconomic positions and development principles, these two spheres of social reproduction are not only separate but also different in many ways. The historic significance of the implementation of the principle of the exchange of labor as a universal criterion governing relations between people regardless of the sphere of labor in which they are active should be underlined. For it is indicative of the depth, complexity, and extent of the process which has to be mastered. What is involved, therefore, is not a mere unilateral act whereby one set of principles regulating reproduction is replaced by another. The practical difficulties along this road are not negligible, as has been shown by practice itself.

In practice the free exchange of labor is not effected through the simple "social purchase of the social services." In practice the free exchange of labor is a complex process of the business integration of the economy and the social services, defining needs, determining possibilities, designing criteria for measuring the contribution of social services to income generation in the economy, determining the capacities and standards of individual social services, and within this context, the prices of individual services which, however, have full meaning precisely and solely within the framework of a broadly conceived practice of the free exchange of labor. With this aim in mind price is an accounting category based on a corresponding economic-social convention.

4.7. Although a social convention is used to determine the prices of services, they are not defined subjectively. For the socioeconomic content of the prices of social services should be based on the criteria of a commodity economy and should ensure that the workers in the social services acquire their income on a footing of equality with the workers in material production.

The basic elements and criteria for determining the prices of social services are:

1. that workers in the social services acquire a total income that will allow the level of their personal incomes to be commensurate to that in material production, taking into account the differences in the qualifications of workers;

2. that on the basis of the same principles as those applied in the economy, workers in the social services earmark funds for public consumption;

3. that from the income acquired through the free exchange of labor, workers in the social services ensure means for expanded reproduction on a level stipulated by agreement in development plans of these services;

4. that the full coverage of material expenditures and depreciation is included in the price of the social services.

These are the basic elements of the economic content of the price of social services. Naturally they are determined in concrete form through self-management agreements and social compacts. But there are two additional elements which have a bearing on prices. They are:

1. The standards of services. They can, of course, be very different. In elementary education, for instance, they can vary up to thirty students per teacher. Or the degree to which schools are supplied with various technical and teaching aids can differ. All this largely determines the standard of services, so that the establishment of standards is an essential element in the process of negotiating the prices of social services.

2. The scope of services also determines the price per unit of services, as does, of course, the overall value of the means which associated labor must pay, as the consumer, to the social services. The scope of services is defined by plan, which should also reflect the scope of citizens' rights to services free of charge.

When prices have been determined, and the development plan

containing all the elements of the formation of prices has been approved, the scope of services and standards as well as provisions for the maintenance and expansion of social institutions, all the elements needed for the valorization of the value of these services are at hand. Thus the scope of the necessary means for the functioning and development of each individual establishment in the social services is determined. This, then, also represents the basis for determining the financial obligations in the form of payments of associated labor as the user of these services.

Such a socioeconomic position of workers in the social services logically stems from the system of self-management. In such conditions and in the sphere of relations between the social services and material production, income becomes a basic mechanism. There is, for instance, no question of the commercialization of social services such as education or health. Solidarity and reciprocity remain the guiding principles in the use of the social services. They are, however, applied in such conditions on the basis of the interests and free options of workers in associated labor, and not through state mediation and state coercion.

With a view to interest-motivated organization of the economy and social services, self-management communities of interest are formed for individual areas: for instance, self-management communities of interest for various levels of education (elementary, intermediate, higher), for health, social welfare, etc. In these communities representatives of the economy and social services decide on programs of development for individual social services and their financing.

As has been shown, the system of financing personal and social consumption differs under conditions of a self-management economic system from that of other economic systems. Essential differences are in question. The purpose is to create an economic framework in which the increase of consumption with a view to fuller and more comprehensive satisfaction of human needs will be the basic motive of production, in which the essential vehicles of development should be the associated workers producing with socially owned means of production. The financing of personal and social consumption under these circumstances is carried out on the basis of the principle of distribution according to work and distribution on the basis of reciprocity and solidarity, with the stipulation that the workers in associated labor decide freely on all essential matters pertaining to financing both these forms of consumption. We are evidently dealing with very profound socioeconomic changes, which cannot be made over a short period of time. They call for an adequate period of time that will allow for the development of a comprehensive economic system which would ensure such a position of consumption.

In relation to such an overall concept of the role of consumption in economic development and the forms of financing it, practice to date has been seriously lagging.

The influence of state organs on income generation in work organizations is still very visible through administrative interventions in determining prices, in the crediting-monetary sector, import and export, and also in determining taxes and contributions meant to meet not only the requirements of the state budget but also to finance social services. Consequently the scope of financing personal and social consumption on the principles of distribution according to work and solidarity and on the basis of direct decision-making on all issues by the work collectives is rather limited. Given such a marked influence of state organs on the income generation of work organizations (via prices, crediting, foreign economic regulations, and the like), the true economic freedom of work collectives in income acquisition through the exchange of goods on the market is still very limited. This is reflected in the process of decision-making on the distribution of income, where the influence of state organs continues to be great, even in terms of the orientation of policy for personal incomes derived from labor. Financial relations between the economy and social services, although institutionally organized on a self-management basis (through the self-management communities of interest), continue to be characterized by fiscal sources of financing social consumption, and less so through the free exchange of labor.

The reasons for practice lagging behind the overall concept of the self-management economic system are numerous. They are an expression of profound socioeconomic transformations which do indeed require a considerable amount of time to be translated into practice. In the implementation of this, in principle, very well-conceived system, a certain number of practical difficulties were encountered, many of which have still not been provided with definitive and satisfactory solutions. For instance, no satisfactory solution has yet been found in practice to the syphoning off of accumulation among economic branches or among work organizations, so that the need for structural changes in the economy has kept the influence of state organs in the field of investment at a high level. Finally, there are objective material limitations to the consistent implementation of the self-management system. That is, on the whole, the economic strength of the Yugoslav economy is low in relation to the concept of a highly developed self-management economic democracy, so that this gives rise to many various contradictions in development, which still cannot be resolved exclusively through democratic self-management agreements and compacts but frequently require the intervention and decisions of the state.

But, despite all the lagging behind of practice in relation to the integrated system as a whole, the progress which has been attained is considerable. This has made possible a noticeable increase of the economic capacity of the Yugoslav economy to effect a very large increase in consumption and in the level of satisfaction of needs and to reduce differences in the level of satisfaction of needs among people. A great deal, however, remains to be done in the implementation of the principle according to which those who work more and better can spend more and can better satisfy their needs, which is an essential element in the integrated economic system of self-management.

Notes

[1]There is a private sector in agriculture, the crafts, catering, and small-scale trade.

[2]When we say that the means of production are "highly developed," we do not mean to say that the overall level of economic development of the Yugoslav economy is high in relation to other countries. But self-management developed in Yugoslavia when the means of production consisted of modern machines, semiautomatic and automatic equipment. Evidently, such means of production can be used in the production process only by associated workers-producers. Otherwise, in terms of the volume of the means of production and their structure, in general economic terms, the Yugoslav economy is quite underdeveloped in comparison with the economies of the developed countries.

[3]The basic economic unit in Yugoslavia into which workers are associated with a view to joint operations, acquisition, and appropriation of income is the "basic organization of associated labor." Such basic organizations of associated labor are further associated to form large composite organizations of associated labor.

[4]Basic relationships in income acquisition and distribution are regulated by law. First of all, by the Law on Associated Labor mentioned above. It is a basic law for regulating essential issues in relations among workers who associate for the purpose of engaging in economic activities with socially owned means of production.

[5]This matter will be discussed at greater length further on.

[6]Self-management Socioeconomic Development of Yugoslavia 1947-1977, Statistical Review, Belgrade, SZS, 1978, with corresponding additional calculations using data in statistical annuals.

[7]Education, health, social welfare, physical education, and other related activities in Yugoslavia come under the social heading of "Social Services."

ABOUT THE AUTHORS

Radmila Stojanović is Professor in the Department of Economics of the University of Belgrade.

Kiro Gligorov is a Member of the Federal Council and former President of the Yugoslav Federal Assembly.

Jakov Sirotković is President of the Yugoslav Academy of Sciences and Arts in Zagreb.

Dragomir Vojnić is Professor and Director of the Economic Institute, Zagreb.

Ivo Perišin is President of the Federal Economic Council in Belgrade.

Branko Mijović is a Councillor of the Yugoslav Banking Association.

Branko Čolanović is President of Jugobanka, Belgrade.

Ljubiša S. Adamović is Chairman of the Department of International Economics at the School of Economics, University of Belgrade.

Vladimir Stipetić is on the Faculty of Economics, University of Zagreb.

Milosav Drulović is President of the Organization of the Machine-Building Industry, Belgrade.

Dušan Brežnik is Professor and Director of the Demographic Institute in Belgrade.

Berislav Šefer is a Member of the Federal Assembly, Belgrade.

For Product Safety Concerns and Information please contact our EU representative GPSR@taylorandfrancis.com
Taylor & Francis Verlag GmbH, Kaufingerstraße 24, 80331 München, Germany

www.ingramcontent.com/pod-product-compliance
Ingram Content Group UK Ltd.
Pitfield, Milton Keynes, MK11 3LW, UK
UKHW010956180926
475701UK00004B/399

* 9 7 8 1 1 3 8 6 3 8 6 2 4 *